THE
OCCULT
IN LANGUAGE
AND LITERATURE

New York Literary Forum acknowledges the support of the Division of Humanities and the Arts,
Hunter College, C. U. N. Y., and its dean Gerald Freund.

THE
OCCULT
IN LANGUAGE
AND LITERATURE

GUEST EDITOR

HERMINE RIFFATERRE

4

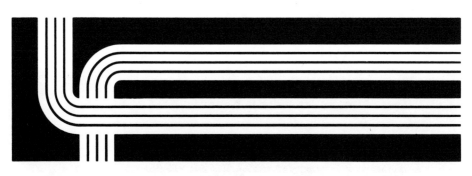

NEW YORK LITERARY FORUM

NEW YORK • 1980

Library of Congress Cataloging in Publication Data

Main entry under title:

The Occult in Language and Literature

    (New York literary forum; v. 4 ISSN 0149-1040)
    Bibliography: p.
    Includes index.
    1. Occultism in Literature--Addresses, essays, lectures. I. Series.

PN49.028   809'.9337   77-18630
ISBN 0-931196-03-5

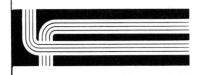 # CONTENTS

Preface vii

PART 1. OCCULT DRAMA

1. The Drama of the Unseen—Turn-of-the-Century Paradigms for Occult Drama 3
   Daniel Gerould and Jadwiga Kosicka

2. Symbolist Drama: Villiers de l'Isle-Adam, Strindberg, and Yeats 43
   Haskell M. Block

PART 2. POETRY OF THE INVISIBLE: THE ROMANTIC PHASE

3. Occultism and the Language of Poetry 51
   Frank Paul Bowman

4. Love-in-Death: Gautier's "morte amoureuse" 65
   Hermine Riffaterre

5. Ghosts, Spirits, and Force: Samuel Taylor Coleridge 75
   Anya Taylor

6. Victor Hugo and Galatea's Flight 87
   Jean Gaudon

PART 3. SUPERNATURAL INTERPRETATIONS

7. Magic in the Writings and Life of Apuleius 103
   Cecil Paige Golann

8. Bloy and the Symbolism of History 111
   Jean-Loup Bourget

PART 4. ASCENT, DEATH, DREAMS . . . .

9. Mallarmé and the "Poison Tutélaire" 125
   James R. Lawler

10. The Dangeruous Game of Dreams: Jean Paul and the Surrealists 133
    Reinhard Kuhn

11. Dark Framing and the Analogical Ascent **147**
    Mary Ann Caws

PART 5. MAGIC WORD PLAY

12. The "Neck Riddle" and Dramatic Form **161**
    B. H. Fussell

13. Occulted Discourse and Threatening Nonsense in Joe
    Orton's *Entertaining Mr. Sloane* **171**
    Maurice Charney

14. Numerology: The Butorian Imagination **179**
    Jennifer Waelti-Walters

PART 6. TEXTS AND DOCUMENTS

15. Stanisław Przybyzewski's *Visitors*, translated by Daniel
    Gerould and Jadwicka Kosicka **197**

    About the Authors **211**

    Bibliography **213**

    Index **215**

Preface

The Occult in Language and Literature, New York Literary Forum, volume 4, explores two distinct occult landscapes: the traditional occult literary motifs that pertain to the supernatural and the occult defined as the hidden power of language. Words can wound and heal more effectively than the practices of magic, alchemy, and numerology. The magic power formerly ascribed to traditional occult wisdom is thus transferred to language. But regardless of the occult genre at hand, *New York Literary Forum* writers stress the utilitarian function: how artists exploit their beliefs for the benefit of their works.

Following the precedent of *Comedy: New Perspectives* and anticipating our forthcoming issues on *Melodrama* and *Shakesperean Comedy,* this current *New York Literary Forum* volume places a strong emphasis on the drama. Part 1, "Occult Drama," deals with the symbolist theater. Daniel Gerould and Jadwiga Kosicka's "Drama of the Unseen—The Turn-of-the-Century Paradigms for Occult Drama" analyzes and interprets the visionary, spiritual, and esoteric currents in symbolist drama and formulates a typology of mystical theater. Examples are drawn from the mainstream of European literature, but the focus in on little known, decadent, bizarre, and disconcerting Russian and Polish fin-de-siècle hidden masterpieces. Haskel Block's "Symbolist Drama: Villiers de l'Isle-Adam, Strindberg, and Yeats " also recognizes the central importance of occultism in the development of a new and disturbing conception of dramatic art.

Part 2, "Poetry of the Invisible: The Romantic Phase," examines occult theories and practices of the Romantic Age. Frank Paul Bowman's "Occultism and the Language of Poetry" reviews occultist and illuminist linguistic theories of the late eighteenth and early nineteenth centuries. Bowman contrasts these speculations with the conventionalist and cratylist traditions and suggests how they still survive today. In "Love-in-Death: Gautier's 'morte amoureuse,' " Hermine Riffaterre claims that Gautier anticipates the surrealist *ready-made* with his use of various occult codes: vampirism, dreams, realism, and illusion. How the poet adapts the occult vocabulary of phantoms, ghosts, and the invisible is also the subject of Anya Taylor's "Ghosts, Spirits, and Force: Samuel Taylor Coleridge." Coleridge transmuted clichés pertaining to disembodied souls to describe personal energy fluctuations, fragmentation of the self, amorous passion, and religious fervor. Jean Gaudon's "Victor Hugo and Galatea's Flight" takes out of the closet Victor Hugo's complicated and outrageous experiences with spiritualism, mediums, photographs, prophecies, "speaking tables," and the mystical power of letters and words. His idiosyncratic use of a rhetoric based not on analogy but on preterition and the accumulation of long enumerations led him to the creation of a truly occult poetry.

In Part 3, "Supernatural Interpretations," it may seem provoking to join Apuleius, a citizen of the North African town of Madura in the second century A.D., and Léon Bloy, a fervent Roman Catholic convert born in 1846 in the French Périgord. Yet, both writers share a common intertext: modern readers who rarely take their ideas seriously. Cecil Golann's "Magic in the Writings and Life of Apuleius" reminds us that although magic was indeed incidental in Latin authors before Apuleius, in Apuleius it is one of major elements. His life and writings indicate that he believed in magic, was preoccupied with it, and may have practiced it on occasion. Jean-Loup Bourget's "Bloy and the Symbolism of History" provides a counterscript to the recent ambiguous French re-readings of Bloy that have focused on the style rather than on the subject. Bloy's apocalyptic conceptions of history again illustrate several essential movements of the turn of the century already presented in Part 1: symbolism, decadence, the occult, and the Catholic renaissance.

With Part 4, "Ascent, Death, Dreams . . . .," the concept of the occult unfolds into a mythical allegory representing closed, hidden, and concealed analogies between things, beings, concepts, and words. James R. Lawler's "Mallarmé and the 'Poison Tutélaire'" explains that the occult presence in Mallarmé ("His own true shade, a tutelary poison") can be traced to Baudelaire and Les Fleurs du mal. By focusing on the affinities between Jean Paul Richter and the surrealists, Reinhard Kuhn's chapter "The Dangerous Game of Dreams: Jean Paul and the Surrealists" explores the essential dangers of the visionary voyage. "Dark Framing and the Analogical Ascent" of Breton, Borges, Daumal, and Dupin allow Mary Ann Caws to develop a typography of surrealist spatial structures.

Part 5, "Magic Word Play," reflects occult language games. In B. H. Fussell's "The 'Neck Riddle' and Dramatic Form," the neck riddle refers to a convention of magic naming whose aim is exorcism and in which language reveals its hidden powers. Plays as different as Oedipus and Waiting for Godot dramatize this common trope. The insight that the seemingly vacuous nonsense of pop culture language harnesses and hides savage and bitter truths is the theory of Maurice Charney's study, "Occulted Discourse and Threatening Nonsense in Joe Orton's Entertaining Mr. Sloane." Finally, Jennifer Waelti-Walters' "Numerology: The Butorian Imagination" initiates the reader into contemporary numerology: Butor exploits numerology not for its divinatory power but for its power to generate prose structure arrangements reminiscent of the series in serial music.

Part 6, "Texts and Documents," presents Visitors, a one-act play by Stanisław Przybyszewski, translated into English for the first time especially for New York Literary Forum by Daniel Gerould and Jadwiga Kosicka. Portraying man in the clutches of unseen diabolic forces, it is a fitting epilogue illustrating many aspects of the aesthetics of the occult.

Appreciation is expressed to Margaret Betz and Tobias Haller, photographers who made the illustrations for chapter 1 possible.

Jeanine Parisier Plottel

PART 1

OCCULT DRAMA

The Drama of the Unseen—
Turn-of-the-Century
Paradigms for Occult Drama

DANIEL GEROULD
JADWIGA KOSICKA

*It is precisely at the moment when positivism is at its heights
that mysticism awakens and the follies of the occult begin.
—But it has always been like that; tail ends of centuries are
all alike. They're periods of uncertainty and confusion. When
materialism rages, then magic begins to thrive. This phenomenon
reappears every hundred years.*

Huysmans, Là-Bas *(1891)*

As our own turn of the century draws closer—and already rumblings are
heard some twenty years in advance of the precise epicenter—we are experiencing a vast revival of interest in the symbolist art and literature of
the last fin de siècle. Esoteric painters and writers, long declared obscure
and consigned to oblivion, have been rehabilitated and publicly acclaimed.
In the field of theatrical performance, rediscovery proceeds at a slower
pace. Burdened with audiences, actors, and a variety of material requisites,
the stage seems at first glance inimical to the visionary.[1]

Yet in our own time we can discern—although still in a highly tentative form— an attempted revival of the sort of spiritual theater that was first proposed at the last turn of the century, doubtful though it may be whether these modern practitioners are fully conscious of all the precedents which they are following. Take, for example, the Om Theater's *The Cosmic Mass*, performed at the Cathedral of St. John in New York as part of the World Spiritual Summit Conference V in October 1975 after having been first presented on the mountain summits of Chamonix-Mont Blanc the previous summer. Combining drama, music, song, dance, and meditation, *The Cosmic Mass* was structured as an immense pageant and processional dedicated to the celebration of spiritual oneness.[2]

Now the very concept of a mystical multimedia spectacle performed among high mountain peaks inevitably leads us back to those extraordinary endeavors to theatricalize the unseen that animated the most advanced European drama in the years around 1900. Contemporary resurgence of occult drama provides a fitting occasion to explore some forgotten turn-of-the-century antecedents, particularly those strange visionary dramas that were created in Eastern Europe as old empires approached the whirlwind of war, revolution, and apocalypse and everyone awaited the coming end of a dying world.

Andrei Bely's *Jaws of Night* and *He Who Has Come*, Valerii Briusov's *The Earth*, Alexander Scriabin's *Prefatory Action* and *Mysterium*, Stanisław Wyspiański's *November Night* and *Acropolis*, Tadeusz Miciński's *The Revolt of the Potemkin* and *Basilissa Teophano*, and Stanisław Przybyszewski's *Visitors*—these are not works that have entered into the mainstream of twentieth-century European drama, and yet it is precisely such hidden masterpieces that can best serve as prototypes of occult theater, by its very nature committed to journeys into the unknown. The often bizarre and disconcerting theatrical forms and postulates put forward by these Russian and Polish fin-de-siècle artists—along with analogical and contrastive models provided by Strindberg, Maeterlinck, and other less familiar Western occultists—will offer sufficiently wide range of examples upon which to base an outline typology and poetics of occult drama.

First, a few preliminary observations setting out the perimeters of our investigation. By occult drama we mean quite simply the visionary, spiritual, and esoteric current in playwriting that flourished throughout all of Europe at the turn of the century. Called by its adherents the "theater of the soul"—a richly allusive phrase suggesting as much a public playhouse for the world soul as an inner stage for the individual psyche— this movement in drama was virtually synonymous with symbolism.[3] Of the relationship between the two, the Russian critic and poet Ellis (L. L. Kobylinsky) wrote in 1910: "The most subtle and delicate form of art, symbolism, has an innate tendency to identify itself with mysticism and the visionary."[4] Interpreting occult along these lines, in the fin-de-siècle context, we shall use the word interchangeably with the term *symbolist*.

Symbolist Playwrights and the Esoteric Tradition

A look at the symbolist playwrights of the period and their filiations with the occult suffices to justify this usage. Above all, it was the Belgian Maurice Maeterlinck in the early 1890s, with his plays and essays delving into unexplained psychic phenomena and mysterious transcendent forces, who first opened the path for the occult drama that then swept the whole of Europe within a decade. Conversant with ancient and modern mystics, including the fourteenth-century Flemish "Ecstatic Doctor," Jan van Ruysbroeck, whom he translated into French, as well as with Indian philosophy, Plotinus, Kant, and Swedenborg, Maeterlinck became the spiritual guide of an entire generation of dramatists.[5]

Without exception, the other symbolist playwrights were students and adepts of esoteric knowledge. Yeats's and Strindberg's contacts with the occult are too well known to need any elaboration here. In his search for spiritual harmony, the Russian novelist and poet Bely became an active member of Rudolph Steiner's anthroposophical community at Dornach, Switzerland, from 1914 to 1916.[6] His friend and associate Briusov, chief spokesman for Russian symbolism, attended seances in Moscow, contributed to the spiritualist journal *Rebus*, and showed a passionate interest in medieval witchcraft, upon which he did extensive research.[7]

The Spanish symbolist Ramón del Valle-Inclán pursued the occult tradition in the folklore of his native Galicia; fascinated by books on magic, he filled his plays and novels with tales of sorcery, demonic possession, curses and spells (especially the evil eye), hypnotism, clairvoyance, and telepathy.[8] Like Valle-Inclán, the Italian poet and playwright Gabriele D'Annunzio avidly collected superstitions and was intrigued by fortune-telling, numerology, astrology, cartomancy, and the other divinatory arts, affirming in 1916 that "our life is a magical work which escapes the scrutiny of reason . . . An occult power directs it, often in opposition to apparent laws"—a declaration of faith that could be subscribed to by all the symbolist playwrights of the fin de siècle.[9]

Przybyszewski was the outstanding Polish satanist at the turn of the century. Nurtured on local superstitions reaching back to the Middle Ages and drawn from childhood to forbidden communication with invisible powers, he dabbled in black magic and devil-worship. From his readings in Trentkowski's *Demonomania* and Kiesewetter's *History of Occultism*, as well as Renaissance demonologists Jean Bodin, Martin Antoine del Rio, and Pierre de Lancre, Przybyszewski conceived the idea of a "synagogue of Satan" (the title of one of his books, taken from the Book of Revelation 2:9) for all those rebellious spirits who are cursed and live in despair; and his disciples at the Peacock Café in Cracow proudly called themselves the "sons of Satan"—an allusion to the master's novel, *Satans Kinder*.[10]

Przybyszewski's fellow countryman Miciński was his exact spiritual opposite. Known as the Magus, he traveled about Europe in quest of enlightenment, studying mysticism in Spain, organizing in Warsaw the Brethren of the Sun, a secret society—similar to the Rosicrucians—devoted to the transformation of man, frequenting Vyacheslav Ivanov's circle in Moscow, and visiting the Emile Jaques-Dalcroze Institute at Hellerau, where he saw Claudel's *L'Annonce faite à Marie.* In both his life and his works, Miciński sought to return to the primal Indo-European religious heritage, by reconciling Christianity, Buddhism, Hinduism, Zoroastrianism, alchemy, the Cabbala, gnosticism, and Persian philosophy. During his years in Paris as a young painter, Miciński's more famous contemporary, Wyspiański, was initiated into the occult sciences by Paul Serusier (Gauguin's friend from Pont-Aven and one of the founders of the Nabis), who gave lectures propagating Plato, Hermes Trismegistus, and hermeneutics in Schuré's version. [11]

But no further evidence is needed at this point to support our claim that the symbolist playwrights were deeply immersed in occult lore. And in any case, we are less interested in the specific mystical beliefs held by these writers than with the uses to which they put them in creating innovative theatrical forms and techniques. In other words, our concern is not with doctrine, but with dramaturgy. Whatever the attitude of the playwright to the tenets of esoteric philosophy—and it may range from total commitment to simple curiosity, or even ironic detachment—as an artist, he imaginatively appropriates mystical precepts and practices in their more theatrical manifestations and makes the occult serve the purposes of drama, not vice versa. The occult dramatist is not necessarily a professional mystic.

The symbolists were attracted to esoteric knowledge primarily because it offered them opportunities for new poetic formulations. In *La Littérature et l'occultisme*, Denis Saurat points out that poets have always been in sympathy with the occultist circles of their age, finding an almost inexhaustible mine of fresh material in the mystic teachings, which have preserved intact the most primordial concepts.

> Occultism is the place of refuge for all vanquished religions and philosophies. For our poets, in opposition to the orthodox culture of their time, there lies a whole world of artistic possibilities. They find in it, living in all the fervor of the initiates, ancient and profound myths, in general little exploited by poets and thus doubly precious.[12]

The great contribution of the turn-of-the-century occult drama has been not to the dissemination of esoteric wisdom, but to the art of the theater, which it has revitalized by expanding conventional notions of what a play is and by liberating stagecraft from nineteenth-century realistic canons. In establishing a new hierarchy of relationships between visible and invisible, outer and inner, known and unknown, the symbolist playwrights have made possible the theatricalization of the unseen, there-

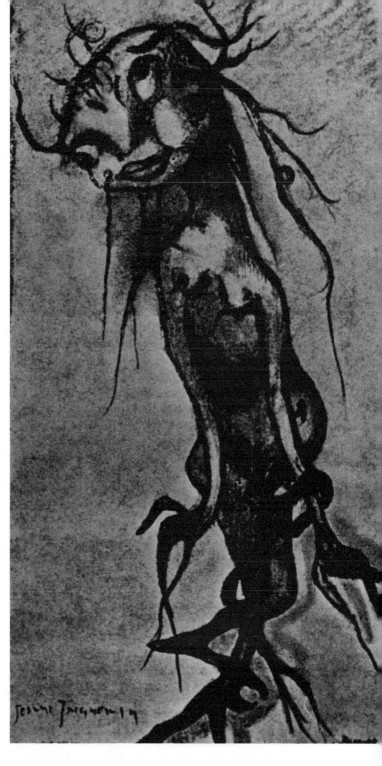

Jeanne Jacquemin's *The Mandrake* (1894). Expelled from the mystical Rosicrucian movement, which accepted only men, Jeanne Jacquemin was the most important woman occult painter of the period. Influenced by Moreau and Redon, she painted heads—for the most part, in pastels—that express an ecstatic longing for the other world.

by adding new dimensions to the old stage world.

The Essence of Occult Drama

I am the god of a mysterious world, the entire world is in my
dreams alone.

Fyodor Sologub

The Church, the sole true Church, is the Cosmos.

Tadeusz Miciński

The occult dramatist's goal is to render theatrically tangible the unseen forces that control man's destiny on earth. To reveal an invisible
world hidden behind the facade of everyday reality and its practical con-
cerns, the playwright must transport audience as well as dramatic characters beyond the personal and public preoccupations that are the subjects
of the traditional genres. Symbolist theater becomes an act of initiation,
leading us—by a process of awakening and transformation—across what
Villiers de l'Isle-Adam calls "the threshold of the occult world"[13] and into heightened states of consciousness, whether these be of a higher of a
lower form of life. Although professional occultists and their followers
tend to believe that spiritual journeys bring enlightenment, not all commerce with otherworldly powers is benign; as well as ascents, there may be
descents, sudden plunges into the dark regions and abysses of the soul
where madness, chaos, and destruction lurk.

To embark upon voyages of discovery toward an unknown world
lying outside our customary temporal and spatial notions, the visionary
playwright is required to create new time and new space rather than to
copy existing models. And here lies the special significance of symbolist
dramaturgy for the theater, a form seemingly bound and circumscribed
by a highly conventionalized, yet "real" sense of time and space—or at
least traditional theory would have us so believe.

Rejecting the confines of the nineteenth-century playhouse, cut off
from eternity, and measured by the petty calculations of an economy-
minded mercantile society anxious to maximize profits and not waste
time or space, the most daring occult dramatists of the turn of the century longed to establish a sacral playing arena on mountain summits and
in holy places. Inspired by the example of Wagner's total theater, two
visionary Polish playwrights voiced similarly grandiose plans around 1900.
Wyspiański projected a stage on "sacred national soil" by the Royal Castle
of Wawel in Cracow overlooking the Vistula and at the same time
dreamed of an enormous theater under the open sky in the Tatra Mountains, with the lofty peaks serving as the wings and the deep blue waters of a
small lake suggesting the auditorium. In the same mountain range, which
he associated with the Himalayas and the origins of ancient Indian religions, Miciński called for the creation of a universal temple of beauty,

Jeanne Jacquemin's *A Head* (1894). According to the critic Rémy de Gourmont, Jacquemin's androgynous figures display "an exquisite putrefaction." Her heads are "so ravaged by suffering that their hideousness becomes superhuman."

"where in an amphitheater of the dead and the living, carved in the mountains, under the azure sky and among the deep forests, there will be revealed the mysteries of life on earth," and where Sanskrit dramas, such as *Shakuntala* could be performed.[14]

At this same period, the Russian composer and mystic Alexander Scriabin first conceived the idea for a vast *Mysterium*, which would represent a synthesis of the arts of music, song, dance, and theater and compose a cosmic symphony of sounds, lights, colors, scents, and tastes. Designed to usher in the end of the world in a flaming conflagration, Scriabin's *Mysterium* was to be given on the banks of the Ganges or at the foot of the Himalayas (the London theosophists recommended Darjeeling), with sunrise and sunset as part of the stage setting, and thousands of spectators seated in a huge, semicircular auditorium with spiral steps facing a semicircle of reflecting water.

Hostile to the conventional theater of his time, the composer was deeply impressed by the rhythmic rendering of a chorus from *Antigone*, as presented at Meyerhold's Studio in 1913, and hoped to use the same technique in his mystery play.[15] As part of his work on the *Mysterium*, Scriabin studied Sanskrit, became a disciple of Yogi Ram Charak, and actually planned a trip to India in the winter of 1914, buying a white suit and pith helmet and spending hours in the sun to prepare himself for the tropical climate. Although he continued to work on the project until his death in 1915, Scriabin was able to complete only a fragmentary sketch of the *Prefatory Action*, which was to last seven days, whereupon, at the end of the twelfth hour of the seventh day, a new race of humans would be born. The *Mysterium* was never realized.[16]

The failure of these visionary artists to create—except in their imaginations—a feasible new playing area outside the theater of commerce might at first suggest that their dream was a futile and unproductive one, worthy of ridicule. But if the theater could not be moved to the mountains and holy places, at least the mountains could be brought into the theater and the secular stage transformed into a sacred arena for ritual performance—and this is precisely what the symbolists did. Emulating Greek, medieval, and Indian models, the turn-of-the-century playwrights made the theater a temple.[17]

And yet, despite these noble efforts, the question naturally arises: Is the occult per se theatrical or suited to visualization? Are the great mysteries too large or too small for the theater as we know it? Here matters of scale and focus become of central importance. Mystical experience takes place either deep within a single consciousness or far outside in the entire cosmos, in both cases leading to a fusion of individual and universal. Stéphane Mallarmé, the poetic presence behind French symbolist theater, recognized these two polar extremes, stating that the ideal drama would be either a vast spectacle of cosmic quest or a minimal presentation involving a single character engaged in soliloquy and mime.[18] The problem for the dramatist—as opposed to the poet or the

Mikalojus Čiurlionis's *Leo, Virgo, Libra,* and *Scorpio* (1907)—from the signs of the zodiac. This visionary Lithuanian artist Mikalojus Čiurlionis (1875-1911) was both a musician and a painter. At the same time that Andrei Bely was writing his four symphonies in rhythmic prose based on musical principles, Čiurlionis attempted to translate his musical ideas into colors and shapes, derived from the analogy of the seven colors of the solar spectrum with the seven tones of the chromatic scale.

novelist, whose imagination remains unfettered—is to find a stage where consciousness can meet cosmos and to escape from cagelike drawing rooms and box sets into a magical universe dominated by the four elements.

But the standard judgment has been that the stage is best suited to purely human interactions, whether personal or social, and inimical to the paranormal and extrarational. [19] For this reason, occult drama—when it is genuinely visionary in form and not simply imitative of traditional genres—inevitably seems odd in shape and lacking in proportion to the untrained eye. From the point of view of ordinary theatrical optics, plays in this mode are too long or too short, there is too much or too little action, and we are too close or too distant from the characters and events. The perspective is disturbing and incommensurate with accepted human dimensions.

Types of Occult Drama

If theatricalization of the unseen is the touchstone of occult drama, then we can discern three broad categories of mystical theater corresponding to the different areas in which the invisible forces are manifested: (1) dramas of eternal human consciousness, such as Maeterlinck produced in *The Interior* and *The Blind*; (2) dramas of cosmic consciousness, as envisaged by Scriabin in the *Mysterium*, with its choir of voices embodying Waves of Life, Awakening Feelings, Mountains, Sunbeam, Forest, and Desert; and (3) dramas of human and cosmic destiny seen in the workings of history—personal, national, or universal—as exemplified by works of Strindberg, Wyspiański, and Miciński. Although the boundaries between these groupings are neither clearly marked nor firmly established, such a rough schema will enable us to chart a typology of occult drama and isolate the unique characteristics of what is by far the least known and most complex species—the historical occult.

The Maeterlinckian Model of Interior Drama of Consciousness. The Maeterlinckian model of interior drama of consciousness takes one of two forms. In the first, revelation of the mysteries occurs in a contemporary setting within the sphere of daily life; in the second, otherworldly powers make themselves manifest in a removed universe of legend or myth. The two subspecies are nonetheless fundamentally alike in their concern with transcendent states of soul and their avoidance of practical mundane affairs.

In the first variety, of which Maeterlinck's *The Intruder* is a good example, an ordinary room with its human community is invaded by a stranger (in this case, death), who—unlike the intruder in realistic social drama—brings not a temporal secret from this world, but an eternal secret from the other world. Within familiar perspectives the old stage space— the drawing room—is made to bear the weigth of the cosmos and reverberate to its invisible forces. Behind banal surfaces there can be glimpsed

the outlines of an occult universe; the contemporary loses its particularized features and becomes transformed into a timeless realm.[20] In the
second variant, represented by *Pelléas and Mélisande*, no pretense as to
actual time or place is maintained. Instead we are transported out of the
present to time immemorial, usually a nebulous Middle Ages where an unearthly atmosphere prevails and invisible presences lurk in every shadow.

In both branches of the Maeterlinckian paradigm, the occult can be
disclosed in human life only to the degree that the arena of performance
moves away from the concrete and the historical toward a dim past or
idealized region. Here the unseen is theatricalized through vagueness and
imprecision, suggestion and removal, with heavy dependence on muted
lighting effects. Because of Maeterlinck's persuasive example, the mystical
quickly became associated with the murky. Symbolist playwrights in
France followed the Belgian master's practice of setting his dramas in ancient castle and shadowy medieval kingdoms. The note by the occult
theoretician and playwright Victor-Emile Michelet at the beginning of his
drama *The Knight Who Wore His Cross* could be used to characterize hundreds of such plays: "The action takes place—if you like—at an indeter-
minate period of the conventional Middle Ages as portrayed in the Chan-
sons de Gestes."[21] As a result of the wide dissemination of this model,
it has been assumed that all symbolist drama must flee the harsh light of
reality and take refuge in a never-never land of obscurity and gloom, thus
giving rise to the accusation—forcefully expressed by John Gassner—that "it is
against the nature of the theatre to exist in a mist and to thrive on vagueness. Drama and theatre are among the most definite of all the arts."[22]

Dramas of Cosmic Consciousness. Rejecting Maeterlinck as a guide,
the French musicologist and occult playwright Edouard Schuré—author
of studies of Wagner and an immensely influential and popular work on
mysticism, *The Great Initiates*—proposed a theoretic model for a universal cosmic drama based on the synthesis of all religions and not dissimi-
liar in spirit from Scriabin's *Mysterium*.[23] An initiatory and redemptive
drama, the "theatre of the soul" proposed by Schuré, should express
the harmony of "the entire religious traditions of East and West" and
demonstrate "the continuity of inspiration in history as an historical
fact."[24] By revealing the bonds between Visible and Invisible in the three
interrelated worlds of Nature, Soul, and Spirit (or the terrestrial, astral,
and divine), the occult dramatist will lead his audience to the door of
initiation and make the world beyond vividly perceptible.

Providing a reconstruction of the sacred drama of Eleusis—the
Hellenic version of the Christian fall and redemption—as the exemplar
of all mystery plays of death and rebirth, Schuré describes how the visionary playwright can dramatize the transmigrations of the soul, its
material incarnations, and earthly trials, preceding ultimate purification
and return to its heavenly home. The two movements of such a drama
are descent into the lower sphere of dense matter and ascent into the
spiritual realm, as Persephone—archetype of the human soul—regains her

position in the upper world. Because for the author of *The Great Initiates* "the theatre affords . . . the joy of metamorphosis and resurrection,"[25] it must present a positive and sympathetic visionary hero who not only seeks initiation, but who actually succeeds in opening the doors of the mystery. Accordingly, Schuré dismisses Maeterlinck's static theater, with its passive, terror-stricken characters, as an inadequate model for occult drama. A genuine pioneer, Maeterlinck has penetrated into the hidden world but wanders there in darkness without any sense of direction. "The occult, in Maeterlinck," Schuré writes, "does not serve to illumine life, it makes it still more incomprehensible."[26]

Schuré's critique of the Maeterlinckian paradigm is from an ideological point of view that proclaims the inevitable victory of the spirit and the transcendent power of spiritual love. But when we turn from the theory to the practice and look at the plays written in this cosmic mode, we find that for the most part such hierophantic dramas of the soul—whether Graeco-mythic or legendary-Christian—fail as theater (although they may be convincing as sacred pageants for true believers) precisely because they are doctrinal rather then poetic in origin. Often written by authors more immersed in the tenets of mysticism than in the imaginative life of drama, these occult thesis plays move too facilely to a preordained conclusion required by esoteric dogma. Anguish and horror can only be fleeting, for a definitive and triumphant solution must resolve all tensions, enlarge consciousness, and usher in a higher life. These initiatory spectacles tend to be little more than hymns of celebration, affirming the harmony of the universe and ending in a cosmic apotheosis that features celestial lights, music, and white-robed chanting figures with uplifted arms.

Two examples of doctrinally inspired cosmic drama should be enough to show the vastness of its aims and the monotonous emptiness of its form. In Fabre des Essart's *Christ the Savior*, "A Gnostic Drama in Three Days," the esoteric Christ preached by the Gnostics and Saint John confronts his enemy Satan, who offers temptations in the form of Spectres that disclose the future crimes of religious wars and inquisitions. After an Angel appears to announce that good as well as evil will result from Christianity, we witness Christ's triumph over Satan in a future earthly paradise, where, clothed in radiant white, all mankind lives in peace and harmony. Digging in the ground, small children unearth an old buried cannon, but no longer recognize what it is, and flowers have grown over the guillotine, fallen into eternal disuse. The City of God has been realized, and the divine millennium come. As Jesus pats the playing youngsters on the head, Mary Magdalene leads a penitent Satan to be forgiven.[27]

Even more grandiose in its effects is Vroncourt de la Ville's *The Mystery Play of Love*, "A Symbolic Hierodrama in Two Acts and Four Tableaux," presented in the style of the medieval revival. Complete with two Eves, the Virgin, Death, Adam, Lucifer, personified vices, and vast choruses, *The Mystery Play of Love* is a sacramental pageant, utilizing Franck's Symphony in D minor and calling for spectacular lighting, as the "Sym-

Mikalojus Čiurlionis's *Castle Fairy Tale* (1907). In his fantastic landscapes, Čiurlionis strove to create another world and a new cosmos. "I should like to create a symphony out of the sound of the waves, the mysterious language of a hundred-year-old forest, the twinkling of the stars, out of our songs and my boundless yearning," he said.

phonic Interlude" after the third tableau makes clear.

> While the two Eves remain locked in each other's arms in a
> mystical ecstasy, a flood tide mounts through the orchestra:
> it is the flood tide of Mercy and Love which invades the world:
> "the presence of God" appears in its most profound and mys-
> terious aspect. And it is like a torrent which sweeps away Evil,
> triumphing over Lucifer and the Vices. Then, an immense calm
> reigns, while up there, in the Heavens, the harmony of the
> movement of the stars resounds, joyous and sparkling. The en-
> tire Creation celebrates.[28]

Lofty in tone and predictable in outcome, ceremonial cosmic drama
looks toward a fixed past, not an uncertain future. Working with precon-
ceived patterns of action, rigidly archetypal characters, and traditional
imagery, the occult playwright in this mode can hardly avoid schematism,
formula, and allegory; the author must depend heavily on music and external elements of spectacle to produce a spiritually uplifting effect.[29]

Dramas of Human and Cosmic Destiny. The third of our paradigms,
the historical occult, offers the least abstract and conventionalized arena
for the theatricalization of the unseen—the stage of history with its inexhaustible supply of particularized character and event. Instead of turning back
to knights, princesses, and ruined castles in dark forests or to the bare
bones of primordial religious myth, the symbolist playwright can also
dramatize the occult in the workings of the historical process—as did
Strindberg with the everyday details of his own life, Wyspiański with the
November 1830 uprising, and Miciński with the revolution of 1905. In
the historical occult, the symbolist imagination ceases to operate in a
void or become an occasion for fleeing from reality and refusing to deal
with social and political issues—the most frequent charges made against
mystical theater. Instead of angelic choirs intoning hymns, historical
personages reenact desperate and violent deeds intractable to simplistic
allegorization, and archetypes are clothed not in white, but in unique
human shapes.

For example, Miciński's *Revolt of the Potemkin*, which deals with
the same events as Sergei Eisenstein's film, is both wildly visionary and
rigorously documentary. The Polish playwright invests with occult
significance realistic details taken from the widest range of sources: songs
of the period, eyewitness accounts of the Russo-Japanese war and Jewish
pogroms, Russian folklore, and newspaper articles, memoirs, and inter-
views on the subject of the mutiny. The antithetical, yet complementary
pair of Christ and Lucifer, who dominate Miciński's drama and give it a
metaphysical dimension, appear not as symbolic figures, but as two actual
Russian officers, Lieutenant Schmidt and Lieutenant Ton. Fusing rather
than opposing the temporal and the eternal, Miciński inscribes historical
time in mystical time; sanctified from the perspective of ultimate things,

contemporary history is raised to the level of myth.

Unlike the cosmic religious dramas in which there is no place for tragedy, the historical occult is permeated with unending tension between real and ideal, human and divine, good and evil. The raw materials of history abound in evidence of contradiction and failure and teach sobering lessons about man's quest for absolutes. The workings of invisible powers in history—whether they be personal, national, or world—bring humanity as much or more pain and torment as consolation and hope of salvation.

August Strindberg, who in fact was a practitioner of all three varieties of the historical occult,[30] can for our purposes be taken as the prime illustration of the psychological visionary, whose laboratory is his own experience in the everyday world—in what Evelyn Underhill calls the "borderland region where the mystical and the psychical meet."[31] In plays such as *To Damascus* and *There Are Crimes and Crimes*, Strindberg theatricalizes the unseen in contemporary daily life through intricate concatenations of events, which are interpreted as signs of the workings of a higher power. The Swedish playwright and occultist transcends the level of immediate reality and uncovers a secret dimension by suggesting mysterious rapports among ordinary happenings. Cause-and-effect plot is subordinated to symmetrical patterning of events, which the author-hero sees as a manifestation of the invisible forces directing his life. As Marcel Réja points out in his preface to the original French edition of *Inferno*, in rejecting causality in favor of coincidence, Strindberg violates common sense and the supposed logic of the theater based upon it. But whereas excessive use of coincidence is regarded as a flaw in all modes of realistic drama, it becomes a crucial device in occult drama.[32]

The two remaining categories of the historical occult, the national and the world, are in many ways similar in form and technique, although different in subject matter. Wyspiański's plays on Polish themes are examples of the former, dealing as they do with questions of national destiny, whereas Miciński's *Potemkin* and *Basilissa*, devoted to significant moments in European history, serve as illustrations of the latter. Together with Bely's apocalyptical dramas, these works are unusually rich in innovative stagecraft and theatrical conception, and it is now time that we turn from classification of types of turn-of-the-century occult drama to specific matters of poetics.

Magical Space

In genuinely visionary drama, the stage becomes neither an imitation of the external world nor a conventional playing area but sacerdotal space, within which the cosmos—or representation of it—is created and structured anew. An extension of the human mind, such invented space is magical, fluid, multilayered, with tendencies to expansion and contraction, existing along shifting planes, given to undulation and pulsation, drawing near and then pulling away. In apparent violation of the law of the theater that mandates only one unchanging point of observation between spectator and presented reality, magical space can accommodate close-ups and long shots at one and the same time, as well as two or more simultaneous actions, as in film or medieval mystery plays. A sudden internal vision, revealing the creative powers of an individual soul, may engulf the stage, as boundaries between subjective and objective are removed and the "I" fills the entire external world.[33]

Take, for example, the mystical fifth act of *The Revolt of the Potemkin*, in which, by a sudden change in perspective offering glimpses of another world, the leaders of the mutiny and crew of the battleship are seen against a cosmic landscape beyond time and space—a device first introduced by Strindberg at the end of *The Dream Play* and *The Ghost Sonata*. Mysteriously transported to a "reef in the midst of the sea which in the darkness glows phosphorescently throughout its blue depths," the epileptic, Christlike hero, Schmidt—clinging to a rock surrounded by strange sea monsters—describes his vision of a Tibetan journey to the mountain temples and holy places. As he speaks, mirages of the giant Himalayas rise up from the sea, the sacred city of Lhasa with its Golden Palaces can be seen, and the ghost of the infant Dalai Lama appears.

Against this background of eternity, the bloody searchlights of the battleship struggle to cut through the darkness, but the *Potemkin* seems to be heading straight for the reef—until at the last moment, saved by the mystic light emanating from the Dalai Lama, the phantom ship glides safely past and continues on its eternal wanderings. Sacral place in Miciński's dramas provides a multidimensional playing arena stretching from the depths of the sea to the highest mountain peaks, from the abysses to the heights, from the kingdom of darkness to the realm of light. On such a magical stage, natural and supernatural worlds intersect and merge.

In the *Shades of the Golden Palace, or Basilissa Teophano*—Miciński's world-historical drama about tenth-century Byzantium, the decline of the empire, and the growing strength of Russia—has dazzling Near Eastern settings, in which each architectural detail is endowed with occult iconographic significance. The interior of Basilissa's palace recalls the brilliant jeweled surface of Gustave Moreau's paintings of Salome at Herod's court.

> *The curtains around the throne are drawn aside. Teophano's radiant face gleams amidst exotic plants; on her head, the mystical city of Lucifer. Like the phosphorescent sea in its murky azure depths, she is immobile, sparkling, with her eyes fixed on distant worlds. She stops by the Basileus's throne and hands him a lotus—then still radiant, she ascends her nearby throne in the shape of a comet made of black agate, amethysts, and topazes; at her feet, steps of priceless black marble, mottled with reddish veins and known as sangarius. A group of priests fan the*

Mikhail Vrubel's *Head of Demon* (1890). Inspired by Lermontov's poem *The Demon,*
Mikhail Vrubel' (1856–1910) made a whole series of visual representations of a brood-
ing, melancholy demon figure with tragic staring eyes. Vrubel', who went mad in
1902, described this demonic image, which came to haunt him, as "a spirit that unites
in itself the male and female appearances, a spirit that is not so much evil as suffering
and wounded, but withal a powerful and noble being."

flames in censers. Black Hindu princesses kneel on the steps,
holding symbols of deities in their hands.[34]

Every scene in *Basilissa Teophano* has as its setting a sacral place
where a cult is celebrated: the Myriandrion Church in Constantinople,
Priapus' Temple, the Palace of Hades in Syria, and, above all, Teophano's
Golden Palace, a vast and mysterious architectural labyrinth. Through
its doors, thresholds, gates, and circular chambers, Miciński's heroes must
pass on their way to glittering cities made of precious minerals. Surrounded by the infinite sea, whose ever-varied sounds are heard throughout the play, the Basilissa's temple has myriads of steps leading down to
dark underground worlds (which have their counterpart aboard the *Potemkin* in the ship's infernal engine and boiler rooms). All matter is alive.

> *The mountains lurk in the darkness.... The stormy wild sea*
> *howls. On a rock very high to the right, the gate of a monas-*
> *tery, above it a black Greek cross. The steps are made out of*
> *rock. Caves, or prisons with bars over the entrances ... A dark*
> *hole in the soil, indicating the proximity of volcanoes.*[35]

By bringing directly on stage sea, mountains, holy places, the four
elements and their transformations, and all manner of minerals (symboliz-
ing artistic creativity and hidden layers of the human psyche), Miciński
creates an occult universe vibrant with the unknown and unknowable
and light years distant from the stuffy drawing rooms of realistic drama.[36]

Visionary Stage Directions

In striking contrast to the practical-minded nineteenth-century playwright like Tom Robertson, who indicated precisely how his famous comedy, *Caste*, was to be performed at the Prince of Wales' Theatre in 1867
by means of stage directions, such as "Bureau, in lower right-hand corner,"
"Crosses to fireplace," and "With elbow on end of mantel-piece, down
stage," the turn-of-the-century occult dramatist in Eastern Europe, who
rarely had an opportunity to see his own plays staged, most often dis-
played a sovereign disregard for all the pragmatic details of scenic realization. And yet at the same time Miciński, along with many of the other
symbolists, does provide extensive stage directions, which are poetically
precise and dramatically essential to the effect of his plays but seem incapable of translation into theatrical terms. For example, the Polish playwright creates a fascinating occult scenario for the following action that
takes place on the deck of the *Potemkin* a few minutes before the mutiny,
but he fails to give any information about how to stage it.

(And suddenly the sun, a new God, beams forth. The golden

*sunbeams are reflected in Wilhelm Ton's eyes, and he tries to
keep his gaze fixed directly on the Unearthly Beyond. His face
assumes an expression of cold, satanic pain, a crown of thorns
stands out quite clearly from the veins on his forehead. But
God stands close by his side. He encircles Wilhelm Ton with the
sky, throws a sheaf of symphonies at his feet—a gigantic Golden
Cross grows in place of the mast. Stepping back, Wilhelm Ton
leans against the gun carriage with his elbow, and calmly looks
at the Vision.)*

WILHELM TON. Oh, Sun, do you wish to transform me into
Paul of Damascus?

*(And Christ, who has thrown himself beneath the wheels of the
cannon, looks up into Wilhelm Ton's eyes and smiles sorrow-
fully—and now it is apparent that it is not Christ, but a woman's
face, plain, exhausted, ghastly pale, with a mystic crown in the
shape of a stonecrop.)*

How, we may ask, are these breathtaking metamorphoses to be presented on stage in the midst of a drama that is to a large extent documentary, sharply focused at an exact moment in history and utilizing the actual words and deeds of historical figures? Leon Schiller, the outstanding
Polish director between two world wars, who successfully brought Miciński's *Potemkin* to the stage in 1926, suggests a way of approaching this
problem; of such anomalous works Schiller declared that their "scenic
shape was a mystery for the authors themselves."[37] For the occult dramatist's imagination to outrun his power of physical realization can hardly
be regarded as a fault, for his very goal is the creation of mysteries. Just
as esoteric theater strives to go beyond the visible world of everyday
reality, so it endeavors to transcend the material limits of the stage.

In pushing dramaturgy beyond the confines of what was considered
possible in the theater of his time, the symbolist playwright like Miciński
pointed the way ahead to an unknown future. Actual realization could
come only a number of years later when notions of the stage and of stagecraft had been enlarged—in part owing to just such pioneering works.
Visionary stage directions are not blueprints for scenic construction or
commands to the director as to how to mount the play—they are appeals
to the imagination, guiding the eye of the beholder like a camera so that
new perceptions are possible. Neither purely theatrical nor purely literary,
visionary stage directions mediate between actual and eventual, real and
ideal, known and unknown; they can serve as inspiration to stage designer
and director, proposing the sort of effect to be produced in the theater,
not the means of achieving it.

The Apocalyptic Mode and the Terror of History

Because of its obsessive concern with ultimate things and historical moments of epochal transformations, Polish and Russian occult drama at the turn of the century was predominantly eschatological—and in this respect it proved an accurate reflection of the spirit of the age. As the czarist empire started to crumble and the first tremors made themselves felt throughout Eastern Europe, apocalypse suddenly seemed immanent in contemporary history, and the Book of Revelation became the basic text of the times. Overwhelmed by a sense of impending catastrophe, preachers of the coming end rose up in all classes of Russian society. The religious philosopher Nicolas Berdyaev has stressed that the approaching millennium was an integral part of Russian popular thought and that the eschatological mentality was a national phenomenon.

> Towards the end of the nineteenth century there developed in Russia an apocalyptic frame of mind which was connected with a sense of the approach of the end of the world and the appearance of the antichrist.[38]

It made little difference whether the millennium would be social, political, or theocratic; the religious and the revolutionary terminology was all the same. Even the historical events of the revolution of 1905 were viewed as fulfilling Biblical prophecies and interpreted in the light of the apocalyptic symbolism; and the imagery, dramatic properties, and stage effects of the New Testament Apocalypse were read into the catastrophic events of the time.[39]

Anticipation of such a spectacular denouement on the world stage could not fail to have repercussions on occult drama. In *The Revolt of the Potemkin*, Miciński dramatized prevailing attitudes toward apocalypse, which effectively bridged the gap between the documentary and the cosmic dimensions of the play. In positing the rapidly approaching end of human history, the eschatological sensibility reunites the temporal with the eternal. Doomsday—an inherently theatrical event—imparts an atmosphere of expectancy and sense of urgency to Eastern European visionary drama; eschatological tension mounts, as the feared, yet longed for event draws near but does not come. Waiting for the Antichrist and the apocalypse is the subject of a number of Russian and Polish plays, including those of Bely, and, most significantly, the act of waiting itself—often for something or someone who nevers appears—becomes a major thematic and structural motif.[40]

Millennarian and chiliastic plays also existed within the French symbolist canon, but because of the attenuated historical consciousness of the Maeterlinck school, which looked nostalgically backwards toward an idealized past, these pseudomedieval mysteries are not genuinely eschatological in that they do not treat the apocalypse as an actual historical event still to come, but simply as a charming legend within an already completed cycle of human culture. Products of a stable bourgeois society that venerate progress and civilization, these Western symbolists could not believe in the imminent destruction of the world, except as a poetic fiction safely located several centuries earlier; unlike their Eastern European counterparts, who were living through the violent and hysterical death throes of a tottering *ancien régime*, they had never known what Mircea Eliade calls the "terror of history" that gives rise to the millennarian movements and apocalyptic visions.[41]   In the preface to his chiliastic play, *The Year 1,000*, the French author Emile Gabory voices the characteristic Western European dichotomy between eschatological myth and modern history.

> History, in our epoch, based on the study of learnedly filtered
> sources, has dethroned legend. It is sometimes a misfortune for
> the Idea. If history has the cold and mathematical rigor of
> science, legend has the golden wings of poetry. The one is the
> daughter of modern times, argumentative and sceptical; the
> other, contemporary with the events, has traversed the ages,
> idealized by the naïve and fertile imagination of our fathers.[42]

Explaining that only a handful of millennarians actually believed that the world would come to an end in the year 1,000, on the basis of a faulty interpretation of a passage in Revelation, Gabory concludes that the apocalypse is only a fable, which, however, can serve as a dramatic subject, his own quasi-allegorical play set in a stylized Middle Ages being one such example.

In Russia, on the contrary, important thinkers, such as Vladimir Solovyov in *A Short Tale about Antichrist*, quite seriously predicted the end of the world and described the coming of the Antichrist—sometimes perceived as the importation of Western civilization and bourgeois capitalism—to be followed by the New Jerusalem, or a social Utopia achieved after bloody revolution and chaos.[43]   Parenthetically, it should be noted that among late nineteenth-century French symbolists, only Alfred Jarry was a true eschatologist; by the initial placement of *Ubu Roi* in the third act of his apocalyptic *Caesar Antichrist*, Jarry shows that he regards Ubu and his bourgeois reign of terror as a contemporary manifestation of the Antichrist in history.[44]

Andrei Bely, the chief Russian representative of the apocalyptic mode, conceived his *Antichrist* in 1898, anticipating by two years Solovyov's work. The only two fragments of Bely's projected mystery ever written—*Jaws of Night* and *He Who Has Come*—have as their theme "the coming of the Antichrist under the mask of Christ."[45]   Although Bely's apocalypse is set in the early Christian period, its portrayal of spiritual confusion, hearkening unto false prophets, and feverish expectation of the end are direct reflections of the apocalyptic temper of the poet's own times. A seismographic recorder of turn-of-the-century cataclysms in the individual, collective, and cosmic spheres, Bely declared that "the gulf over which we are hanging is deeper and darker than we think," and his Antichrist plays are modern dramas of the abyss.[46]

In *Jaws of Night* and *He Who Has Come*, the entire universe—heavens above, hell below, earth posed precariously between—grows animate. Scenic images of constellations and comets, sky, surf, wind, precious stones, and flowers—along with sudden bursts of light creating strange, momentary epiphanies—express psychic states of spiritual illumination and its terrifying opposite, deprivation of divine light. Through multimedia techniques, Bely evokes a cosmic awareness—both the wonder and the dread—of the boundless expanses of the universe, comparable to that found in Scriabin's later music and in Mikhail Vrubel's many paintings and drawings of the Demon (based on Lermontov's narrative poem).[47] Except for interminable waiting for a redeemer—who may be no redeemer, who may never come, who may already have come unnoticed—Bely's plays have no action other than the symphony of shapes, colors, and sounds that constitutes their magical poetic texture—as is effectively illustrated by the opening of *He Who Has Come*.

> *The stage represents a small enclosed arena surrounded by sheer black cliffs, as though made of labradorite, which give off a greenish-blue glow. Amidst the cliffs there is a barely visible path with steps carved in the rock. From beyond the cliffs the two golden domes of the Temple of Glory shine. To the right of the spectators, the arena comes to an end with the seashore, for the sound of the surf can be heard, and a huge rock in lonely isolation protrudes onto the arena, evidently cast there by a storm. To the right also, between the black cliff and the sea there is a passageway. In this passageway the golden heavens are visible. Still higher it is azure. Amid the pale satin azure, a comet is etched with misty contours, although it is still day. Its tail blends with the sky.*
>
> *The rays of the sun flood the area with their amber-golden light. Soon the rays of the sun begin to pour off with an amber pink. Up to the rising of the curtain, singing is heard, which soon dies out somewhere in the distance, although a far-off echo of songs, like a sigh made by the breeze, carries through the silence. Mikhail and Sergei, two disciples of those awaiting the end, stand in long yellowish white clothes, facing one another against the background. Their long russet curls fall over their shoulders.*

Here the setting and spectacle are the drama itself, not separate elements detachable from it. Throughout the play this brilliant and dynamic picture of apocalyptic expectancy will glow and pulsate at different levels

Mikalojus Čiurlionis's *Rex* (1909). Čiurlionis talked of "painting" his sonatas and called his exhibits "concerts" in an effort to synthesize the arts. In 1910 he suffered a mental breakdown and in 1911 at the age of 35 died in a psychiatric clinic near Warsaw.

of intensity; Bely has found a pictorial equivalent of the eschatological sensibility.

Science Fiction and Apocalypse

In *New Worlds for Old*, David Ketterer argues that "the apocalyptic imagination . . . finds its purest outlet in science fiction," maintaining that "religion, mysticism, and science fiction concern themselves—in different ways, to be sure—with the same ground, the unknown. The shared object of desire is the revelation of a genuine, hitherto hidden, reality."[48] We should not, therefore, be surprised to find a variety of apocalyptic drama, futurological and cautionary in nature, that deals with the extinction of life on earth owing to a great catastrophe brought about by innovations in science or technology.

An important turn-of-the-century example is Valerii Briusov's *The Earth*, subtitled "A Tragedy of Future Times," first conceived in 1890 and completed in 1904, which depicts the self-destruction of advanced technological civilization after mankind has cut itself off from the natural world and radically transformed the human environment by creating a huge enclosed city with a special roof that blocks out the sky and air.[49] One of the strange sects to spring up in this sterile, artificial atmosphere is the Order of Deliverers, who worship death and darkness, thereby hoping to free humanity from the scourge of life and all its earthly passions. Led by the Sage, a rival group urges a return to the sun and stars that must inevitably shine above the black dome that shuts them in. Aspiring to restore man to his rightful place in the universe, the Sage actually brings about the apocalypse when he orders the dome to be slid back; the blazing light of the sun kills all the inhabitants of the city within a few minutes. In the final moments of the play, as the antiseptic lid is about to be rolled open, Teotl, leader of the Order of Deliverers, addresses the terrified crowd.

> TEOTL. On your knees, all you people! Pray! Pray! Pray to Death That Approaches! The deliverance of the entire earth will be accomplished in one moment! There will be no more sorrow, no more desire, no more horror, no more illusory bliss. All you people, you are worthy of your ancestors! At one blow you are destroying yourselves and all future generations as well. Soon, oh, soon there will be nothing left here! No great thoughts, no creative achievements, no wild passions! Nothing! Nothing! Nothing!
>
> YOUNG MAN *(in ecstasy, in an exultant tone of voice, at the sound of which some people turn around).* You are mistaken, Teotl! We are not the last humans left! There are other halls down here! True humanity lives there! Life on

Alberto Martini's *The Destruction of the Earth* (1910). Martini's illustration of the last scene of Valerii Briusov's drama *The Earth* shows the apocalyptic end of mankind. Influenced by Dürer and Cranach as well as by Moreau and Redon, Alberto Martini (1876–1954) was the most important illustrator and engraver working in the symbolist tradition. His fantastic, macabre, and grotesque engravings portray the most terrifying aspects of an hallucinatory and invisible universe, as in his long series of dramatic illustrations for Poe's stories.

this earth has been entrusted to it! It will represent the
Earth before the Creator. And as for us—we are just a
wretched mob who have gone astray in these dark halls, like
a branch cut off from its stem. Let us perish so that the
Earth can remain alive!

*(With a cracking noise, the dome swings open. A beam of sun-
light floods the hall. Total silence.)*

FIRST MAN. I'm going blind!
SECOND MAN. It is a fiery angel blowing his golden trumpet!
SOMEONE IN THE CROWD. Oh, Lord! Lord of our fathers!
ALMOST EVERYONE. Teach us how to pray, oh, Lord!
TEOTL *(in a suppliant tone of voice).* I see your commanding
    face, oh, Death! . . . Oh, Sun! Sun! Your rays will never pierce
    through the darkness into which I am plunging!

*(He staggers, clutching his breast. Many people start to moan.
And then in a wild frenzy, they all get up off their knees. They try
to shout, but their voices fail them. Others laugh dementedly.
Throwing their arms around one another, they convulsively embrace their neighbors. Teotl continues to bless the crowd.
Then he falls down, and slowly, very slowly, the entire hall,
now silenced, turns into a cemetery of motionless wizened
bodies upon which there shines through the open dome the
deep sky and, like an angel blowing a golden trumpet, the blazing sun. . .)*

The symbolist critic Ellis, who considered the play Briusov's masterpiece and a great philosophical drama in a class with Goethe's *Faust*,
points out that *The Earth* is based on Plato's allegory of the cave, the
Egyptian Book of the Dead, and the Assyrian cosmological myths and
rituals.[50]

Coincidentia Oppositorum

The apocalypse awaited by the Russian and Polish symbolists was ex-
pected to bring not only the end of the old world but also the beginning
of the new age—in Mircea Eliade's words, "the end of one humanity, followed by the apparition of a new humanity."[51] By its very nature the
turn of the century points in two different directions, and the apocalyptic
syndrome with its cycle of birth, death, and resurrection is dualistic. Bely
described the sense of eschatological tension felt by members of his generation in the following terms: "The failure of the old ways is experienced
as the End of the World; the tidings of the new era—as the Second Coming.

We sensed the apocalyptic rhythm of the time. Towards the Beginning we strive through the end."[52] It is only natural that the apocalyptic occult dramatists at the fin de siècle, caught between two epochs at the point where past and future intersect, should make extensive use of dualistic and antithetical pairs, such as Christ and Antichrist, light and dark, heights and depths (found throughout the Book of Revelation) and strive for unity of polar opposites.

What the great fifteenth-century mystic, churchman, philosopher, mathematician, and political theorist, Nicholas of Cusa, called *coincidentia oppositorum* (or union of contraries in God) became an essential technique of turn-of-the-century occult dramatists, whereby the mystery of totality finds affirmation and "ultimate reality is defined by pairs of opposites."[53] The plays of Bely and Miciński are structured dualistically through the use of striking iconographic extremes in setting, character, and situation. Instead of the optimistic and univocal denouements that render doctrinal cosmic drama flabby, unresolved tension is maintained throughout these Russian and Polish works by ambivalence between paired antipodal possibilities.[54]

Sharing Heraclitus' notion that all things carry with them their opposite, Bely in his *Antichrist* plays penetrates to the primordial state in which contraries exist as complementary aspects of a single reality. Viewed with metaphysical irony, cosmos and chaos, creation and destruction, Christ and Antichrist are seen as inseparably linked and even indistinguishable at times. In *He Who Has Come*, members of the commune awaiting the end fall into dissension as to whether "He Who Has Come" is Christ or Antichrist; and although the prophet Ilya declares that the millennium has already begun, life goes on as before and the waiting continues. In *Jaws of Night*, the saintly old prophet with luminous clothes and electrically charged hair may actually be an evil magician, preaching a false messiah and luring the children to night and death.

Following the Gnostic myth that God and the Devil are blood brothers, Micinski in *The Revolt of the Potemkin* develops the *coincidentia oppositorum*, central to all his work, that Lucifer—"the elder brother of Christ in his pre-eternal existence"—must complete what God alone could not successfully accomplish.[55] In turn-of-the-century eschatology, as God ceased to be regarded as the judge and became the accused, going on trial for having created an unhappy and destructive race of men, Lucifer was rehabilitated as the champion of poor and downtrodden humanity.[56] Like Prometheus, Miciński's revolutionary Lucifer—embodied in the nihilistic Lieutenant Ton—identifies with human misery and challenges God in the hopes of destroying his imperfect creation and building a new earthly paradise free from suffering. Master only of the material world and its knowledge, acting not out of love, but will to power, the Luciferian Ton (a direct descendent of Dostoevsky's Ivan Karamazov and Kirillov) brings only disaster with his utopian schemes. To create a new world, the wisdom and energy of Lucifer must be combined with the faith of Christ in a synthesis of two opposite, yet complementary forces within man.[57]

Like the rotten meat served to the sailors and the entire rotten *ancien régime*, the human condition itself—as portrayed in *The Revolt of the Potemkin*—is subject to decay, disease, and death unless it is redeemed by a transcendent spiritual goal. In the Walpurgis Night of Act III, during which Odessa is looted and burned, Miciński presents the grotesque underside of the revolutionary saga—a polar opposite of divine aspiration—in the form of the Putrescent Man in the Garbage Can (half a century before Beckett's *Endgame*), the Syphilitic Madonna, and the Unknown Figure proclaiming his vision of a world ruled over by microbes. Lucifer curses and longs for God, rebels and creates the darkness that will lead men back to Christ's light.

Everywhere in Miciński's *Potemkin*, the informing principle is *coincidentia oppositorum*. Responsible for consuming the old port, the fire—associated with apocalypse—is a self-immolating conflagration that annihilates and purifies at the same time. The sea—symbol of life and death, as well as of the strength and desolation of the soul—is *mare tenebrarum* (sea of darkness), the flood that devours and the flood that renews.[58] Ever-present are contradictory aspects, both creative and destructive, of the mysterious elements and powers active in the universe, as the phantom ship of the soul passes by on its endless journey.

Mythic Incarnations and Historical Syncretism

The opposition between legend and history felt by Western European authors ceases to exist in the dramas of the Polish symbolists. For Stanisław Wyspiański, obsessed with national issues, ancient Greek mythology comes to life in Polish history. The myth which Wyspiański's Polish heroes embody is not known to them in advance; it is only by acting out the time-honored story that they gradually become modern incarnations of legend. The myth lives again through their deeds. Wyspiański's characters are not abstract archetypes; rather, as historical figures participating in a ritual experience, they become initiates in an action that acquires its significance once it is sanctified by being raised to the level of myth.

Wyspiański's drama about the first great Polish uprising against czarist oppression, *November Night*, takes place at a precise historical place and hour—Warsaw on the night of November 29, 1830—with a cast of characters, including Grand Duke Constantine, Governor General of Poland, and members of the Cadets Corps who led the rebellion; and yet at the same time the events of the insurrection are presented within the eternal context of the ancient myth of Demeter and Persephone, advocated by Schuré as the essential sacred drama. Through juxtaposition and synchronism, the nineteenth-century Polish soldiers become Greek warriors, playthings in the hands of Homeric gods, and the 1830 uprising turns into an Eleusinian mystery of vegetation.[59]

Mikhail Vrubel's *Head of a Prophet* (1904). A visionary artist drawn to the mysterious world of legend and fairy tale, Vrubel' was deeply influenced by Byzantine art, worked in mosaics and icons, and undertook reconstructions of medieval frescoes. In all his art, Vrubel' created a strange vision of a second, higher reality.

The moment is night, a magical time of dreams, memories, and associations reaching back to roots of human consciousness, and the principal place, to which the action constantly returns, is a windswept autumnal park, where the conspirators meet to begin their ill-fated revolt. In this elemental setting, dead leaves—a classic symbolist motif introduced by Maeterlinck, but here put to startling new use—swirl under the feet of the doomed officers who will win no other laurels.[60] At the same time, the gloomy park becomes the borderland between Earth and Hades where the goddess Demeter says farewell to her daughter, Persephone, who every year must descend into the underworld—only to return each spring, bringing hope of deliverance from pain and death. As the immortals converse, the two dialogues—human and divine—become intercut, the Polish cadets taking up the words of the mythic litany without realizing that they are entering into the occult world and reenacting the Eleusinian rites. The seasonal death of nature (and its longed-for resurrection)—embodied in the withered leaves—is the eternal mystery confronting the officers who await their destiny in the autumnal park.

In Wyspiański's visionary mythopoetic awareness, past times and present times, Greek myth and modern history coexist in an eternal moment. Seeing the entire world and its history as a whole, rather than scientifically compartmentalized, the occult playwright is able to make daring leaps and surprising linkages that open unexpected theatrical vistas and free the stage from the bounds of time and space. In a second drama of death and rebirth, *Acropolis* (written in 1903, but not performed in its original form until 1926), Wyspiański fashions a syncretism of Judaic, Greek, and Christian religious mythology through a series of correspondences—a central device of symbolist poetics—whereby the Old Testament, Homer, and Polish history are fused.[61]

By setting *Acropolis* in the royal castle and cathedral of Wawel overlooking the city of Cracow and the river Vistula, Wyspiański, who had a double vocation as painter and playwright, was able to make the entire action of the drama grow out of visual images associated with the sacral place. Instead of human characters (none ever appears in the work), sculptured figures in wood and marble from the cathedral architecture and heroes woven on tapestries depicting scenes from the Bible and from Homer come to life and reenact their eternal stories at the magical hour of midnight preceding Easter Sunday. Utilizing the syncretic theory advanced by Schuré that all known religions contain one and the same esoteric doctrine, Wyspiański links Easter to pagan rites of seasonal renewal and the primordial rhythms of nature. By occult analogue, Poland is the living Troy, Wawel becomes the Acropolis on the holy hill of Athens, and the sacred rivers Jordan and Scamander flow again in waters of the Vistula. Resurrection, awaited as a spiritual, biological, and national event, comes in an apocalyptic ending, when, amidst thunder and the extinction of the old world, a luminous Christ-Apollo appears at dawn in the chariot of the sun drawn by four white horses to the pealing of the cathedral bells.[62]

Black Occultism and the Demonic Universe

So far in our charting of the range of occult drama at the turn of the century, we have dealt only with models that portray ascending spiritual quests, no matter how doubtful or ambiguous their outcomes may be. A final paradigm remains to be discussed—the Satanic occult—a flamboyant subgenre that shows the purely negative impact commerce with the unknown can have on certain human psyches.

One of the great fascinations that esoteric lore held for fin-de-siècle writers lay in its cult of black magic, demonology, Satan worship, vampirism, and sacrilege—themes first popularized in French poetry of the 1880s and then quickly taken over by fiction and drama.[63] In the years around 1900 Satanism became a European craze, promulgated from Spain to Poland and Russia.[64] One popular theatrical variant, inspired by Huysmans's *Là-Bas* and the contemporary vogue for blasphemous ceremonies, was the black mass play. Designed to shock and titillate, these pornographic dramas are only pseudo-occult travesties of the genuinely demonic, cleverly exploited for profit.

Consider, for example, Roland Brevannes's *Black Masses*, presented at the Théâtre de la Bodinière in 1904, which in a series of sensational tableaux presents infernal practices down the ages. In Part I, The Black Mass in the Middle Ages, we watch the notorious Gilles de Rais (Bluebeard) practicing alchemy in his laboratory and longing for more little boys and girls to torture; the height of pleasure, he says, would be "to caress a woman with hands reddened in her child's blood." During a witches' Sabbath in a graveyard while a frightful storm rages, a beautiful young sorceress removes all her clothes, setting in motion an abandoned orgy in which male and female sorcerers, demons, and monstrous animals all rub against the phallic black goat and couple on the ground. Part II, the Black Mass in the Age of Louis XIV, is celebrated by the evil Abbé Guiborg on the bare torso of Madame de Montespan. In the third and final section of the drama, the Black Mass in the Twentieth Century, at a private party given by Axel Wartz, decadent young men lounge on tiger skins, embrace, and crown one another with roses. The author himself views the supposedly infernal proceedings with irony, as can be seen from the comic denouement when the Prefect of Police arrives and demands to know what is going on.

> AXEL. We were getting ready to celebrate a modernized black mass.
> PREFECT OF POLICE. In the Middle Ages that would have warranted burning at the stake; under Louis XIV, exile or the Bastille.

Stanisław Wyspiański's *The Eleusinian Mysteries* (1892). Poet, painter, playwright, book illustrator, and maker of stained-glass windows, Stanisław Wyspiański (1869–1907) studied in Paris in the early 1890s. In 1892, under Edouard Schuré's influence, Wyspiański did a sketch for a theater curtain in Cracow, which he submitted for a competition, plus two pastels to serve as part of a triptych. The theme is the Eleusinian mysteries as described by Schuré in *The Great Initiates,* the seasonal myth of death and resurrection about Demeter and her daughter, Persephone, abducted by Hades.

Stanisław Wyspiański's *Fire* and *Air* (1897). Wyspiański's drawings of *Fire* and *Air* (from *The Four Elements,* 1897, in crayon) reveal the artist's ability to animate the cosmic forces that direct human life.

AXEL. And nowadays?

PREFECT OF POLICE. I'm a good devil; permit me to see the show.

AXEL. Let the festivities continue![65]

In his brochure *Sadism, Satanism, and Gnosis,* the occultist Fabre des Essarts points out that Satanism—once a tragic protest against the iniquities of God's created universe (as in Miciński's Luciferianism)—has degenerated into lascivious farce or elegant, aesthetic pornography.[66] After 1900, at least in France, Satanism is little more than an excuse for public nudity, and the devil becomes a character in vaudeville or opera, until the macabre reality of World War I brings to an end the fashion for demonic make-believe.[67]

A far different form of black occult drama is represented by Stanisław Przybyszewski's dramatic epilogue in one act, *Visitors,* which we offer as a fitting epilogue to this study.[68] In the truly demonic universe of *Visitors,* man is in the clutches of unseen diabolic forces, which first awaken him to a consciousness of evil and then drive him to suicide as the only way out of a hopeless dilemma. As portrayed in Przybyszewski's dark and sinister drama, human nature appears to be the creation of a wily Satanic spirit hostile to Adam-Everyman, who is guilty without even knowing why, simply for following the promptings of his heart. *Visitors* dramatizes a frightening personal apocalypse that becomes cosmic in implication, for the microcosmic individual psyche and timeless realm of the unconscious are expressive of the larger universe ruled over by fiendish powers.

In 1899, Przybyszewski read a lecture, entitled "The Mystical in Maeterlinck," after the first Cracow performance of *The Interior.* Written not long afterwards, *Visitors* is an inner drama that undoubtedly reflects the influence of the Belgian playwright, even though Przybyszewski was no admirer of Maeterlinck's dramatic vision or style. Depicting—as did Maeterlinck—the unknown forces within man that act as a palpable fatality, the Polish dramatist sought to penetrate deeper and find an innovative theatrical form capable of expressing the naked soul—outside time, independent of environment, beyond experience and reality. A remarkable anticipation of depth psychology in its embodiment of what Jung would call the shadow and R. D. Laing the divided self, *Visitors* avoids all discursive analysis and renders in vivid theatrical shapes the indefinable atmosphere of anxiety generated by an hysterically obsessed psyche.[69]

Like "The Dance of Life" and other paintings and engravings done by Przybyszewski's friend Edvard Munch at this same period, *Visitors* projects a world of eros and guilt against a stark, empty background dominated by primal imagery of earth, water, sun, moon, and mountains. Instead of serving as a healing power to soothe disordered passions, the the music for the ball in the mansion of the soul is a cacophonous dance of death futilely employed to drown out and deaden the painful voice of conscience that torments its owner. Not only the music, but the entire

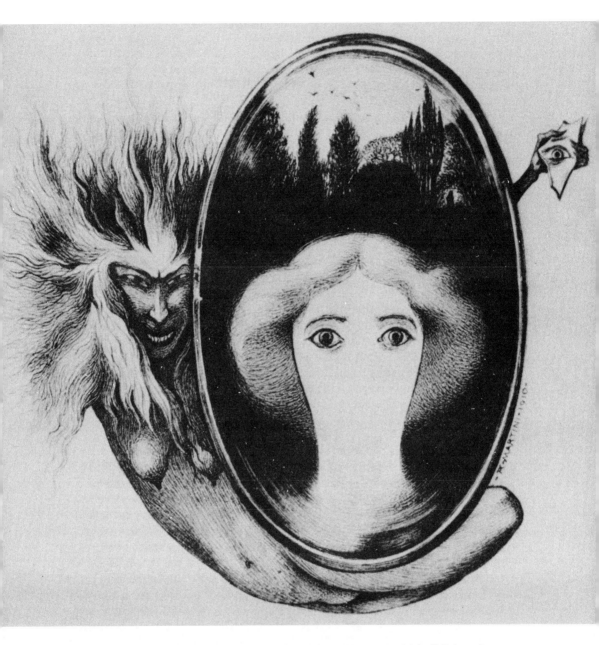

Alberto Martini's *In the Mirror* (1910). Martini's illustration for Valerii Briusov's story *The Mirror* (1910) represents a demonic rendering of the theme of the double.

orchestration of sounds—Adam's sardonic laugh, the Visitor's infernal chuckle, the Stranger's convulsive giggle, the dry cackling of the Old Men, the gasps and sighs of Pola and Bela, and the uneasy murmurs from the couples in the mansion—create a hellish vocalization of the demonic universe. Przybyszewski's occult drama moves not toward spiritual illumination, but total darkness, as all the lights in the house of the psyche are forever extinguished.

An original variation on the dual themes of the double and the shadow, which were often combined in nineteenth-century fantastic fiction, *Visitors* externalizes Adam's shadow as an astral or phantom double that has become detached from his body, only to reappear when the moment of his death draws near.[70] In occult doctrine, demonic apparitions, phantoms, ghosts, and doubles correspond to the real beings that inhabit the astral or lower plane of the invisible world. Returning to the source of its being, the shadow now exacts revenge on the creature who once had projected it. Hating and fearing his divided self, which he has attempted to repress and destroy, Adam must now confront himself, as his life, his marriage, and his psyche come to pieces.[71]

The paranoia of the persecuting double, so forcefully portrayed in *Visitors*, calls to mind Przybyszewski's onetime friend, August Strindberg, who during the Inferno crisis (1894-1897) came to regard the Polish Satanist as his deadliest enemy, intent on destroying him. Identifying with the terrifying Przybyszewski, whom he regarded as the personification of his own guilty conscience, the Swedish author—like Adam in *Visitors*—experienced premonitions of disaster, torment for imagined sins, and sensations of suffocation, as his hated other self drove him relentlessly to suicide. Victim of an astral double existence comparable to Adam's relationship to the Visitor, Strindberg in his descent into an inferno of madness and despair, maintained that "happiness must be punished," feeling that he was "always being accused without knowing why" and suffering from "remorse for bad deeds" even when he had committed no known crime. In the light of the close personal and artistic interplay between Strindberg and Przybyszewski, *Visitors* can be interpreted as a dramatic depiction of neurotic states of anxiety shared by these twin souls, pursued by the same demons and subject to corresponding hallucinations.[72]

But these biographical details should not be taken as exhausting or even limiting the meanings of *Visitors;* rather they illustrate the range of its allusiveness and universality. Przybyszewski's dramatic epilogue has many other resonances and affinities. The setting and atmosphere of the play can be traced back to Poe's poem "The Haunted Palace" in which a stately mansion where once joyous spirits swayed musically has been invaded by a "hideous throng" who "move fantastically to a discordant melody." The persecuting shadow and punishment for uncommitted crimes are common themes in fin-de-siècle occult literature, as witness the observation from one of Miciński's novels, "Everything in life exacts its vengeance, and punishment must take place even where there has been no crime," and the final stanza of his poem, "Christmas Eve."

> But a threatening Shadow follows me everywhere,
> and I do not know when I shall be freed
> from this darkness—by God's deliverance.[73]

Visitors also had its impact in the theater, most notably influencing Leonid Andreyev's *Black Maskers* (1908), in which Lorenzo's castle becomes filled with strange visitors who attend a masked ball, while the host's shadow forces him to recognize his deceitful life and drives him to suicide as the only escape.

Using purely theatrical means, in *Visitors* Przybyszewski accomplished what he himself had declared to be Munch's goal: "to express, in fine, the naked psychological state, not mythologically, that is, by means of sensory metaphors, but directly in its coloristic equivalent.[74] In this short masterpiece of occult drama, the demonic world of psychic phenomena comes alive as powerfully as in a painting by Munch.

Notes

1. Detailed accounts of occult performances of works of Aleister Crowley, Gurdjieff, and Rudolph Steiner can be found in the Occult and Bizarre Issue of *The Drama Review*, 22, No. 2 (June 1978).

2. Florence A. Falk, *"The Cosmic Mass:* Reflections on a Spiritual Theatre," *Anima*, 2, No. 2, pp. 40-41. We are grateful to Elinor Fuchs for acquainting us with this unusual production.

3. Among those who used the term "theater of the soul," notable are Maeterlinck, Strindberg, Schuré, Wyspiański, Evreinov, and Sologub.

4. Ellis, *Russkiye Simvolisty* (Moscow: Musaget', 1910), p. 229.

5. For Maeterlinck's occult studies and beliefs, see Bettina Knapp, *Maurice Maeterlinck* (Boston: Twayne, 1975), pp. 42-43, 137-147.

6. For Bely's estimate of Steiner as man of the theater, see Andrei Belyi, "The Man, Rudolph Steiner as Stage-Director and Actor," *Journal for Anthroposophy*, No. 27 (Spring 1978), pp. 27-38.

7. Oleg A Maslenikov, *The Frenzied Poets* (New York: Greenwood Press, 1968), pp. 117-118. Briusov's occult novel, *The Fiery Angel* gives such a convincing picture of sixteenth-century magic and alchemy that it was once taken for a Russian translation of an authentic German text of the period.

8. Emma Susana Speratti-Piñero, *El occultisme en Valle-Inclán* (London: Coleccion Tamesis, 1974). We are indebted to Rosemary Weiss for information about Valle-Inclán and the occult.

9. Gabriele D'Annunzio, "La Leda senza cigno: Ritratto d'Ignota," in *Poesie: Teatro: Prose* (Milan-Naples; Riccardo Ricciardi, 1966), p. 1010.

10. Przybyszewski wrote many of his early works in German during his years in Berlin, where he was one of the editors of the occult periodical *Metaphysische Rundschau*. There he studied Egyptian hieroglyphics and immersed himself in the Cabbala, the Apocalypse, and the enigmas of the philosopher's stone. See Alain Mercier, *Les Sources esotériques et occultes de la poésie symboliste: 1870-1914* (Paris: A. - G. Nizet, 1974), II, 93-96, and Alfred Wysocki, *Sprzed pół wieku* (Cracow: Wydawnictwo Literackie, 1974), pp. 46-48.

11. For Miciński's lifelong association with the occult, see Jerzy Tynecki,

Incijacje mistyka (Łódź: Wydawnictwo Łódzkie, 1976); on the influence of Parisian occult circles on Wyspiański, there is extensive evidence in Zdzisław Kępiński, "Stanisław Wyspiański—malarz i myśliciel," *Sztuka*, 6, No. 4 (November-December 1977), pp. 11-43.

12. Denis Saurat, *La Littérature et l'occultisme* (Paris: Rieder, 1929), pp. 71-72.

13. Auguste Villiers de l'Isle-Adam, *Axël,* ed. Pierre Mariel (Paris: La Colombe, 1960), p. 204.

14. *Myśl teatralna Młodej Polski,* ed. Irena Sławińska and Stefan Kruk (Warsaw: Wydawnictwa Artystyczne i Filmowe, 1966), pp. 435, 197. Indian drama enjoyed a great vogue at the turn of the century; *Shakuntala* was staged by Lugné-Poe at the Théâtre de l'Ouevre in 1895, at the Berlin Schauspielhaus in 1903, and at Tairov's Kamerny Teatr as the opening production in 1914.

15. Vera Verigina, "Po dorogam iskanii," in *Vstrechi s Meyerholden* (Moscow: Vserossiiskoye Teatral'noye Obshchestvo, 1967), p. 58.

16. B. O. Schloltzer, "Misteria," *A. Skriabin,* Vol. I (Berlin: Grani, 1923), pp. 172-338, and Faubion Bowers, *The New Scriabin* (New York: St. Martin's, 1973), pp. 72-73, 92-100, 124-126. The Soviet composer Alexander Nemtin completed his reconstruction of the *Prefatory Action* in 1970-1972.

17. See Miciński's essay, "The Theatre-Temple," trans. Daniel Gerould and Jadwiga Kosicka, *yale/theatre,* 7, No. 1 (Fall 1975), pp. 66-67.

18. Haskell M. Block, "Mallarmé and the Materialization of the Abstract in Modern Drama," in *Aux sources de la vérité du théâtre moderne: Actes du Colloque de London (Canada), 1972,* ed. James B. Sanders (Paris: Minard, 1974), pp. 42-43.

19. "Drama is naturally hostile to fantasy," according to J. R. Tolkien in *Tree and Leaf* (New York: Houghton Mifflin, 1965), p. 49.

20. This variety of esoteric drama soon filtered down to a popular level, as witness *Les Invisibles (Invisible Presences),* one of the many collaborations between Grand Guignol master André de Lorde and the celebrated psychologist Alfred Binet. In this one-act play set in a mental institution, the insane are revealed to have contact with the dead through extrasensory perception.

21. Victor-Emile Michelet, *Théâtre,* Vol. I (Paris: Pythagore, 1932).

22. John Gassner, *Directions in Modern Theatre* (New York: Holt, Rinehart, and Winston, 1965), p. 148.

23. Schuré developed his ideas on drama in a number of books and articles, including *Le Drame musical: Richard Wagner—Son oeuvre et son idée* (Paris, 1895); "Le Théâtre de l'élite et son avenir," *La Revue,* November 1 and 15, 1901: and *Le Théâtre initiateur: La Genèse de la tragédie: Le Drame d'Eleusis* (Paris: Perrin, 1926).

24. Edouard Schuré, *The Genesis of Tragedy and the Sacred Drama of Eleusis,* trans. Fred Rothwell (London/New York: Rudolf Steiner Publishing Company, 1936), p. 14.

25. Ibid., p. 154.

26. Edouard Schuré, "Maeterlinck et le théâtre du rêve," *Précurseurs et Révoltés* (Paris: Perrin, 1904), p. 239.

27. Fabre des Essarts, *Le Christ sauveur* (Paris: Librairie Générale des Sciences Occultes, 1907).

28. R. Vroncourt de la Ville, *Le Mystère de l'Amour* (Tours: Chez l'Auteur à l'Oisellerie Nostre-Dame, 1912), p. 80.

29. Most of the plays of Steiner and Schuré fall into this category, whereas writers like Mallarmé and Villiers de l'Isle-Adam cautioned against allegory as incompatible with symbolism.

30. Strindberg's national history plays, such as *Gustavus Vasa* and *Eric XIV,* reveal the workings of invisible powers in the Swedish past; in a series of world-historical dramas about Luther, Moses, Socrates, and Christ, Strindberg attempted—somewhat less successfully—to disclose such forces operating on a universal scale.

31. Evelyn Underhill, *Mysticism* (New York: Dutton, 1961), p. 149.

32. Marcel Réja, "Préface" to Auguste Strindberg, *Inferno* (Paris: Mercure de France, 1966), p. 13.

33. On magical space in Miciński's plays see Elżbieta Rzewuska, *O dramaturgii*

Tadeusza Micińskiego (Wrocław: Ossolineum, 1977), pp. 137-139,152-156, and Edward Balcerzan, *Oprócz głosu* (Warsaw: PIW, 1977), pp. 61-82.

34. Tadeusz Miciński, *Bazilissa Teofanu* (Cracow, 1909). p. 188.

35. Ibid., p. 85.

36. Although Ibsen is often accused of making what Francis Fergusson calls the "tasteless parlor" a preferred setting for much late nineteenth-century drama, it should be remembered that *Brand*, and later *The Master Builder* and *When We Dead Awaken*, established an important precedent for the symbolists' use of mountains and high places on stage.

37. Leon Schiller, *Teatr Ogromny*, ed. Zbigniew Raszewski (Warsaw: Czytelnik, 1961), p. 143.

38. Nicolas Berdyaev, *The Russian Idea* (Boston: Beacon Press, 1962), p. 204.

39. Samuel D. Cioran, *The Apocalyptic Symbolism of Andrei Belyi* (The Hague: Mouton, 1973), p. 13.

41. In his essay "The Tragic Theatre," Yeats calls this device "the celebration of waiting."

42. Mircea Eliade, *Aspects du mythe* (Paris: Gallimard, 1963), p. 88. "Paradise will be regained. All millennarian and eschatalogical movements show signs of optimism. They react against the terror of history with a force which only utter despair can call forth."

42. Emile Gabory, *L'An Mille* (Paris: Aux Bureaux de la Revue des Poètes, 1911), p. 5. The author explains that he published his work, written five years earlier, only after two other dramas with the same title and subject matter had appeared. In 1947, Jules Romains produced his own version, *L'An Mil*, which is not a true apocalyptic play, but rather a sardonic comedy in which a clever swindler uses the end of the world as a ruse to buy up property at low prices.

43. Czesław Miłosz, "Science Fiction and the Coming of the Antichrist," *Emperor of the Earth* (Berkeley: University of California, 1977), pp. 15-31.

44. Two other French plays that dramatize the eschatological mentality are Carlos Larronde's *Le Mystère de la fin du monde* (written 1911, published 1917) and Antonin Artaud's *Le Jet de sang* (1927).

45. Andrei Bely, *Na Rubezhe dvukh stoleti* (Moscow-Leningrad: Zemlyai Fabrika, 1930), pp. 401-402.

46. Daniel C. Gerould, "Andrei Bely: Russian Symbolist," *Performing Arts Journal*, 3, No. 2 (Fall 1978), pp. 25-29. A translation of *Jaws of Night* appears in the same issue. For valuable information about Bely as a dramatist, see Zoya Yurieff, "A. Bely and A. Chekhov," and George Kalbouses, "Andrey Bely and the Modernist Movement in Russian Drama," in *Andrey Bely: A Critical Review*, ed. Gerald Janeck (Lexington, Ky.: University of Kentucky Press, 1978), pp. 44-55 and 146-155.

47. A. D. Alekseyev, "Russkaya muzyka v predoktyabr'skie gody," in *Russkaya Khudozhestvennaya Kul'tura Kontsa XIX-Nachala XX Veka*, Vol. 3 (Moscow: Nauka, 1977), p. 278.

48. David Ketterer, *New Worlds for Old: The Apocalyptic Imagination, Science Fiction, and American Literature* (Garden City, New York: Anchor/Doubleday, 1974), pp. 15, 91.

49. Briusov wrote a number of science fiction stories and plays, including *The World of Seven Generations* (1923), the name of a comet destined to collide with earth and destroy human civilization.

50. Ellis, op. cit., pp. 196-197. Influenced by *The Earth*, Konstantin Stanislavskii began work on an apocalyptic drama, *The Comet, a Fantasy in Four Acts* (1908). Stanislavskii's play, of which only some fragments of Act II exist, begins at the point where Briusov's ends, with the final catastrophe.

51. Mircea Eliade, *Aspects du mythe* (Paris: Gallimard, 1963), p. 72.

52. Bely, cited by Cioran, op. cit., p. 22.

53. Mircea Eliade, *The Two and the One*, trans. J. M. Cohen (New York: Harper & Row, 1965), p. 95. Chapter 2, "Mephistopheles and the Androgyne or the Mystery of the Whole," is devoted to *coincidentia oppositorum*.

54. Rzewuska discusses *coincidentia oppositorum* in the plays of Miciński, and Cioran refers to its use in Bely's works without calling it by that name. In her book

on Maeterlinck, Knapp mentions the Belgian playwright's employment of the device, describing it as *complexio* or *conjunctio oppositorum.*

55. Miciński, *Father Faust*, p. 113, quoted by Sue Ashton Fines, "Lucifer, Man and Christ in the Works of Tadeusz Miciński," Ph. D. dissertation, Stanford University, 1974, p. 83.

56. Adam Ważyk, "U Modernistow," *Twórczóść,* No. 8 (August 1977), pp. 83-84.

57. In her thesis, Fines discusses at length Miciński's Luciferianism as it evolves throughout the poet's entire career.

58. Hélène Tuzet, *Le Cosmos et l'imagination* (Paris: José Corti, 1965), pp. 447-448.

59. Tymon Terlecki, "Stanisław Wyspiański and the Poetics of Symbolist Drama," *The Polish Review,* 15, No. 4 (Autumn 1970), p. 57.

60. Jan Nowakowski, *Wyspiański* (Cracow: Wydawnictwo Literackie, 1972), pp. 114-143.

61. Terlecki, op. cit., pp. 60-61. See also Claude Backvis, *Le Dramaturge Stanislas Wyspiański* (Paris: Presses Universitaires, 1952), pp. 253-254.

62. In the Grotowski-Szajna production of *Acropolis,* by a comparable process of association the action was transferred to Auschwitz, not far from Cracow, and a new historical dimension became added to Wyspiański's play.

63. Mercier, op. cit., I, p. 240.

64. See, for example, the collection, *Satanizm* (Moscow: Zeno, 1913).

65. Roland Brevannes, *Les Messes noires* (Paris: Bernard, n.d.). Anatolii Kamenskii's *Chernaya Messa (The Black Mass),* based on Huysmans, is likewise a pretext for presenting orgies on stage.

66. Fabre des Essarts, *Sadisme, Satanisme, et Gnose* (Paris: Bodin, 1906).

67. Roland Villeneuve, *Le Diable: Erotologie de Satan* (Paris: J.-J. Pauvert, 1963), pp. 218.222.

68. Published and performed in Polish in 1901, *Visitors* was twice translated into Russian, in 1903 and 1904, and selected for production by Meyerhold at his Theatre Studio in 1906, although never actually produced there. See A. Volzhskii, "Stanisław Przybyszewski," *Voprosy zhizni,* No. 9 (1905), pp. 133-134 and No. 10 (1905), p. 248.

69. Herman Maxime, "Maeterlinck et Przybyszewski," *Revue d'histoire de la philosophie et d'histoire génèrale de la civilisation* (July-September 1942), pp. 258-267.

70. Theodore Ziolkowski, *Disenchanted Images* (Princeton: Princeton University Press, 1977), p. 236, and Ralph Tymms, *Doubles in Literary Psychology* (Cambridge, England: Bowes & Bowes, 1949), pp. 17, 25.

71. J. Peterkiewicz, "Cast in Glass and Shadow," *New Literary History,* 5, No. 2 (1974), pp. 353-363.

72. Gunnar Brandell, *Strindberg in Inferno,* trans. Barry Jacobs (Cambridge, Mass.: Harvard University Press, 1974), pp. 84-89, 107, 120, and Evert Sprinchorn, "The Zola of the Occult," in *Strindberg and the Modern Theatre* (Uddevalla, Sweden: The Strindberg Society, 1975), pp. 108-114.

73. Tadeusz Miciński, *Poezje wybrane,* ed. Piotr Kuncewicz (Warsaw: Ludowa Spółdzielnia Wydawnicza, 1976), p. 64.

74. Stanisław Przybyszewski, *Na drogach duszy,* p. 59, cited by Maria Podraza-Kwiatkowska, *Symbolizm i Symbolika w Poezji Młodej Polski* (Cracow: Wydawnictwo Literackie, 1975), p. 44.

Symbolist Drama: Villiers de l'Isle-Adam, Strindberg, and Yeats

HASKELL M. BLOCK

Occultism in early modern drama reflects the symbolist conception of art as at once concealment and revelation and as the expression of the dynamic interplay of visible and invisible planes of reality. For the symbolist playwrights, the great exemplar of the dramatization of occult experience is Goethe's *Faust*. In his elaboration of drama as a vast cosmic quest, Goethe makes no distinction between natural and supernatural experience. The substantial reality of occult powers is not argued in his play; it is asserted as given. In this respect, *Faust* defines the role of occultism in the work of Goethe's successors. Of course, playwrights of occult persuasion of the later nineteenth-century drew freely on the esoteric beliefs and practices of their time, but underlying their efforts is the example of Goethe's prodigious dramatization of the heights and depths of human experience.

Perhaps the entire course of modern drama could be explained as a series of responses to the strategies of *Faust* and their alternatives. In a more restricted context, we can see the plays of Villiers de l'Isle-Adam, Strindberg, and Yeats as explorations of esoteric self-knowledge as well as of the mysteries of creation. The symbolist poet and playwright defined the theater as inherently spiritual. As Mallarmé put it, "Le Théâtre est d'essence supérieure." The preoccupation with ceremony and ritual in symbolist drama is not simply a response to Wagner or to the mystical and religious impulses of the time; it expresses a deliberate effort to recover the notion of theater as a sacred mystery, wherein the acting place is not merely a physical stage but a temple of spiritual revelation and communion.

Axël

We should not view the theater of Villiers and his successors solely as a reaction to scientific positivism and the dominance of a drama of representational reality. Their theater constitutes an assertion as well as a repudiation, an embattled expression of faith in the power of art to impart mystical experience. For Villiers, as E. Drougard has shown *(Revue Belge de philologie et d'histoire*, 10 [1931], 505-530), the breviary of occultism was the *Dogme et rituel de la haute-magie* of Eliphas Lévi, and many passages from that work were incorporated verbatim into *Axël*. Strindberg experimented with alchemy, telepathy, magnetism, and other forms of mystical or magical experience. He claimed in a letter of 1896 that his role "seems to be to provide the link between science on the one side and occultism and religion on the other." He viewed himself as called upon to be "the Zola of Occultism" and steeped himself in the writings of Swedenborg ("the Buddha of the North"), as well as in the mystical fiction of Balzac and the theosophy of Péladan. Yeats similarly claimed that "the mystical life" was the center of his being and based his private symbolism in his early work not only on literary forebears such as Blake but also on the spiritualism of the Hermetic Society of Dublin and the London order of the Golden Dawn. The mysticism of fin-de-siècle drama is no mere fashion or convention but a totally committed personal utterance.

Villiers described *Axël* as a "tragédie métaphysique," abstract and intellectual, directed primarily to the mind, and with the theatrical action of secondary interest. The performance of the play in 1894 required over five hours. Much of the drama consists of long debates between Axël and the Commandeur or long elaborations of doctrine by Axël's spiritual guide, Maître Janus. Villiers seems constrained to demonstrate what his followers could assume. The preachment of Maître Janus conforms to the doctrine of the Rosicrucian text that Axël studies: *"Tout verbe, dans le cercle de son action, crée ce qu'il exprime"* (In the circle of its action, every verb creates what it expresses). (Villiers de l'Isle-Adam, *Axël* [Paris: 1960], p. 106). Axël's progress is one of growing self-knowledge and self-realization, as a disciple of Maître Janus and in conformity with his own nature and destiny. His meeting with Sara is foreordained. As Maître Janus declares at the end of "Le Monde occulte," "l'Œuvre s'accomplit." The fate of the lovers is predestined. Their suicide is a repudiation of the meaningless flux of the here and now for the sake of eternal life hereafter. Axël's justification for the love-death is human as well as divine; by its very nature, the intensity of the love he and Sara have known cannot last. We must recognize that, despite its length, Villiers's play remains an unfinished work. He was particularly distressed over the ending; evidently, he planned to extend the action into the life of the lovers after death in order to harmonize his occultism and orthodox Christianity. For Villiers's admirers, *Axël* is a sacred book, not literature but scripture. Late in life, Yeats, who attended the premiere of *Axël* in Paris, remarked: "It did not move me because I thought it a great masterpiece, but because it seemed part of a religious rite, the ceremony perhaps of some secret Order wherein my generation had been initiated."

Strindberg and Yeats

The structure of the mystical drama of the turn of the century is almost always enclosed within a pattern of spiritual initiation. Axël moves through a series of stages of purification wherein he proves himself a true disciple of Maître Janus, even in spite of Axël's categorical renunciation of "la Lumière, l'Espérance et la Vie" as defined by the Maître. In Strindberg's *The Road to Damascus*, the Stranger comes to learn the necessity of struggle and suffering in man's tortuous quest for peace. Similiarly, in *The Ghost Sonata*, the student, Arkenholtz, comes to view the world as a place of illusion and pain and to recognize that what seems to be beautiful and good is in fact ugly and evil. Both the Stranger and the student undergo a spiritual transformation that makes it possible for them to appeal beyond the limits of the here and now to ultimate redemption hereafter. A similar pattern of inner transformation shapes many of the plays of Yeats. In part inspired by *Axël*, *The Shadowy Waters* moves from the realm of dream and expectation to the celebration of love as a life beyond life. Dectora and Forgael renounce treasure and the claims of common life to move toward death and immortality.

By its very nature, symbolist drama reflects the interplay of natural and supernatural events. After Sara refuses to take the veil, Soeur Laudation would strike her but finds her hand stayed in flight, "comme secrètement immobilisée." Strindberg's Stranger is pursued everywhere by invisible dark powers, whereas Arkenholtz, as a Sunday child, can see invisible presences such as the milkmaid or the corpse of the Consul, "wrapped in a winding sheet," coming out of the door and into the street. In Yeats's *The Shadowy Waters*, Forgael's harp is enchanted and holds his sailors in awe. As one of them remarks, "It is said that when he plays upon it he has power over all the listeners, with or without the body, seen or unseen, and any man that listens grows to be as mad as himself." Examples of supernatural enchantment abound in many of Yeats's plays. We need only glance at the *Four Plays for Dancers*. In *At the Hawk's Well*,

Cuchulain is transfixed by the dance of the Guardian of the Well. In *The Only Jealousy of Emer*, the Figure and the Ghost of the hero interact with the women who love him. The play itself refuses any distinction between everyday and occult experience.

The quest for magic in symbolist drama is inseparable from the use of magic. The supernatural and the occult function not as spectacular effects but as the revelation of sacred truth. It is in religious and ritualistic contexts that supernatural events acquire their fullest significance. At the climax of Strindberg's *Charles XII*, which occurs on the battlefield in Norway, while the king seems to be praying in the trenches, the king's followers try to explain his conduct that has ruined their country. To the query "Are you aware that we are talking as if he were dead?" the prophet Swedenborg exclaims, "He *is* dead!" A moment later the cry resounds, "The king is shot!" The death is an act of supernatural punishment; as Swedenborg declares, the bullet came not from the fortress but from Heaven. Early in the play the king is described as a dead man still walking the earth. His fatal moment is made wholly credible as part of a realistic military situation. The presence of the seer, Swedenborg, at the scene provides supernatural sanction for the king's death as the working out of divine predestination. Yeats's plays provide similar acts of climactic revelation. Perhaps the most striking example is *The Resurrection*, wherein the formal stylization of the plays for dancers provides a frame for an essentially realistic account of the aftermath of Christ's burial. As in *Axël*, much of the drama consists of long debates, in this instance between a Greek and a Hebrew, who are hoping to protect Christ's disciples from a frenzied mob of worshippers of Dionysus. The two argue over the identity of Christ, and their dispute extends, by implication, to the scope and limits of human knowledge. Their Syrian colleague arrives with an account of Christ's resurrection and reappearance that raises the further question of the credibility of what one claims to have seen. Only the Syrian is able to accept the operation of the irrational, "outside knowledge, outside order." As the debate continues, punctuated by the revels of the worshippers of Dionysus, the figure of Christ moves through the curtain and across the room. The Greek draws out the enormous significance of the event—"God and man die each other's life, live each other's death"—followed by the Musicians' song of the vanity of all human endeavor. The climax of Yeats's drama constitutes an almost overwhelming experience, even though the tendency of the audience might be to redefine the events of the play rationalistically.

Mysticiam and Reality

At first glance, the occultism of the playwrights at hand would seem to constitute a flight from the rational world, a repudiation of objectively verifiable norms of experience. A larger view of their plays would suggest

A drawing of a chimera by Gustave Moreau (1826-1898)

that mysticism in the theater may heighten rather than diminish our perception of reality. The preoccupation with inner life in early modern drama led not only to a revival of subterranean currents of esoteric thought, but also to a recognition of the dramatic importance of dreams, visions, hallucinations, and other forms of psychic disequilibrium. Particularly in the later work of Strindberg, the language of nightmare becomes that of everyday reality. In this process, it is not possible to separate Strindberg's occultism from his expressionistic art. As Strindberg declared in an essay of 1896, "imaginations, fancies and dreams possess a kind of reality ... we are all of us spiritual somnambulists. ..." Occultism is here the very groundwork of a new dramatic art. In *The Road to Damascus, A Dream Play, The Ghost Sonata,* and similar works, Strindberg's explorations of occult experience are part and parcel of his portrayals of psychic disorganization and destruction, wherein the crises of individual demoralization express at the same time the fundamental crises and cleavages of a whole society.

Occultism may be said to provide its own drama in the theater. By extending the acting place from the stage to the cosmos, the symbolist playwrights moved toward the abolition of the theater as most audiences know it. The fact that the transformation of life and art for which these playwrights hoped did not take place does not invalidate their effort or diminish the significance of their art. Without seeming to repudiate traditional Christianity, their plays redefined the spiritual function of drama. In an age of scientism and demystification, their mystical art can still disturb and even overwhelm the spectator or reader. In the early modern theater, occultism at its best finds expression in a drama of intensity, sweep, and imaginative energy that will not release its hold on our attention.

PART 2

POETRY
OF THE INVISIBLE:
THE ROMANTIC PHASE

Occultism
and the Language of Poetry

FRANK PAUL BOWMAN

Just as the infinite intelligence is manifested by the un-created Word, by the Logos which determines it in God, all intelligence is manifested by a word which determines it in the intellecting being. And since intelligence is one in its essence, just as the truth, which is intelligence's goal and end, is one, so the word is also one in its essence, and all language is a participant of the infinite language, of the divine logos.[1]

Lamennais

"Oyant jadis l'ange/Donner un sens plus pur aux mots de la tribu" (Hearing in another age the angel gives a purer sense to the words of the tribe)— so Mallarmé describes the parallel the hydra-mob drew when faced with Poe's poetry, implying that this was indeed what Poe had done or at least tried to do and, less directly, that this was what Mallarmé was doing in writing Poe's epitaph.[2] Léon Cellier asked repeatedly that we study the "occult sources" of symbolist poetic theory and practice, following the model of Auguste Viatte's famous *Sources occultes du romantisme*, suggesting that the occult-illuminist tradition informed symbolist poetic theory as Viatte had indeed proved that it informed Romanticism. With respect to poetic language—the nature and sense of words and grammar—the tradition in some ways did, and in some perhaps more important ways it did not. No self-respecting occultist could write Mallarmé's line; he would have to rewrite it to read: "Hearing now as ever the man of desire restore a purer sense to the words of the human race." Writings on occultism and the illuminist tradition, often apologetic in both senses of the term, tend to "tirer la couverture," to claim that all comes from the Tradition, the Cabbala, Saint-Martin, whatever source one wills.

My concern here is with occultist theories of language as expounded in France during the Romantic age and with the question of how much those theories may have affected later poetic practice, particularly that of Mallarmé and the symbolists. My illuminist version of the famed passage from "Le Tombeau d'Edgar Poe" pinpoints some of the problems. For the illuminist tradition, the purer sense is not something to be created, but something to be restored, something that has been lost. That restoration is a continuing task, which takes place throughout all of history (just as, of course, the corruption and degradation of language can take place throughout all of history). It is the words not of the tribe but of the human race—all language—that must be restored. Finally, the task of restoration is performed not by an angel nor by the poet—though, as we shall see, the poet may have a particular and even preeminent function in the task—but by the man of desire, he who yearns for and seeks the divine and absolute and has been initiated into the illuminist vision. Man alone is both free and gifted with thought; all of nature thinks, and indeed an illuminist may well maintain that all of nature has a language, but man alone is free and he alone has the power to restore language to its primordial purity.

The basic tenets of occultism are rather simple, though of course each school, each representative of the tradition emphasizes or develops certain common convictions.

At the beginning, all was unity; this unity has been lost, fractured. The restoration of unity and the obliteration of differences are the tasks of men and the end of history. From this principle stems a preference for modes of thought that are unifying, for synthesis rather than analysis, or at least for a dialectic that can synthesize differences, for the intuitive perceptions of unity rather than the categorizations of reason. This preference often leads to an appreciation of the "poor in spirit," who in their innocence perceive a truth hidden from educated intellectuals. Certain mechanisms of language, in particular allegory and metaphor, are especially apt at embodying the perception of unity. All creation emanates from the Divine (creation is not, then, *ex nihilo*) and, because of the Fall (of angels, then of man/woman), is more or less separated from the Divine. This emanation-separation is represented by one form or another of the great chain of being, with man always at the center but with the Divine present to some degree throughout the chain. God is in everything—trees, babbling brooks, stones—but these things are not divine. They must be restored to their divine status by man, that free and thinking microcosm of God. The term *panentheism* describes more accurately than pantheism this presence of the divine, but it alas has not been widely adopted. However, the poem reads: "Tongues in trees, books in the running brooks, sermons in stones, and good in everything." This presence of the divine in all creation is conceived of as a presence of language because of the very mechanism of creation, where God emanates from his Being to the Sophia or uncreated Wisdom and then the Logos, Word, or created Wisdom, which is thus present in all creation, but corrupted since the Fall. The illuminist tradition, with its fondness for synthesis, associates rather than dissociates the divine Word, the Platonic logos, the Johanine logos, language as such (including human language and also the language of all creation) and, when the tradition is Christianized, the Christ as the Word incarnate in history. Language, like creation, is divine in origin; it has lost in large part its original purity and unity and yet retains traces of that origin. These traces may be found in the four aspects of language: in sounds (vowels, consonants, monemes), in words, in syntactic and/or grammatical structures, and in writing itself (letters, hieroglyphs, and so on). Illuminist linguistics, like any linguistics, examines all four. The story of Babel represents the destruction of linguistic unity just as the apostolic gift of tongues or glossolalia is a vision of an at least partial restoration of that unity. This fractioning of language is an historical phenomenon and is reversible in history—hence the development of an illuminist philology with its etymological quest for traces or remnants of the divine and an illuminist comparative linguistics that seeks what different languages have in common with, or rather retain of, their divine origin. Usually, though not always, Hebrew is considered the language closest to the divine. During the first half of the nineteenth century in particular, illuminist thought is preoccupied with an historical and comparative study of language. Illuminists on language are always "essentialists"; that is, they are convinced that linguistic signs are or should be motivated, as opposed to "conventionalists," who consider linguistic signs to be unmotivated or arbitrary, the results of historical and/or social convention.

Other aspects of illuminist thought are less central to the problem of language, but it is important to note that all religious systems and myths are studied from a similar perspective. They all offer, in their varied forms, different expressions of the same unity. This syncretism is assured by an allegorical reading of sacred literature, of liturgies, of myths. The universally discerned essential pattern is one of Fall, initiation via a new revelation and expiatory suffering, which results in transfigurative metamorphosis or beatific vision and so on. (Alchemy and astrology are susceptible of a similar analysis.) This pattern or redemptive process is repeated in history until the end of time. The nineteenth century is perhaps distinct from earlier illuminism in the high degree of importance it attaches to woman's role not only in the Fall but also in the redemptive process; a study in the illuminist origins of women's liberation (Esquiros, A.-L. Constant, Enfantin in France) would be of considerable interest.

The illuminist tradition is richer and more varied than the preceding schematic analysis may suggest. I should like now to present four instances of illuminist discourse on language: the grand master Jacob Boehme; the "unknown philosopher" Louis-Claude de Saint-Martin, who was, in fact, very well known and influential in nineteenth-century France; Louis de Bonald, because of his synthesis of illuminist notions of language and traditionalism; finally Steinmetz, an unknown author of the 1840s, whom I have chosen for his representative value. In conclusion, I shall try to contrast (a most unilluminist approach) these theories of language with the two other mainstreams of Romantic thought on language, those of the conventionalist and the mimologist, and raise certain questions about the importance of each for modern poetic theory and practice.

Boehme, Saint-Martin, Bonald, and Steinmetz

Jacob Boehme, like all illuminists, was fascinated by the first verse of the Gospel according to Saint John and concluded from a meditation on it and on Genesis that the Word was both the objectivation of God and the means of the creation of the visible world. Thus, there is a mutual, essential relation between the representation of the Word in the spirit and its incarnation in creation; the Word proffered by God continues to live both in our mind and in objects. The names Adam gave to animals and to creation before the Fall (the Adamic language) were translations of the divine Word, signatures; for Adam, knowing the virtues of beings, gave them their correct names. This correctness was perverted by the Fall, but the Adamic signatures can still be partially read in the words we use for things. For the language of nature—the Word in creation—also exists, and letters, words, and syllables reflect its secrets and significations. Since man is created in God's image and his spirit partakes immediately of the divine spirit, letters, and so on, are figurations of this divine centrum; by them, man participates in the qualities that constitute the world (by the letter S, for example, with fire). Our intellection of natural language lets us understand the divine acts demonstrated by the letters, and Boehme provided exemplary readings of the Our Father and the first chapter of Genesis in terms of this intelligence of natural language.

Wolfgang Kayser has exhaustively studied the origins of Boehme's theories in classical, patristic, and medieval thought, including Boehme's debt to the Cabbala. Boehme synthesizes various currents, combining in particular Neoplatonic theories of the logos and meditations on Adamic language; later illuminism mostly embroiders on his synthesis. God becomes the eternal orator; all creation is an oration or prayer; all life is the action of the Word. Thus, all creation is a symbolic cipher, the hieroglyph of a superior reality. The natural language is found in the signatures of things and in the Word within us. Man can know the being of things and learn to give them their true names, and language is the depository of man's resemblance to God,

Louis-Claude de Saint-Martin has been called the "Luther of occultism" and perhaps merits the title several ways, not only because he was impatient with certain superstitious practices curried in some occultist circles and because he preferred instead to emphasize the essential elements of illuminist theory but also because of his considerable skills as a writer. *L'Homme de désir*, perhaps the most moving of his texts, can still be read with pleasure as well as appreciation. Saint-Martiin frequently discusses the problem of language; perhaps his fullest exposition is in *Des erreurs et de la vérité* (1775). Man's major resource is the attributes contained in his knowledge of language, for language gives him the power to communicate his thought, to enter into commerce with his fellows, and to make them sensitive to his thoughts and affections (Saint-Martin draws a sad portrait of the insufficiency of the substitutes for language among animals and deaf-mutes). If language has this power of communication, however, it must be because languages are common to all men, because, that is, all men possess the same signs. Indeed, if language is now fragmented, our desire to learn other languages is a sign of our drive toward unity—though Saint-Martin would consider it a better task to purify one's mother tongue rather than to seek to restore unity through the acquisition of multiple languages. An introspective analysis of man himself proves that he is meant to possess only one language and, therefore, that the multitude of languages are the effect of habit and convention, perpetuating mankind's loss of unity.

Saint-Martin distinguishes between two sorts of language: an interior, mute language, contained within us, and the demonstrative and perceptible language by which we communicate with others. The former is the "mother" of the latter but is itself the voice and expression of a principle that is outside us and that is a manifestation of the Divine. Because this principle is one and governs all interior language, that language should take the same form everywhere and follow identical structures; the true intellectual language of man is everywhere the same and essentially one. But if the principle is one and the mother or interior language is one, then perceptible language should also be one, which it obviously is not. The variations of perceptible language, however, reflect a deficiency located, not in it, but in the mother language within us. This deficiency is produced by our misuse of the will and the imagination, which has impeded or perverted the operations of the principle. As a result, perceptible language has been considerably altered. Man, who no longer perceives things in their true nature, has given them names that came from him and that, as they are no longer analogous with the thing named, cannot designate unequivocally; this incapacity gives rise to misunderstandings, inaccuracies, and so on. The variety of language is thus a proof of the inadequacy of language and a demonstration of the great distance between man and the spiritual principle that should govern him. The picture, however, is not totally black; words may be largely conventional rather than essential, but potentially they can still offer fairly sure signs of the beings represented. Man's natural tendency is to express a thing by the sign or word that seems most analogous. We experience pleasure and admiration when offered signs, expressions, and figures that bring us close to the nature or essence of the objects being evoked and that make us conceive them better, for then every production or object comes closer to the ideal of being presented by its proper name, the name that is linked to its essence. The task of every man is to learn and use the true names; as we shall see, the true poet for Saint-Martin is the one who excels at this task.

Language is not something discovered or invented by man, but the true attribute of men, a divine gift, of which sufficient vestiges remain so that man can return to his source or origin, to purity and unity. Saint-Martin notes that many do not agree and cites the problem of the child brought up in solitude or by animals—a child dear to eighteenth-century linguistic speculation. That child admittedly does not speak the natural or essential language. Saint-Martin uses the child to refute both Descartes and Locke. On the one hand, the child proves that in our present state of privation, we can do nothing without the aid of an exterior reaction, without, that is, the aid of our fellow men who also labor at their rehabilitation. We must help one another in restoring our faculties, including our linguistic faculties; both nature and the law of the mind call us to live in society. (Other illuminists also emphasize the "social" aspects of the language problem.) Experiments with a child raised in isolation are doomed to failure; it is as if you placed a seed on a stone, and then the seed did not grow, and then you made comments on the seed—which rather takes care of the Cartesian innate ideas. On the other hand, the fact that the child does not produce a language also shows that the universal language is not a "natural" product of our structures and perceptions but must be a divine gift—which takes care of Locke or rather of the *idéologues* such as Destutt de Tracy and Garat, with whom Saint-Martin debated at the Ecole Normale. He does concede that the child will achieve an elemental system that will let him express pleasure and pain, but animals also possess that language of sensation, whereas true language seeks to express not sensation, but thought. The distinction, however, is one of degree rather than kind, and the degree depends on where the being is in the great chain. One must grant a degree of language even to the least of created beings, a language that is nothing other then the expression of their faculties.

This, one might note, is not quite "sermons in stones," for the faculties of the stones, according to Saint-Martin, are not really adequate for the practice of sacred eloquence. Martinism distinguishes between the developments of the *coeli enarrant* theme—"the heavens declare the Glory of God, and the firmament proclaimeth His handywork," the perception of the divine in the harmonies of creation, on the one hand, and, on the other, the presence of the logos throughout the chain of being. Romantic poets such as Gérard de Nerval and Victor Hugo tend to confuse or, at least, fuse the two.

Saint-Martin is confident that the possibility exists of restoring the "essentiality" of language, of recovering the fixed and invariable language of the principle. It has not been totally lost; it is present in all men and nations and is the source of the true principles of justice. It does and must use our human, physical organs and senses: the ear and the eye because writing lets us communicate with those distant from us (although for Saint-Martin writing only indicates, offers a dead explication, whereas speech is a living explication; I know not what he would have thought of tapes and records). The study of etymologies can lead us back to prelapsarian language. More importantly, we can purify our own language by the spiritual *ascesis* Saint-Martin ever recommends, which is rather quietist. We must abandon our own will—our "property"—and desire the will of that active and intelligent Cause, which should govern man and the universe. To demonstrate this survival of the essential language in humanity, he cites a syntagmatic example—for grammar, more than words, retains and manifests the inherent order. In order to express any complete notion of a thought, one needs an active noun or pronoun, a verb, and a passive noun or pronoun; this grammatical law is invariable and essential, for it reflects the ternary of agent, action, and product. (The significance of the ternary in Martinism and its relation to the Trinity are too complex to discuss here, but it is a very essential—in both senses of the word—concept.) Other parts of speech are accessory; they supplement these three, and their usage and position vary greatly from speaker to speaker and from language to language. The accessories, in short, have been more corrupted than the basics. (One of Saint-Martin's great virtues is that, unlike many illuminists, he never succumbs to the delight of the accessory and returns unerringly to the basics.)

I leave aside his developments on the six cases and the six major modifications of matter, as well as on gender, to emphasize two points. First, Martinism is a very active and demanding spirituality; in the *Tableau naturel*, Saint-Martin provides a quite similar statement of his linguistic theories but concludes with what amounts to an appeal for linguistic action. The present variety, corruption, and obscurity of language are the products and proofs of our ignorance, sloth, and prevarication (Saint-Martin avoids "sin," a word he considered obfuscatory). We can know the forms and numbers of the essential signs. Indeed, we cannot utter a single word, write a single letter, that does not to a degree manifest the supreme Agent. The question is, To what degree? All use of language becomes charged with moral value.

The other noteworthy point is that poets are those who manifest the supreme Agent to the highest degree in their use of language. Poetry is not the true and unique language, yet it is the nearest equivalent. It is the most sublime production of man's faculties, which draws him closest to his principle and which, by the transports it provokes, best proves to him the dignity of his origins. This proclamation of the precellence of poetry is somewhat circular in the sense that Saint-Martin clearly does not have in mind the contemporary satirical or didactic verse of Voltaire or the descriptive nature poetry of Saint-Lambert or even the earlier poetry of the Renaissance, but rather his own ideal of poetry. He does define elsewhere the qualities of this poetry in a way that prefigures Romantic practice and also echoes pre-Romantic poetics: poetry is not a question of fixed form or rhyme and rhythm; rather, it differs from prose by the very nature of its language. Poetic language is essentially prophetic because it recalls man's origin and mission and also because it presents not the beautiful but rather the sublime, which englobes the ugly—not only honey but also gall, *miel* and *fiel*; he provides a very developed spiritual (as opposed to mimetic) justification for the presence of the ugly in "true poetry." The models cited or evoked, to my knowledge, are all Biblical.

Maine de Biran, the most noteworthy of French philosophers in the early nineteenth century, labeled Louis de Bonald a *"histrion en philosophie"*—a clown, and a bad one at that, whose excess makes his artifice all too evident. Indeed, Bonald's single-minded devotion to the task of explaining, justifying, and thereby destroying the Revolution of 1789 in order to turn the clock back to an ideal feudal age is so overriding that it is at times hard to take him seriously. He has neither the whimsy and wit of Montlosier nor the ambiguity and precious little of the radicalism of Joseph de Maistre, to name his two great conservative contemporaries. Yet for illuminist linguistic theory, he is, I suspect, of great importance, and that for two reasons. The first is that he historicizes that theory or, more accurately, associates the philosophy of language and the philosophy of history and derives from the illuminist meditation on language a theory of history and hence of politics. Others will do likewise, either echoing or refuting him. The other reason is that he "Catholicizes" the illuminist theories of language, utters them from a declared Roman Catholic position, and thereafter (perhaps not only because of Bonald—Ballanche and Maistre are tributaries) the discourse of French Catholicism on Word and language becomes profoundly marked by the basic illuminist tenets and will remain so throughout the Romantic age.

Bonald discusses language in the *Discours préliminaire* of his *Législation primitive* (1802), and again in his *Recherches philosophiques sur les premiers objets des connaissance morales* (1818), but his theses do not change. Language is, and remains, of divine origin, but man knows it not immediately because of a contact with the divine but mediately through society, which is of divine institution and mediates or transmits language to man. Thus, he rejects both Malebranche, who proposed that man had direct communication with eternal Reason, and Condillac, who failed to note the divine origins of society and hence of social language. Man is indeed created in the image of God, and just as God is only known by His Word *(Verbe)*—the expression and image of His substance—so man, finite intelligence, is only known by his word *(parole)*, the true expression of his spirit. Society, however, transmits that language to man and thereby transmits to him the knowledge of all moral truths that are innate not in man, but in society (to a greater or lesser degree). Man, in acquiring language, which subsists perpetually in society, acquires moral and religious truth. Thus, any society with an articulated language has a knowledge of God, of the future life, and so on. Bonald carries this idea quite far; the three grammatical persons (again, like Saint-Martin, he prefers to demonstrate the essential nature of language via an analysis of syntax, rather than of words or sounds) reflect not only the divine Trinity and the structure of the family, but also the structure of society, that is, king, nobles, and people—the latter, like children, should obey. When the people took power in France, they immediately created linguistic disorder. This will become a common theme among French rightists: the revolution destroyed not only institutions but also language, creating bad grammar and neologisms and even confusing grammatical persons (Bonald cites Molière's servant's "j'avions" as exemplary of the bad grammar of democracy, where the individual claims to speak for the collectivity.) Victor Hugo, in his "Réponse à un acte d'accusation" and more particularly its "Suite" ("Sequel"), will take up the challenge, assert the revolutionary right to neologisms, and claim that the destruction of the barriers between the levels of style is a good thing. Hugo was for linguistic change, whereas, of course, Bonald was against it, except so far as that change represented a purifying return to prerevolutionary usage.

Bonald's linguistic theories presuppose a universal revelation to all society of divine truth and hence of language, which he propounded together with Maistre and which Lamennais developed as an apologetic argument in his *Essai sur l'indifférence.* By so doing, they gave great impulse within French Catholicism to the kind of syncretist reading of religions and myths characteristic of illuminism—and indeed to the analysis of language as the vehicle of the expression of religious truth. Only in the late 1830s will a renewed attention to the distinction between natural revelation and supernatural revelation dampen. (and then, to a limited extent) this syncretist quest for Aztec trinities, Chinese incarnations, American Indian resurrections, and so on. Meanwhile, theories such as Bonald's gave rise to immense speculations about philology and comparative linguistics. The leading figure here was Baron Eckstein (affectionately known as "Baron Sanskrit"), who, convinced of the essential relations between language, the divine, and the created world, wrote and published a whole periodical, *Le Catholique*, devoted to demonstrating that relation in detail.

Finally, Bonald's position attaches a great deal of importance to language because it precedes thought. "Man must think his word before he can speak his thought," as he succinctly put it—which seemed to him yet another proof that man cannot have invented language. This is the sense he gives to *"si orem lingua, spiritus meus orat"* (if my tongue prays, my spirit prays); all prayer, for Bonald, seemingly must be verbal, as is all thought; we can only think and pray by language, an instrument God gave to society when He instituted it and that society transmits to us.

The early nineteenth century knew endless variations on this theme of the divine origin of language, and it would be interesting to trace them through Fabre d'Olivet and his reconstruction of Hebrew, through Lamennais, Bautain, Blanc Saint-Bonnet, Lacuria, the great French Swedenborgian Edouard Richer, and many others. I prefer to cite a tempered statement from the 1840s because it represents what I think was the common core of the doctrine. In the *Université catholique* for 1842 (XIII, 112 ff.), Steinmetz, in a "Cours de physiologie" offers a lengthy analysis of language as an instrument of faith, of the essential relations between language and thought, and of the degradation of that relation. Language is the instrument of the order of faith, is the source of all thought, and is endowed with inherent power that fecundates intelligence. This is true not only of spoken language, but of all creation, because all creatures announce or proclaim the glory of God—even inorganic nature possesses language. Man probably received this powerful instrument in a state of perfection at the time of his creation; some have maintained that he only received the potential of language as a gift, but even if one accepts that theory, there can be no development of intelligence without language. Everything we know, including the most recent discoveries of philology and linguistics, leads to the belief in the existence of a divine primitive language. Steinmetz then examines the imperfections of savage language, where the divine gift is in a state of notable corruption. (For him and the *Université catholique*, all civilization is necessarily Christian, and the heathen is barbaric). They have lost the art of writing, they have lost words, their language systems are embedded in the material order of concrete metaphors, they cannot express abstract ideas, and they use polysyllabic words to express simple numbers. After painting this sad, if rather imperialistic, picture, Steinmetz insists on man's responsibility to use properly the divine gift of language and quotes Matthew (12:36-37) about the punishment of individuals and societies that misuse language. The spirit of evil seeks to corrupt language, particularly by blasphemy and sarcasm. His strictures concerning blasphemy are not unexpected. Sarcasm, he maintains, denatures the meaning of words and attributes bad qualities to the good; the theater is a center of the misuse of language. Happily, God created the Catholic church as the guardian of the truth and of truth in language . . . A similar and even more complicated and metaphysical theory of language is offered by R. Bossey in the same periodical (1841, XII, 1 ff.). The *Université catholique* is not an illuminist publication; in the 1840s, it is the major periodical of French Catholic intellectuals—lay and clerical.

"L'Apparition" by Gustave Moreau (1826-1898), in the Musée Gustave Moreau, Paris

Illuminism, Conventionalism, and "Cratylism"

The illuminist tradition of language as being divine in origin is, of course, not the only linguistic theory propounded in early nineteenth-century France. Oversimplifying, one could divide the speculations on language into three tendencies: the illuminist, the conventionalist, and the "cratylist" or mimologist. The conventionalists, perhaps best represented by Destutt de Tracy in his *Eléments d'idéologie* (1801-1815), continue the Condillac tradition. Language is of human invention, provoked by our sense perceptions and developed by our faculties, and natural signs are refined and developed by the needs of survival, of society, and so on. It is noteworthy, however, that Destutt de Tracy also has a Utopian dream of a perfected language that would possess the referential certitude of the language of mathematics, where all misunderstanding and ambiguity would disappear; he, also, dreams of a transparency between thought and language.

Cratylism can, of course, enter into an illuminist theory of language but, as Gérard Genette has noted, is usually presented during the late eighteenth and early nineteenth centuries as an alternative explanation of the origin of language. Charles Nodier, the great exponent of mimologism in Romantic France, posits an origin in onomatopoeic imitation transformed and developed by metaphor and metonymy; poetry once again becomes the highest or purest form of language but for reasons quite different from those advanced by Louis-Claude de Saint-Martin. Nodier's theory is based on a series of "horizontal" harmonies among sounds, colors, forms, whereas in illuminist language theory the correspondences are vertical, between matter, man, and the divine.

Things are never all that simple, and Baudelaire's famed "Correspondances" discusses both. Modern poetry, with Nerval, Baudelaire, Hugo of the exile years, and their symbolist successors, thus faced a rich inheritance of theories of language. How much does it owe to illuminist theory? Parallels are tempting, but I think there are also problems. Illuminism is concerned with syntax; the poets were perhaps more preoccupied with the nature of the word. Mallarmé's debts to George Cox and Cox's debt to Nodier are well known; *Les Mots anglais*, Chapter IX of Victor Hugo's *Les Travailleurs de la mer*, Nerval's *Pandora*, those premonitions of *Finnegans Wake* rather represent explosions of cratylism à la Nodier, of horizontal correspondences among words with little if any verticality. Illuminist language theory posits the existence of the divine and seeks a restoration of the unity between that divine, language, and the created world. Hugo also sought such a restoration, but he posited that words as they are contain the Word, refused any hierarchial notion of language, and proposed the inherent goodness of what was normally labeled evil language. In the "Suite" to the "Réponse à un acte d'accusation," which requires and merits close reading, he refuses to say who created language. And Mallarmé's famed flower, absent from every bouquet, contradicts by its absence the illuminist dream of restoring creation in divine harmony. So far as symbolist poetics moves toward the notion that a poem must be, not mean, it creates a chasm between itself and the illuminist tradition. Signs are potentially motivated for both mimologists and illuminists, but Romantic illuminism is deeply marked by a Christian heritage on the one hand (whence the ease with which its tenets were adapted by such Catholics as Maistre, Ballanche, Bonald) and a belief in progress partly conceived of as a restoration of language. (A study of the evolution of A.-L. Constant, alias Eliphas Lévi, as he moves from Christian illuminism to a quite different kind of occultism, would probably help understand this historical change.) Christian illuminism surely survives, but its great twentieth-century exponent is not André Breton but Teilhard de Chardin. For Mallarmé, the poet becomes an angel, seemingly ex officio; for Saint-Martin, the poet is a man who desires God and the will of God. Mallarmé's poet gives a purer sense to the word and thereby separates it from all created bouquets; Saint-Martin's poet restores a purer sense in the word and thereby seeks to reunite created bouquets with the divine. The social dimensions of illuminist linguistic theory are largely absent from symbolist poetics. Mallarmé's poet is concerned with the words of the tribe; Saint-Martin's, with the words of the entire human race so far as the Word is at the origin of all creation. This constitutes a considerable change in perspective, the consequences of which are perhaps best illustrated in Rimbaud's *Alchimie du Verbe*—"l'histoire d'une de mes folies."

Notes

1. Lamennais, *Esquisse d'une philosophie* (1843), II, 222. Translation here, as throughout, my own, and not without problems as the French series "Logos-Verbe-Parole-Langue-Langage-Mot" does not correspond to the English "logos-word-language"; I have tried to solve the problem by a rather liberal use of capitals.

2. This essay owes much to many conversations with Karl Uitti and Jacques Seebacher. I have only scratched the surface of French Romantic theories on language and of the "divine origin" theories. Gordon Winant Hewes, *Language Origins, a Bibliography* (The Hague: Mouton, 1975), indexes "Divine origin of language" as well as "Origin of language theories" and "Eighteenth century theories" but not nineteenth; the listing is rich but far from complete. Karl Uitti, in *Linguistics and Literary Theory* (New York: Prentice-Hall, 1969), set the framework for investigations such as this. George Steiner, *After Babel* (Oxford: Oxford Univ. Press, 1975), presents a most rewarding study of myths about language. Gérard Genette's *Mimologiques, Voyage en Cratyle* (Paris: Seuil, 1976) is an absolutely remarkable study of cratylism through the ages, with an excellent chapter on Nodier. Also of use is Dell Hymes, ed., *Studies in the History of Linguistics* (Bloomington: Indiana Univ. Press, 1974) but the "divine origin" theories merit the kind of attention Genette has given the cratylists. On Boehme, an excellent article by Wolfgang Kayser, here used in its French translation, is "La doctrine du langage natural chez Jacob Boehme et ses sources," in *Poétique*, No. 11 (1972), pp. 337-365. On Saint-Martin, Robert Amadou's *Louis-Claude de Saint-Martin* (Paris: 1962) remains perhaps the best introduction but should be supplemented by later studies by Amadou, Nicole Chaquin, Léon Cellier, and Annie Becq. Becq's study on "Les traditions ésotériques" in *Histoire littéraire de la France*, Vol.7, (Paris: Editions Sociales, 1976), is a masterful synthesis, but Auguste Viatte, *Les Sources occultes du romantisme* (1928) has not been replaced. The only outstanding pertinent monograph is Cellier's study of *Fabre d'Olivet* (1953). French Romantic

thought on language, literature, aesthetics, the imagination, and particularly the mystical tradition in that thought has only recently begun to receive serious attention. Notable are Pierre Albouy, *La Création mythologique chez Victor Hugo* (1963); Hermine Riffaterre, *L'Orphisme dans la littérature romantique* (1970); Brian Juden, *Traditions orphiques et tendances mystiques dans le romantisme française* (1971); Paul Bénichou, *Le Sacre de l'écrivain* (1973) and *Le Temps de prophètes* (1977). To these should be added the many articles, prefaces, and studies of the late and much regretted Léon Cellier.

4

Love-in-Death:
Gautier's "morte amoureuse"

HERMINE RIFFATERRE

The myth of the "morte amoureuse," the dead woman in love, is a recurrent theme in Gautier's works.[1] The tragic quality of Eros and Thanatos fascinated him. Again and again the theme appears—sometimes
treated in a serious vein, sometimes in a lightly parodic manner: A woman
died yesterday or long ago (it matters not when) and returns to haunt
the narrator or the protagonist. The lady knocking at the smoker's door
in the story "Pipe d'opium"[2] ("Opium Pipe"), the young nun hovering
over the evenings of an idle rich man in *Spirite*[3] ("Spiritist") hypothesize
a world beyond. The haunted man is torn from his leisured bourgeois
smugness and precipitated into a quest of the ideal, for which his cult of
dilettante intellectualism has not prepared him. There is the vampirism of
the novella "La Morte amoureuse"[4] ("The Dead Woman in Love"), in
which "une morte" makes herself so desirable that the man who saw her
in a vision chooses to let himself bleed to death rather than lose the dream.
I think that neither Gautier's morbid tendencies nor the decadent extrem-
ism of the Romantics is sufficient explanation of his theme. This is not
mere literary fashion; the vampirism of the myth reflects deeper motifs.

It permits us to fathom the depths of an important source of Gautier's inspiration and perhaps to witness a stable law of poetic effort. For example, the theme may also be linked to an aesthetic of imagination, of which it is simply a variant.

Proof of both the vampire myth's power and of its sublimation in our author lies in the fact that the myth becomes language. Content may be lost, but the discourse is maintained. We know that the *Roman de la momie* ("The Novel of the Mummy") is the love story of Tahoser, the pharaoh's widow, buried by the Red Sea. The story is interred with the mummy in her underground grave; the prologue relates the discovery of the tomb; mummy and embalming motifs are the subjects for another tale, in a realistic vein, about the victory of beauty over death. This fiction uses the vampirism code for its discourse: the corpse is so well preserved (by an ancient and long-lost embalming art) that the young woman seems asleep. This mummy is not shriveled up—"racornie"—like other mummies; she had "conservé l'élasticité de la chair . . . les paupières encore frangées de leurs longs cils faisaient briller entre leurs lignes d'antimonies des yeux d'émail lustrés des humides lueurs de la vie"[5] (she had retained the elasticity of living flesh . . . the eyelids, still fringed with their long lashes, made her eyes sparkle between their metallic outlines, enamel eyes shining with the moist glow of life). Readers of Bram Stoker will recognize an "Undead" lying asleep in her coffin. And the mouth: "la bouche colorée d'une faible rougeur, avait gardé ses plis imperceptibles, et sur les lèvres voluptueusement modulées, voltigeait un mélancolique et mystérieux sourire" *(Roman de la momie,* 58-59) (the mouth, faintly tinted red, had retained its barely perceptible ridges, and over the voluptuously modeled lips hovered a melancholy and mysterious smile). We are reminded of an always-threatening mythical archetype: the crimson living mouth of the vampire Clarimonde in "La Morte amoureuse"; the mouth of the bloodless, waxlike ghost *(revenante)* in the "Pipe d'opium"—these were live mouths. "Tout en elle était mort: la bouche seule, fraîche comme une grenade en fleur, étincelait d'une vie riche et pourprée, et souriante à demi."[6] (Everything about her was dead; only her mouth, fresh as a blossoming pomegranate, glistened with a rich and carmine life, half smiling.) This mouth returned the kiss placed on it by the visitor to the grave.

The archaeological discovery itself gave rise to a tale about the dead who returned to life: "Ils tirèrent le cartonnage de sa boîte et le dressèrent contre une paroi.... Spectacle étrange que ce maillot funèbre à masque doré, se tenant debout comme un spectre matériel, et reprenant une fausse attitude de vie, après avoir gardé si longtemps la pose horizontale de la mort sur un lit de basalte, au coeur d'une montagne éventrée par une curiosité impie" *(Roman de la momie,* 50).　(They removed the bundle from its box and propped it up against a wall. . . . Strange spectacle, this funereal shroud with its gilded mask, standing there like a corporeal ghost, feigning to be alive again. It had lain there so long, stretched out as in death, upon a bed of basalt, in the heart of a mountain that had been disemboweled by an impious curiosity.)

To reinforce this impression, the Egyptologist is described as an expert on funeral rites, endowed with a bestial expression; Lord Evandale, expedition leader, is compared to Osiris: "son stick rappelait le sceptre" (his stick was like the scepter). Twice, therefore, an unlikely detail reveals the thrust of the repressed myth. Under the guise of comparisons and metaphors, the sketched-in necromantic ritual becomes rhetorical descriptive device and actual style.

Love Transcending Death

The discussion thus far has been about sublimation; now it remains to try to find its key in a significant episode illustrated by two variants of the myth. Commentators, from Van der Tuin to Albert Smith, agree that these variants exhibit characteristics completely unlike those found in Gautier. The two texts with these variants are the novella "La Morte amoureuse" (let me stress the word *novella* to differentiate the actual text from the potential myth) and *Spirite*, written at the end of Gautier's career.

In both these stories, the occasion of love at first sight and the encounter that consecrates the dead woman's love for a living man, the setting is a religious ordination. In the novella, Romuald, the hero, still chaste, innocent of sexual desire, has given himself up wholly to the love of God. In the course of the ordination ceremony, as the seminarian becomes the priest, sexuality is revealed to him. At the precise moment when his vows are separating him forever from the world and condemning him to a hopeless virginity, he sees Clarimonde, the beautiful vampire, and falls madly in love with her. Actually, the entire ceremony expresses the struggle between postulancy and the Satanic attraction of the courtesan. This struggle is augmented by Clarimonde's jealousy; she will later avenge herself by taking her future love captive under the pretense of receiving the last rites from his hand. Note that the seductress, who seems very much alive, is in fact *dead*; her victim's reprieve is temporary, and he escapes through a symbolic death. He is now a priest; as far as the world is concerned, it is the same as if he were dead.

In *Spirite*, the young woman gives herself spiritually to the hero, Guy de Malivert (whom she believes incapable of marrying), on the very day she takes her vows. But even before her actual death, at the time of the symbolic death of the novice who becomes a nun, at the very moment when her hair is being cut (this series of funereal images she calls "toilette du condamné, contact d'une hache"—153 [the beauty ritual of the condemned, the fall of the axe]), she faints, as though predicting her real death. Just as she takes up the veil—"Linceul symbolique qui me faisait morte au monde" (symbolic shroud that would make me dead as far as the world is concerned)—at that precise moment, she gives herself to the hero in spirit and vows to be his beyond the grave. This vow will be fulfilled later on and will lure its prey from the living world.

This double coincidence, of course, is no accident. Its intertext is the famous scene in *René*, where the hero watches his sister as she takes the veil and hears her confess aloud her incestuous passion for him, her brother. This confession is uttered at the very moment of her symbolic death; beneath the "suaire" that transforms her into a woman who is "dead," she is still capable of feeling mortal love. In Gautier as in Chateaubriand, the mouth of such a woman who was dead, but in love, is a metaphor; it is an oblique reference to the crossing of another boundary, another transgression: the incest taboo. In 1933, Van der Tuin remarked on the role played by the poet's sister (in his study on the *Evolution psychologique, esthétique et littéraire de Gautier*). We are thus tempted to see that the essential motif is love transcending death at the precise moment of death's triumph; as in Chateaubriand and as in Mallarmé, this love is a sublimation of repressed incest.

The Dream versus Reality

I come now to a second aspect of the myth that I believe is characteristic of Gautier's art. Rather than examine his psychology, I refer to the special qualities of his text, such as the technique he employs to convey the impression of verisimilitude. This technique is twofold: first, there is the possibility that an anomaly exists. Even if it does not, the idea of an anomaly cannot be rejected, so that even the incredulous allow themselves to become ensnared little by little. Second, there is the important role of *detail* in the narration. Let us begin by analyzing the first aspect of this technique. The question of an anomaly always comes up when we deal with the fantastic; in the same way, the bizarre, the abnormal, and the unbelievable are so presented that the reader is unable to make up his mind whether he is faced with a dream, a hallucination, or reality—if the last, then something truly supernatural.

In Gautier, this dilemma is almost always confined to the halfway state between sleeping and waking. In the myth of the *morte amoureuse*, the object or target of the dead woman's ardor or desire always ends up by actually substituting the dream for the waking state, that is, reality. In the novella "La Morte amoureuse," a country priest is seduced by a vampire. Not only does he believe himself to be dreaming that he has become the lover of the courtesan Clarimonde but he dreams also that he is leading a life of luxury in a Venetian palazzo, far away from his humble parishioners. His dreams soon carry him away completely, and he begins to believe that he is a wealthy and fashionable Venetian jet-setter, who is afflicted with a recurrent nightmare, in which he is a wretched priest forbidden carnal pleasures. His "real" life is thus the life generated by the repression of his true desires. In other texts, every time the dead woman is glimpsed by the man who loves her, a kind of nostalgia overtakes him:

it is not long before the lover is convinced that his real life is but that of an exile. His actual life, that is, the life presented as real at the beginning of the story or novel, becomes for the reader the spring-board to verisimilitude or truth. This is particularly clear in the case of Guy dé Malivert, the protagonist of *Spirite*. There are more light and more sun in his nocturnal dreams than there are in the daytime for him. Because it is an accepted fact that dreams have no sunshine, the reader must conclude that there has been a juxtaposition, a permutation from the oneiric to the actual. In the *Roman de la momie*, Lord Evandale remains a bachelor, although he is one of the most eligible men in England; this proves to the reader that his true life has been transposed to ancient Egypt, where he has found the Pharaoh's wife, the woman whose mummy he unearthed (305-306).

It is important to emphasize here that this technique is also characteristic of a formula for aesthetics and metaphysics that has been given by Charles Nodier:

> L'impression de cette vie de l'homme que le sommeil usurpe sur sa vie positive, comme pour lui révéler une autre existence et d'autres facultés. . . . La vie du sommeil est bien plus solennelle que l'autre . . . le sommeil est non seulement l'état le plus puissant, mais encore le plus lucide de la pensée, sinon dans les illusions passagères dont il l'enveloppe, du moins dans les perceptions qui en dérivent. . . . Cette mort intermittente, où il lui (à l'esprit) est permis de reposer dans sa propre essence et à l'abri de toutes les influences de la personnalité de convention que la société nous a faite.[7]
>
> (The impression of man's life that sleep is a thief, encroaching on his real life as if to reveal to him another existence and other capabilities. . . . The life of sleep is much more solemn than the other. . . . Sleep is not only the most powerful state of thought, it is also the most lucid, if not in the passing illusions that clothe it, at least in the perceptions that derive from it. . . . This intermittent death, where he [his spirit] is permitted to rest in his own essence, sheltered from all the influences of the conventional personality society has imposed on us.)

This formula is the key to the integration of myth and art: as a tale of marvelous adventure, the myth serves as narrative support for the quest of the ideal. It is used as a variant of a structure whose constant is the search for beauty. It is not by chance that the hero of *Spirite*, visiting Greece with his invisible seductress, suddenly contemplates "the Parthenon as it was in the days of its splendors" (205). In Gautier, this myth has the unique characteristic of never turning into a horror story, ending with a sinister awakening to confront the avid succubus at last unmasked (the *Albertus* parody apart): this dream is wholly positive. Even the funeral is a source of beauty; or, if you prefer, death = love = beauty; or, in the words of *Spirite*, the myth and its vision "rappelle [nt] . . . les beautés que font entrevoir les magies du rêve, l'imagination des poètes, et le génie des peintres (86)" (remind us of the beauties that we are allowed to perceive through the magic of dream, the imagination of poets, and the genius of painters).

The Little Detail That Is True

Next, the role of *detail* is considered. Each apparition and each visitation are given versimilitude by the device of the "petit fait vrai," (little detail that is true), in the manner of Stendhal. Each time the protagonist thinks he is prey to an illusion, some tangible object that he sees during the vision, an object already noticed before the vision, gives silent witness when he wakes up: this is concrete proof that he has not invented the whole thing. However, there are two different types of detail. First, there is the detail that gives the illusion of reality and is itself invaded by the vision. All the elements that looked like mere decor become metonymic of the dead woman's presence within this decor. For example, "les plis des rideaux prenaient l'aspect de vêtements féminins et semblaient palpiter comme agités par le mouvement d'un corps" *(Spirite*, 58) (the folds of the curtains took on the appearance of feminine clothing and seemed to rustle, as if stirred by the movement of a body). Moving curtains are frightening; this is an ordinary experience. Another example is even more convincing by its very exaggeration. It is almost a parody of itself, and it underlines the main purpose of the system. In "La Cafetière" ("The Coffee Pot"), the elegant shape of a rather prosaic object becomes the profile of the vampire. In other words, the "petit fait vrai," impregnating the enamored dead woman, is evidence of erotic paranoia rather than of the actual experience: the absent woman saturates the whole decor, and everything that is visible bears witness to the invisible. The nonmotivation of the "petit fait vrai," its irrelevance to the plot and the story, its function as objective marker, are characteristics of what may be termed the mystery's discourse.[8]

The second category of details giving the illusion of versimilitude is perhaps more interesting because it has links with the aesthetics that made Gautier the embodiment of the Parnassian writer. This type of detail must seem as natural, as normal, and as ordinary as possible. In context it is essentially the symbol of what is most perishable and most transitory. The paradox is that the anomaly is manifested right at the peak of the norm—according to the rule Gautier himself attributed to Hoffmann, master of the fantastic:

> Vous voyez un intérieur allemand, planche de sapin bien frotté au grès, murailles blanches, un clavecin dans un coin, une table à thé au milieu, tout ce qu'il y a de plus simple et de plus uni au

A romantic variant of a vampire archetype by Gustave Doré (1833-1883)
for Dante's *Inferno*

monde; mais une corde du clavecin se casse toute seule avec un son qui ressemble à un soupir de femme. . . . La tranquillité du lecteur est déjà troublée, et il prend en défiance cet intérieur si calme et si bon. Hoffman a beau assurer que cette corde n'est véritablement pas autre chose qu'une corde trop tendue qui s'est rompue comme cela arrive tous les jours, le lecteur ne veut rien croire.[9]

(You see a German interior, pinewood well polished with sandstone, white walls, a harpsichord in the corner, a tea table in the center, the plainest and simplest place in the world; but then a string of the harpsichord breaks all by itself, with a sound like a woman sighing. . . . The reader's tranquillity is already disturbed, and he becomes suspicious of this room, so nice and quiet. It is useless for Hoffmann to assure us that this string is in fact nothing but a string stretched too tight, that it has snapped, as happens every day; the reader will have none of it.)

Nor is this all. Not only do the ordinary and the extraordinary still coincide so that the illusion of reality is maintained, but the perishable and the eternal also coincide. The most transitory, evanescent traces of the dead woman in love become a monument to her beauty or better still, a monument to beauty itself. In the *Roman de la monie*, the first sign of proclaiming the immortality of buried beauty, is a 30-century-old footprint in the dust of the hypogeum (35, 36). In the "Pipe d'opium," the smoker, intoxicated by the drug, hallucinates and sees the dead woman's foot (420). At first, this detail merely suggests suspense, but then it becomes an object of beauty: the foot is compared to the marble of an ancient statue. Although this anatomical reference may seem quite insignificant, it actually suggests a polarization, almost an aesthetic fetishism; (the title *Le Pied de la momie* indicates as much): reverie and amorous madness seize upon these vestiges of a departed body. Elsewhere the daydream will dwell upon the reflection of a face in a mirror, a reflection that is so faint that it is impossible to know which eye has seen it—the eye of the flesh or the eye of the soul. Elsewhere again, a perfume plays this role.

In *Giselle*, the ballet whose libretto Gautier wrote for the dancer Carlotta Grisi, the myth is adapted to the genre, and *la morte amoureuse* becomes a dancer beyond the grave. We know the motif is not due to chance in Gautier because ghost dancers appear also in "La Cafetière" of the *Jeunes-France*, and "Inès de Sierra" in *Emaux et Camées*. After Giselle dies, her heart broken by an unfaithful lover, she becomes a "Willi," that is to say, in the Germanic mythology that Heine made fashionable in France, a sort of waltzing undine who entices each of her victims to dance until the unhappy wretch falls into the water and drowns. Her mother, assuming the anticipated role of the *mater dolorosa* (grieving mother) tells her:

> Tu iras au bal de minuit avec une robe de clair de lune. Tu en-
> traîneras les voyageurs dans la ronde fatale, et tu les précipiteras
> dans l'eau glaciale du lac, tout haletants et tout ruisselants de
> sueur. Tu seras un vampire de la dance! [*Souvenirs de théâtre,
> 101*].

> (You will go to the midnight ball in a dress of moonlight . . .
> you will draw travelers to join in the fatal dance, and you will
> throw them in the icy water of the lake, panting and streaming
> with sweat. You will be a vampire of the dance!)

Now she is dead but still passionate; as she herself says, "Il est si bon
de sentir une tiède larme pénétrer sous terre jusqu'à [moi], et tomber
d'un oeil brûlant sur [mon] coeur glacé" (109) it is so good to feel a
warm tear sink down through the earth until it reaches me, to feel it fall
from a burning eye upon my icy heart). When her lover loses his way near
her grave at the edge of the swamp, she pulls him into the dance; she ma-
terializes out of the fog; only the light of the day saves him. The first sign
he gets of Giselle's presence is her footprint; need one point out that a
dancer's foot is by definition an art object or an instrument of art? But
the imprint of a beauty persisting beyond death, the betraying vestige
stressed in the libretto, is a faint, sweet aroma first described as a mystery
and then at last revealed as the incarnation of the vampire's soul: "Une
rose qu'il cueille sur la tombe, une rose où l'âme de Giselle a laissé son
chaste parfum, voilà désormais tout ce qui reste au comte Albrecht de la
pauvre villageoise" (110). (A rose that he picks on her grave, and still
clinging to the rose the chaste perfume of Giselle's soul, henceforth this
is all Count Albrecht will have left of the poor village girl.) Whether or
not we are dealing with a flower (and such flowers, by definition, become
wilted, lose their petals and their scent), we have here simultaneously the
permanence of the symbolic object, the character as a sign of beauty, and
the paradox of its frailty carried to the extreme.

The detail manifesting the presence of the invisible and its tangible
proof is always the locus of a paradox. Impermanence becomes the marker
of permanence; the ephemeral becomes the eternal monument to a moment of erotic pleasure and expresses itself through the conventions of
amorous discourse. The most revealing formula in this connection is always the most antithetical: "effleurer ces cheveux plus durables que les
empires, plus solides que des monuments de granit" *(Roman de la momie,*
p. 60) (touch lightly this hair more durable than empires, more solid than
granite monuments). The reader will recognize the parallel to Gautier's
most famous verses, to the "l'Art" stanza in *Emaux et Camées*, summariz-
ing his philosophy of artifice:

Tout passe.—l'art robuste
Seul a l'éternité,
   Le buste
Survit à la cité.

In the light of this analogy, we must conclude that the lesson Gautier wished to teach us was not the dramatic rather aleatory lesson of the survival of the object, after the collapse of an entire civilization. That would only show his liking for antithesis. The truth is that it is necessary to isolate an object in order to describe it. Here the metonymic proliferation of amorous paranoia is but a pretext for choosing the insignificant and unmotivated detail. The description of such detail will strengthen its paradoxical impact and give it the insignificance that will make it a vehicle of symbolism.

Should we wish to classify this technique, the Parnassian label would be just an obvious borrowing from literary nomenclature. We must keep Romanticism, for the story—the narrative pretext—is drawn from that reservoir of archetypes. It seems to me that it is also important to note that the use of such details anticipates the surrealist object, the *ready-made:* by merely isolating the object, by merely *uttering* this object, the writer transforms it into a work of art.

Notes

1. The literal translation of "la morte amoureuse" is "the dead woman in love." I shall use *morte amoureuse* throughout this chapter.
2. Théophile Gautier, "La Pipe d'opium," *Romans et Contes* (Paris: Bibliothèque Charpentier), pp. 415-427.
3. Gautier, *Spirite: Nouvelle fantastique* (Paris: Nizet, 1970), p. 44.
4. Gautier, "La Morte amoureuse," *Nouvelles* (Paris: Bibliothèque Charpentier, 1967), pp. 263-295. In "Notes sur le fantastique (textes de Théophile Gautier)," an article in *Littérature* (December 1972), pp. 3-23, Jean Bellemin-Noël gives a psychoanalytical interpretation of "La Morte amoureuse" and most of the nouvellas examined in this chapter. These women vampires and the fantastic in general are regarded as symbols of castration by women. One can also find an ideological treatment of "La Morte amoureuse" and the other "fantastic" Gautier novellas in Decottignies, "A propos de 'La Morte amoureuse' de Théophile Gautier: Fiction et Idéologie dans le récit fantastique," *Revue d'Histoire Littéraire de la France* (1972), pp. 616-625. For Gautier and the literature of the fantastic, see Albert B. Smith, *Théophile Gautier and the Fantastic* (Jackson, Miss.: Univ. Press of Mississippi, 1977).
5. Gautier, *Le Roman de la momie* (Paris: Bibliothèque Charpentier), p. 58.
6. Gautier, "La Pipe d'opium," *Romans et Contes,* p. 424.
7. Charles Nodier in Albert Béguin's *L'Ame romantique et le rêve* (Paris: Corti, 1939), p. 340.
8. Gautier, "Contes humoristique: La Cafetière," *Les Jeunes-France* (Paris: Bibliothèque Charpentier, 1873), p. 259.
9. Gautier, "Les Contes d'Hoffmann," *Souvenirs de théâtre* (Paris), p. 44.

5

Ghosts, Spirits, and Force: Samuel Taylor Coleridge

ANYA TAYLOR

The *Philosophical Lectures* of 1818 amply document Coleridge's intention to reject the occult in its many Neoplatonic, Gothic, and folkloric forms.[1] In Coleridge's view, the occult—because it aims to achieve illumination all at once and because it assumes an inextricable intermingling of spirit and matter—makes communion with divine power too easy and leads at worst to the worship of self. It is, therefore, surprising to notice, as Kathleen Coburn observed in her 1949 introduction to these lectures, how often Coleridge recurs to theories that we habitually group under the term *occult*—theories of analogous universes, of correspondences among things and thoughts, and of the outgoing and effective energies of mind, as these theories are enunciated by Plotinus, Psellus, Agrippa, Bruno, Ficino, and in the seemingly congruent formulations in non-European cultures—and how often Coleridge describes these theories with partial sympathy.[2]

Much in these theories foreshadows important elements in Romantic conceptions of "imagination" and of "self." These theories, taken together, are roughly equivalent to what Coleridge calls the "Plotino-platonic philosophy," a philosophy that does not lull "the Soul into an indolence of mere attention . . . but rouses it to acts and energies of creative Thought, & Recognition—of conscious re-production of states of Being."[3] So rousing is this philosophy that "no man worthy the name of man can read the many extracts from Proclus, Porphyry, Plotinus, &c . . . . without an ahndung, an inward omening, of a system congruous with his nature & thence attracting it."[4] Whatever theoretical criticisms Coleridge has, he nevertheless praises the energy roused up by this philosophy and its inspiration to "conscious re-production of states of Being"; he believes that we are drawn naturally to such theories because they correspond to our deepest, most active, powers of mind. Moreover, Coleridge continues to investigate the occult long into what those who compartmentalize his life would call his devoutly Christian, specifically Trinitarian, period; even where he works to establish Christian principles, as in *The Friend*, he turns nevertheless to this subject, claiming that he "had long wished to devote an entire work to the subject of Dreams, Visions, Ghosts, Witchcraft, etc.," a work that was to have taken the form of a "psychology." In preparation for such a work, he claims to have so filled a whole memorandum book with records of ghostly phenomena that ironically he has ceased to believe in them.[5]

Given his complex stance in relation to the occult, we may wonder what purpose these continuing studies served in the development of Coleridge's wide-ranging and influential thought. I want to suggest that Coleridge, whose Christianity rejected idolatry and whose curiosity about science encouraged skepticism, nevertheless persisted in investigating these subliminal communications, these outgoings of force, and these vanishings of ghostly beings in his poems and in his speculative thought because they seemed to contribute to his knowledge of being and because they helped to explain the mysterious fluctuations of power and powerlessness within each individual and among individuals. Ghosts, dreams, visions, witchcraft, active powers, energies, and conscious reproduction of states of Being: these phenomena will, he hopes, converge into a discovery of what we are and of where our life lies hidden.

The Basis of Coleridge's Supernatural Beliefs

Coleridge's preoccupation with invisible powers—with invisibility and with potency—has its intellectual origin in his profound understanding of the value and also the limitation of the eighteenth-century skeptical philosophers. Along with his arguments against the mind's passivity and in favor of a view of the outgoing, energetic apprehensiveness of thought came a less often emphasized argument against the eighteenth-century insistence in "visibility," the deathly hold of the sense of sight. Coleridge clarifies this opposition to the criterion of "visibility" in "The Statesman's Manual," an opposition that he had long intuited. In the Manual he explains that "the leading differences between mechanic and vital philosophy may all be drawn from one point: namely, that the former demanding for every mode and act of existence real or possible *visibility*, knows only of distance and nearness, composition . . . and decomposition, in short the relations of unproductive particles to each other. . . . This is the philosophy of death, and only of a dead nature can it hold good."[6] By flattening everything into the dimensions of the seen and by demanding that all conceptions be picturable, the empirical philosophers banish the invisible powers as being by definition nonexistent because invisible, and thus they cut the link between values and their invisible ground. Like Thomas probing the wounds of the risen Christ, these "Laodiceans in spirit"[7] ask for sensuous proof before they will believe. At their touch, the invisible powers evaporate and with them, Coleridge seems to believe, the freedom of the spirit, which depends upon the postulation of an invisible world.

Despite his own frequently voiced skepticism, Coleridge believes in some deep corner of his heart that "demonstrated Truths are inferior in kind of certainty to the Indemonstrable out of which the former are deduced"[8] and that an invisible grounding may validate a truth more permanently than a visible one. "Those whispers just as you have fallen or are falling asleep—what are they and whence?"[9] asks Coleridge with his persistent curiosity about the margins of consciousness, the borders between the visible and the invisible, where certainties may be hidden.[10] Not only in the famous supernatural poems where invisible voices sing, strange powers radiate from one speaker to his listener, a mother's spirit hovers and warns, and dreams are read with uncanny telepathy, but even in his views of the workings of thought, Coleridge peers toward the invisible. Dorothy Emmett has hinted that there are more spirits in Coleridge's philosophy than rational religionists would concede, that his "notion of Ideas as dynamic powers . . . sounds like primitive animism, but this does not mean it should be dismissed. Primitive animism may not be all nonsense, but that is another story."[11]

Some of Coleridge's interest in the invisible phenomena may have arisen, then, in reaction to the visibility demanded by the eighteenth-century philosophers as proof of reality. At the same time, a good part of his concern with power, with powers, and with potency in general, with the outward moving of inward energy, may have been inspired by his readings of these philosophers, particularly because his interest in ghosts and spirits arises from his heightened sensitivity to the systole and diastole of power as a personally felt reality. From David Hume, in particular, he may have learned about the subjective projection of power, for Hume, that most thoroughly skeptical of eighteenth-century philosophers, argues in *The Enquiry* that we have fancied all spiritual power as a reflection of our own inward power when it is most intense.[12] For Hume, the imaginary nature of such analogies indicates their foolishness; for Coleridge, however, the radiations of analogy provide vitality to the universe around us and constitute the central interest of our thought.[13] Coleridge had an eighteenth-century precedent for criticizing Hume's perspective in Bishop Berkeley's dialogue *Alciphron*, where the Humean Alciphron mocks the "mere prejudice" that there are spirits by saying, "Men frame an idea of chimera in their own minds, and then fall down and worship it."[14] In the dialogue the skeptic is refuted by a full panoply of Neoplatonic spirit lore.

Aspects of the Supernatural in Coleridge's Writings

Beginning like these real and fictional skeptics with a subjectively felt projection of power, Coleridge himself observes the waxing and waning energies of his own personality and sees them as having analogies in the spirit world.[15] On occasion he feels that he has "such a power of Life within me. . . that none could die whom I intensely loved." These experiences of radiating energies suggest to him that "there may be unions and connections out of the visible world" *(Collected Letters*, I, 490).[16] On other occasions, he is overcome with his own weakness, with a feeling of being emptied out. These experiences come to him in the form of a haunting, as if, like his Christabel, he had been sapped of his substance by an invisible parasite. He writes of "a sense of weakness—a haunting sense" that he has "power not strength"; this feeling of emptiness is "as fair a statement of my habitual Haunting, as I could give before the Tribunal of Heaven" *(Collected Letters*, II, 509). By contrast, he admires Wordsworth's power: "Strong in Thyself and powerful to give strength."[17] There is other evidence, too, that Coleridge knows in his own life the waxing and waning of force; when it waxes, he feels his own subjective being irradiating the world outside him and seeming even to preempt its natural processes; when it wanes, he feels his "I" overwhelmed by the contrary opaque forces of the objects of his senses, and these objects become more powerful than he. In such personal fluctuations he roots his theoretical meditations on the alternating authority of subject and object.

How does one discuss these alternations of force or give names to invisible fluctuations that seem to follow irrational impulses of their own, often glimpsed in dreams? Coleridge calls the poems "Phantom" and "Phantom or Fact" "fragments from the life of dreams";[15] by using this vocabulary from the world of spirits, he can perhaps begin to comprehend the workings of the subconscious and conscious mind. Not limiting his use of this vocabulary to the overtly supernatural poems, Coleridge writes, for example, in his late poem "Human Life":

> Why waste thy sighs, and thy lamenting voices,
> Image of Image, Ghost of Ghostly Elf [*CP*, p. 426; ll. 22-23]

In "Limbo," he cries in disgust,

The sole true Something—This! In Limbo's Den
It frightens Ghosts, as here Ghosts frighten men. *[CP*, p.
429, ll. 1-2]

In a late fragment, number 22, he worries still about these shadowy fragments:

> The body,
> Eternal Shadow of the finite Soul,
> The Soul's self-symbol, its image of itself
> Its own yet not itself. [*CP*, p. 498]

He is concerned with "phantoms of sublimity," with "angel visitants," and with motions as abrupt "as Spirits vanish."[19]

Ghosts and spirits are images for how we feel about ourselves in moods of power or weakness, either capable and effective or vulnerable and subject to the influences of other powers. The notebooks indicate that Coleridge often analyzes himself in these terms, where, for example, he becomes a ghost in relation to the substantial men of the world around him *(Notebooks*, 3324); he is different in substance from them because he seems to evaporate or blur; but in his ghostliness lies his genius. Similarly in *Notebooks*, 1241, he plans "Poems.—Ghost of a mountain/ the forms seizing my body, as I passed, became realities—I, a Ghost, till I had reconquered my substance." Here the mountains, like the substantial men of the world, begin as Ghosts; then by a sort of thickening of the air, they absorb his substance and leave him insubstantial, until he, in turn, can reassert his force and reclaim his substance. Elsewhere *(Notebooks*, 3026) shadows gather to make up the substance of self. In these instances and others, Coleridge uses a vocabularly of occult spirits and ghosts for dealing with interior events, for indicating that we are conscious of fragments within ourselves. Phantoms, spectres. and ghosts become ways of speaking about the splitness of our being and about our ability to step back and forth into and out of this shifting entity, to imagine ourselves as other to ourselves, by virtue of being multiple. As the personality thins and thickens from ghost to substance and back again, the self-conscious spirit becomes increasingly split, containing a multeity of projected and absorbed phantasms. These refracted images eventually become the basis for Coleridge's proofs that we are spirits, a proof presented most carefully in the *Biographia Literaria*, to which we will return.

Coleridge extends these interior fluctuations to human relations; a number of his poems examine passionate tangles of love and power by using terms from the occult interchange of forces. In dealing with such difficult situations, whose dynamics are often glimpsed in throbbing silences, Coleridge unearths an area of feeling that Wordsworth, for instance, finds less central than the elemental sorrows of parent and child. Man and woman, woman and woman, in Coleridge's poems possess each other like spirits and ghosts. Where Wordsworth preferred solitary figures already abandoned and battered by poverty and war, Coleridge broods upon sexual relations that become ultimately spiritual relations, based perhaps on the mutual diminishments of his own thwarted loves. He finds in love a field of force that waxes and wanes, a trouble to his dreams, that takes shape as a multitude of fiends,

> a fiendish crowd,
> Of shapes and thoughts that tortured me:
> A lurid light, a trampling throng,
> Sense of intolerable wrong,
> And whom I scorned, those only strong! [*CP*, p. 389; ll. 16-20]

Coleridge often describes this power struggle in occult terms. In "The Three Graves," written in collaboration with Wordsworth and never finished, he captures the eery power of desire. In a note to the poem written in 1817, he confesses that at the time of the writing of the poem he "was less averse to such subjects than at present" and that after "reading Bryan Edwards's account of the effect of the *Oby* witchcraft on the Negroes in the West Indies, and Hearne's deeply interesting anecdotes of similar workings on the imagination of the Copper Indians," he "conceived the design of showing that instances of this kind are not peculiar to savage or barbarous peoples" *(CP*, p. 269). In "The Three Graves" a mother wishes to possess her daughter's lover, subverts the daughter, and then curses her. The poem is rife with ominous silences and radiations of feeling. For example, the mother and prospective son-in-law hear the girl above them decking the bridal bed; the mother, aghast at the imminence of the event, is propelled to act to keep the man herself. Ordering the daughter away, she cries:

> "Would ye come here, ye maiden vile.
>   And rob me of my mate?"
> And on her child the mother scowled
>   A deadly leer of hate.
>
> Fast rooted to the spot, you guess,
>   The wretched maiden stood,
> As pale as any ghost of night
>   That wanteth flesh and blood.
>
> She did not groan, she did not fall,
>   She did not shed a tear,
> Nor did she cry, "Oh! mother, why
>   May I not enter here?"

> But wildly up the stairs she ran,
>   As if her sense was fled,
> And then her trembling limbs she threw
>   Upon the bridal bed. [*CP*, p. 272; ll. 78-93]

In the midst of the melodrama Coleridge deals with passions too unaccountable to present except as expanding potencies, flashing eyes, fierce hates, and invisible methods of destroying the force of others. Like Christabel, the child is unable to speak in her own defense; transfixed by invisible radiations, she becomes "as pale as any ghost." The impassioned mother, denouncing the daughter, proposes to the lover and is answered with a maniacal laugh. The mother's vengeful curse sounds in the upper room (ll. 134-145), and the girl is doomed; she hears it and "the bed beneath her stirred" (l. 149). The mother curses the daughter to barrenness, haunting the marriage bed. Because of this passionate history, expressed in the ballad tradition of supernatural and uncanny powers, the graves of these haunted beings are surrounded with ghosts (l. 217), with wandering spirits (l. 207), and with howling fiends (l. 209). Physiological symptoms of decline are explained in terms of occult changes. After the wedding

> The shade o'er-flushed her limbs with heat—
>   Then came a chill like death,
> And when the merry bells rang out,
>   They seemed to stop her breath. [*CP*, p.277; ll. 252-255]

Listless and joyless, the young couple waste away, haunted by the mother's rage and by the efficient words of her curses.

> She had a sore grief of her own,
>   A haunting in her brain. [*CP*, p. 281; ll. 428-429]

Convulsion, compulsion, melancholia, and hallucination combine with a change of form so that the daughter, while wasting, takes on the look of her mother, the power invading her, as Christabel similarly took on the aspect of Geraldine, squinting and hissing: the husband, dreaming of tearing out a woman's heart, suddenly dies. Such a series of hauntings and cursings seems to us extreme, but Coleridge tries to deal with the inscrutable ways in which the omnipotence of one mind imposes on the fragility of another, in which one substance absorbs another, leaving a ghost, and that ghost reflecting the shadow of the powerful hostile substance. This is a problem that, as we saw, concerned him in his own subjective life, and it is one of the ways in which he saw the ancient traditions of occult force still operating. Other poems on love reveal a similar use of this occult vocabulary. In "The Picture; or, The Lover's Resolution" the lovers like departed waves meet,

Each in the other lost and found: and see
Placeless, as spirits, one soft water-sun
Throbbing within them, heart at once and eye! [*CP*, p. 373;
ll. 127-129]

Similarly, in "The Exchange" the lovers become identical, trembling together, having exchanged not only their vows, but even their personalities:

I strove to act the man—in vain!
We had exchanged our hearts indeed. [*CP*, p. 391; ll. 7-8]

In the last stanza of "Lewti," the poet imagines inhabiting another's dream,

Oh! that she saw me in a dream,
    And dreamt that I had died for care;
All pale and wasted I would seem,
    Yet fair withal, as spirits are! *[CP*, p. 256; ll. 76-79]

However sinister these relations and interchanges sometimes are, they expand the range of the soul's life and allow us to see its vitality in a highly charged state. In *Coleridge and the Idea of Love*, Anthony John Harding discerns that images of phantoms and spectres are often connected with images of the loved one, as the lover's soul opens to include the shadow of the loved one or the loved one becomes the substance of the lover's ghost. Harding indicates that these fragments gather together to form that difficult being, the original self; the desire to escape from himself and yet to be multiple within himself combine to re-create the individual self in a higher form.[20]

Why do these images surround the condition of love? In the exalted and complex meaning that Coleridge gives to this term, love arouses in each soul such a series of vital dreams, reflections of the life of self with others, that spirits seem to interchange their essential natures. This proliferation of parts in a state of mind that brings the whole soul of man into activity allows us to glimpse inside ourselves the intricate realities of our spiritual beings. We know this intricacy most intensely when we have stepped over into this state by an act of will, mingled with desire and leading ultimately to God. In this state we are most fully and transparently ourselves. We are spirits and essences, volatile and free. The strange intensities of love, Coleridge writes in *Notebooks*, 3372, teach us about the psychology of superstition, and he finds himself thinking of his own love for Asra as an aching in his eyes toward vacancy—"yea, even when the Beloved is present, seeming to look thro' her and asking for her very Self within or even beyond her apparent Form" (*Notebooks*, 3370).

An illustration by Gustave Doré (1833-1883) for the verse by Coleridge

A speck, a mist, a shape, I wist!
And still it neared and neared.

Coleridge's Philosophy Concerning the Supernatural

Coleridge does not say that there are ghosts, but that there are states of mind when we feel such presences intensely. Given the imaginative shaping of our sense of our lives by the primary imagination at all times, such an intense feeling of reality may be real enough. Because our feelings about the fragmentation, hollowness, or fullness of our own selves constitute our immediate sense of self, we need images to convey this sense. For Coleridge those ancient terms of the spirit world, which have now been partially modified in the fictive terminology of psychoanalysis, serve that purpose. Not only that, but the vocabulary of shadows, spectres, and ghosts, (more closely resembling Jung's psychological terminology than Freud's) helps him analyze the psychic being with a view toward proving the soul autonomous. For fundamental to Coleridge's difficulties with radiating energies is the question of how he exists as more than matter. Struggling to define his own spiritual being in the midst of his expanding and contracting energies, he comes to make this kaleidoscopic multiplicity a basis for his proof that we are spirits. In the *Biographia* he seems to believe that the fact that we conceive of ourselves as split is, in part, what makes us different from the objects of our contemplation, which, by being objects merely and not at the same time self-conscious subjects, are fixed and dead. We who contemplate them, however, contemplate ourselves in all that we conceive, thus including within us both subject and object. He writes of the spirit as a "self-duplication," when the soul represents itself to itself as both subject and object of its own contemplation. Unlike nonspiritual objects, it refracts its being into "modes and repetitions of itself";[21] it sees everywhere a "reflex of itself," duplicating, echoing, and repeating its being in shadows. These multiple refractions of the self lead Coleridge to intuit a divine ground of Being, which roots these refractions in eternity. We are spirits, then, to the extent that we envision aspects of ourselves, and, recognizing our own fragmentation, go on to imagine the fragments to be ghosts and apparitions that give evidence of "unions and connections out of the visible world."

Coleridge's interest in power, force, and energy as figured in spirits has affinities with many other nineteenth-century investigations, and yet his chiefly differs from these by bringing the accessions and evaporations of power into balance under a Christian reconciliation. Though he knows Fichte's theory of egoismus, for example, so premonitory of Nietzsche's, he ridicules it as trying to be all in all, the root and conjugation of being, without reference to God;[22] and even as he follows closely and sometimes copies German *Naturphilosophen*, he strives to bring the magnetism of their polarities under a third, divine, term. His concern with power and powerlessness, imaginatively represented as substance and shadow, seems to bear a close affinity to the theories of William Butler Yeats, later developed in part out of Nietzsche's antinomies. But the antithetical and primary masks are not theories for Coleridge as much as agonized feelings of powerlessness and power, spirit and substance, an agony occasionally resolved in moments of unity. For Coleridge's concern with spirits is not theoretical or archaic but is at the core of his own personal life and of his faith. He must solve the problem of spirits and ghosts, as he solves the problem of being a more than material substance. If we are in some sense spirits, passing in and out of unions and connections beyond the visible world, our element is not matter or air or anything else measurable by the senses. Our element is freedom: "the medium by which spirits understand each other is not the surrounding air, but the freedom which they possess in common, as the common ethereal element of their being, the tremulous reciprocations of which propagate themselves even to the inmost soul."[23] In poems, philosophical speculations, and in private notes, these "tremulous reciprocations" are an essential indication for him of our more than animal life and of an immortality that must be because we intuitively yearn for it beyond our visible substance. Thus, topics usually considered "occult" serve Coleridge as aids to faith.

Notes

1. *The Philosophical Lectures,* ed. Kathleen Coburn (London: Pilot Press, 1949), for example, pp. 92, 250, 282. Among critics who stress this rejection, see Owen Barfield, *What Coleridge Thought* (Middletown: Wesleyan Univ. Press, 1971), p. 25.

2. *Philosophical Lectures,* pp. 144-147.

3. *The Notebooks of Samuel Taylor Coleridge,* ed. Kathleen Coburn (New York: Pantheon, 1957-   ), III, 3935.

4. Ibid.

5. *The Friend,* ed. Barbara E. Rooke, in *The Collected Works of Samuel Taylor Coleridge,* ed. Kathleen Coburn (Princeton: Princeton Univ. Press, 1969), IV, 1, p. 146.

6. *Lay Sermons,* ed. R. J. White, in *The Collected Works,* ed. Kathleen Coburn (Princeton: Princeton Univ. Press, 1972), VI, p. 89.

7. *Lay Sermons,* p. 93. For Coleridge's belief that realities can be conceived without being perceived or pictured, see the *Biographia Literaria,* ed. George Watson (London: Dent, 1965), p. 157. See also his remark to Wedgwood, in Letter 383, *Collected Letters,* ed. E. L. Griggs (Oxford: Clarendon, 1956-   ), II, that "to assert that a thing is so and so, and to assert that it *cannot* be demonstrated *not* to be so and so, form articles of belief widely different from each other."

8. *Notebooks,* 3783.

9. Ibid., 2470.

10. See Angus Fletcher, " 'Positive Negation': Threshold, Sequence, and Personification in Coleridge," in *New Perspectives on Coleridge and Wordsworth,* ed. Geoffrey Hartman (New York: Columbia Univ. Press, 1972), pp. 133-136.

11. Dorothy Emmett, "Coleridge on Powers in Mind and Nature," in *Coleridge's Variety,* ed. John Beer (Pittsburgh: Pittsburgh Univ. Press, 1974), p. 170. Emmett, p. 177, cites F. J. A. Hort for an early appreciation of the seriousness of Coleridge's interest in spirits. In his new edition of Coleridge's *Verse* (London: Faber, 1972), pp. 18-20, William Empson overestimates not so much the extent of Coleridge's interest in spirits, but of his actual belief in them.

12. David Hume, *The Enquiry Concerning Human Understanding,* in *The Empiricists,* ed. Richard Haylor (Garden City, N.Y.; Anchor Books, 1974), pp. 352-370.

13. For a study of the importance of analogies for Coleridge, see Reeve Parker, *Coleridge's Meditative Art* (Ithaca, N.Y.: Cornell Univ. Press, 1975).

14. George Berkeley, "Alciphron, or The Minute Philosopher," *The Works*, ed. A. A. Luce and T. E. Jessup (1954; reprint ed., London: Nelson, 1964), III, dialogue, iv, p. 141. Such skeptical "Minute Philosophers" may have influenced Coleridge's term *Little-ists*.

15. See Richard Haven, *Patterns of Consciousness: An Essay on Coleridge* (Amherst: Univ. of Massachusetts Press, 1969), for a richly documented theory of the ramifications throughout Coleridge's thought of his subjective experiences.

16. The letter, to Thomas Poole from Germany, May 6, 1799, discusses his reaction to the death of his son Berkeley, whose death he felt he might have prevented by his own "Power of Life." An earlier letter to Poole, on October 16, 1797, describes his superstitious intuition of his father's death in a dream.

17. *The Poems of Samuel Taylor Coleridge*, ed. E. H. Coleridge (London: Oxford Univ. Press, 1917), p. 408; l. 103.

18. *The Poems* (referred to in the text as *CP*), p. 485; l. 18.

19. *The Poems*, p. 393, note. Tormented figures like Cain *(CP*, pp. 290-291) and overly imaginative ones like Martin Luther *(The Friend*, I, p. 140) live surrounded by ghosts and shapes and succumb to "those unconscious half-sleeps . . . which is the *true witching time* . . . the fruitful matrix of Ghosts."

20. Anthony John Harding, *Coleridge and the Idea of Love: Aspects of Relationship in Coleridge's Thought and Writing* (Cambridge, England: Cambridge Univ. Press, 1974), pp. 36-41; 85-90; 119-121.

21. *Biographia*, ed. Watson, chap. XII, theses III, VIII, IX, pp. 150-154.

22. *Biographia*, ed. Watson, chap. IX, p. 86, note.

23. *Biographia*, ed. Watson, chap. XII, p. 140.

Victor Hugo
and Galatea's Flight

JEAN GAUDON

Between 1852 and 1855, during his first exile, Victor Hugo posed a number of times for his elder son, Charles, who was a gifted photographer. Under one of the prints, which represents him in a typically meditative posture, hands clasped, eyes closed, head slightly bent, the poet wrote: "Victor Hugo listening to God."

This combination of arrogance and passivity is typical of Hugo's relationship with the unknown: it is a rough approximation of a major poetic theme, that of the poet as "contemplator"[1] and also the source of a severe distortion of his image. For a number of critics, brought up in the pervasive anti-Hugolian faith, which is characteristic of our century, this is the face of a man who thought of himself as God's chosen interlocutor and who dabbled in spiritualism, deceiving himself into believing that he could also converse with Shakespeare or Jesus Christ. Even André Breton, who was on the whole sympathetic toward Victor Hugo and who favoured all forms of irrational behavior that could be identified as presurrealist, sniggered.[2]

The Significance of the "Speaking Tables"

It might be tempting to push the ungainly skeleton into the closet of anecdotal history and leave it there, under the pretext that great men have failings that have little to do with their greatness, but this would be ill-advised. The whole story, in which photographs, prophecies of the "speaking tables," and poems are inextricably mixed, has, indeed, a significance that extends far beyond biographical curiosity.

The practice of consulting the "speaking tables" was introduced into the Hugo household in September 1853 by a visitor from Paris, Delphine de Girardin, a well-known society figure and a prolific writer, who had succumbed to the latest craze, lampooned by Daumier in a series of caricatures: *La Fluidomanie.* For the small group of exiles gathered around the dining-room table at Marine-Terrace, spiritualism was part of their attempt to fight alienation, along with the reading of Parisian newspapers and the preservation of their urban, typically French habits. There was also the dim hope that some sort of communication with the beyond would bring back the soul of Léopoldine, Hugo's eldest daughter, whose accidental death ten years earlier was still a source of sorrow: a few vague words, during the first successful session, had created the illusion.[3]

After the initial shock, Hugo was more curious, even inquisitive, than passionate. His professions of faith were always qualified. The realization that the quality of the table's message seemed to depend almost entirely on the presence of Charles Hugo, who was as good a "medium"[4] as he was a photographer, puzzled him. In a very rational manner he was tempted, at the beginning at least, to make Charles more or less consciously responsible for what was being dictated by the table. In her journal, Adèle, the poet's second daughter, recorded a conversation of September 21, 1853, in which Hugo said to Charles: "It is simply your intelligence multiplied fivefold by magnetism that agitates the table and makes it say what is in your mind."[5] However, the increasing richness and complexity of the table's discourse affected Hugo's thinking, and this kind of enlightened rationalism was soon replaced by an attitude of guarded belief. Something, he thought, could not be explained away by semirational notions like magnetism: some kind of influence, an undefinable spiritual force, was making itself felt through this inefficient and wasteful means. The mode of communication was, indeed, cumbersome; and one marvels that purely spiritual creatures, having shed all trace of matter, should communicate through a Victorian table. However, it could not originate, at least for Hugo himself, in his son's psyche; and it had to come from the outside, that is, an undefined area, beyond the reaches of the senses, where the spirits of the dead and, perhaps, some superior beings, such as angels, dwelled. As to the real identity of the spirits who took on great historic names, like Aeschylus, Marat, Shakespeare, or abstract ones, like Drama, the Shadow of the Sepulchre or Death, Hugo leaned towards disbelief: "I believe strongly in the phenomenon of the tables, but I would

The name surrounding the ruins—an allegory of the mystical power of a name
A drawing by Victor Hugo (*Album Chenay* and Musée Victor Hugo)

not vouch for the identity of Joan of Arc, Spartacus, Caesar, or Tiberius who seem to take part in it. It is more likely a spirit who assumes those names to get us interested."[6] On the whole, Hugo's attitude toward this particular problem remained constant. When it was announced that Shakespeare would dictate a play, Hugo decided to stay away from the sessions and even not to read the text in order to avoid for himself any suspicion of interference, but this precaution did not entail any kind of recognition of "Shakespeare's" identity. In spite of the excitement of the participants, there was, for Hugo himself, no alternative to doubt. In his usual courteous manner, he asked a question that was to remain unanswered: "We sometimes have doubts about the absolute and real identity of those who talk to us. You, who are the very incarnation of light, of happiness, of kindness, do you possess, in the world where you live, some way of totally convincing us that you really are those under whose names you communicate with us? Or must you leave us, in this respect, with our doubts?"[7]

In spite of the irrationality that seems to characterize both the discussion and the practice of spiritualism, it is rather remarkable that Hugo should attempt to remain within the boundaries of rational discourse. When confronted by systematic doubters, like his younger son, François-Victor, he would call upon a Cartesian notion, that of evidence, and contend that every "phenomenon" ought to be explained: to dismiss it without examination would be arbitrary and unscientific and a serious sin against the nineteenth-century notion of progress. On this particular point, Hugo's position remained the same throughout the years: "The unknown cannot be penetrated by our vocabulary. To deny its existence does not get rid of it. Surnaturalism is immanent. What we see of nature is infinitesimal. The prodigious, multiple Being escapes almost immediately our short terrestrial gaze. Why not pursue it a little more? All these things, spiritualism, somnambulism, catalepsy, biology, convulsionaries, mediums, second sight, turning or speaking tables, invisible knocks, people who have themselves buried alive, fire-eaters, snake charmers, and so on, all these phenomena that it is so easy to make fun of ought to be examined from a realistic angle. There might well be in them a certain amount of perception. If you neglect these facts, beware: the charlatans will soon take over, together with the imbeciles. There is nothing between science and ignorance."[8]

This enumeration is a little disturbing and, I suggest, voluntarily so. Hugo is fully aware that fire-eaters and snake charmers have a very low status among the priests of the unknown. He is fully aware that his mentioning them among other, more respectable forms of "surnaturalism" will be understood as pure provocation. Biased readers, who believe in scientific explanations and whose robust rationalism could, perhaps, envisage a scientific study of somnambulism, are confronted with all possible forms of what is normally considered as irrational, a grotesque array of phenomena that they will find ridiculous, far-fetched, or simply debasing. They will then be faced with an alternative: they will either refuse to envisage these phenomena and will prove that their prejudices are stronger than the thirst for knowledge or recognize that they have as yet no valid explanation.

The belief that some kind of explanation would one day be available and that every form of unaccountable manifestation would eventually become an object of scientific observation had no repercussion on the actual assessment of the experiment that was being conducted. It is probably significant that the strange list of supernatural/natural phenomena dates from 1864, ten years after the period of experimentation, at a time when the "speaking tables" had lost most of their impact and when Hugo was quite disillusioned with them. Their inclusion in the list raises some obvious questions that Hugo may not have wanted to raise. Contrary to the other manifestations of a yet unexplained character, they were not only a challenge to reason, but they also provided their own explanation of themselves and a coherent view of the whole hidden universe. Although mysterious in themselves, they advertised their message as an answer to all mysteries. Moreover, whereas the "unknown" remains so because of the inadequacy of our vocabulary, the "speaking tables" perform a linguistic act, using this same vocabulary to communicate with us. The fact that they cannot be accounted for by any rational means may be an obstacle to their credibility, but their message is there, for everybody to ponder, and it is a verbal message. This puts the "speaking tables" in a special category, apart from the other "phenomena," together with another human activity that Hugo called poetry.

This strange kinship has nothing to do with what is normally described as influence or even interference. Although the point could have been argued in a more subtle manner, Hugo's opinion on this matter was clear: "God does not need a piece of timber to assist Shakespeare or Calderon."[9] But even if the table is not, for the poet, an auxiliary (or vice versa), both activities follow the same pattern in the production of the message and imply an exterior origin. An incident, which took place during one of the sessions, illustrates this point. When the table referred to the "seer" (le voyant), Victor Hugo, who was used to the appellation, thought wrongly that it referred to him and was a little humiliated to discover that the "seer" was, for the "spirits," his son, Charles. The confusion was understandable. Medium and poet are, in this particular framework, both passive conductors of some unknown, unidentifiable force. The poet is a "tripod," that is, the *place* where something is being spoken, where another voice is being heard. "God dictated, I wrote," says Hugo at the beginning of "A celle qui est restée en France" (To the one who remained in France).[10] Hugo's major *ars poetica*, "Les Mages," written during the last months of the "speaking tables" episode, evokes the mythical figure of the poet who writes with a quill fallen from the wing of an angel, unaware, perhaps of his own existence ("Ils sont. Savent-ils ce qu'ils sont?" [They are. Do they know what they are?]), a madman who says that he is a seer ("A ces fous qui disent: Je vois!" [To the mad who say: I see])." The photograph, with its self-incriminating inscription, was just that: the oblique confession of a madman, a poet.

Whatever the hierarchy between the spiritualist and the poetic message—and Hugo might have had mixed feelings on the subject—the problem of veracity or, rather, credibility has its importance. Those two different discourses, which often converge so much that one is constantly tempted to explain one by the other, share the same malediction. They are no more credible and not much easier to integrate into a coherent, rational view of the world than the antics of the snake charmers or the fire-eaters. The message itself might be impressive. It is nonetheless as good as void. No proof is ever available.

The "speaking tables" episode appears, in this respect, as a particularly paradoxical one; even more outrageously remote from common sense than poetic activity, it might also provide the participants—and the poet himself is not only a participant, but perhaps the chosen interlocutor— with the ultimate weapon against doubt. For a brief moment Hugo, leaving aside his lofty messianic attitude, totally in keeping with his optimistic, progressive view of the history of mankind, asks for proof, *hic et nunc* (here and now), posturing as the Torquemada of the spirits, trying to make them confess and to corner them into proving that they are telling the "truth." He even mused with the idea of making them lift all doubts, once and for all, and proposed a bargain: "We should ask the mysterious Beings who speak to us to divulge to us three secrets: how to cure rabies, how to steer balloons, and the location of a gold lode in Australia. We would send the three secrets to the Academy of Sciences in a sealed envelope and we would say: we are going to publish a book, dictated by the tables, and we have asked from these tables three secrets, which are in the sealed envelope. If the three secrets are verified, then our book will be proved true. If not, it will be false."[12]

Naturally, Hugo was not naïve enough to put the spirits to the test. He knew only too well that the rules of the game were incompatible with this unrefined procedure. But what about poetry? Who is going to prove to the Academy that the poet, as Hugo sees him, is really a "seer"? The message, coming from the "speaking tables," might have served two purposes, in proving that the poet was as right as the tables themselves or, at least, that he was elected. But there is no direct way of verifying the poet's credentials.

Hugo — "Illuminist" Tradition and the New Rhetoric

The absence of poetry from the enumeration of "phenomena," in spite of its obvious affinities with the most respectable of them, might have two meanings. On the one hand, it could easily be explained away by Hugo's unwillingness to list an elevated, quasi-divine endeavor together

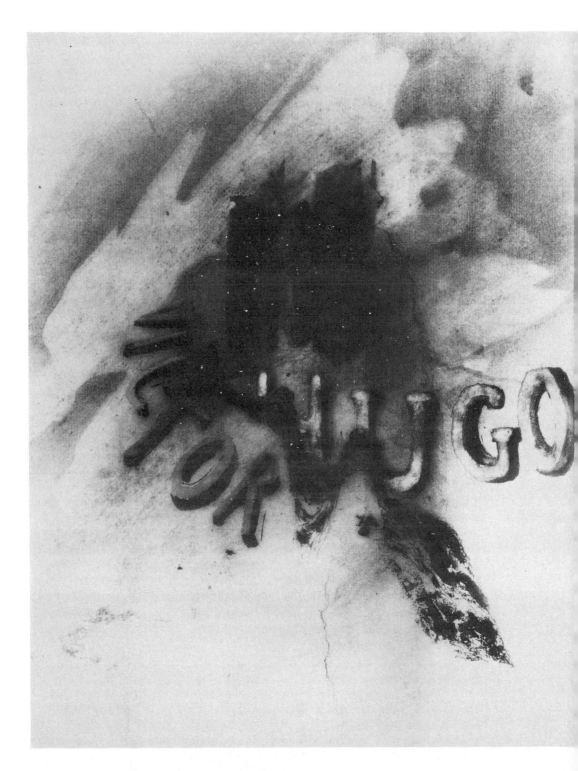

Another mystical drawing of a city in ruins by Hugo

with the strange activities of shady characters. But it could also denote another kind of uneasiness: an obscure feeling that the "scientific" chances of accounting for the mysteries of fire-eating or even for the knocks Hugo sometimes heard during his sleepless nights in Jersey were far greater than those of establishing the powers of the poet in his relationship with the occult. On the surface, Hugo's belief in the future rationalization of every unexplicable phenomenon was unshakable: "Electricity was, for a long time, part of surnaturalism. It took the numerous experiments of Clairaut to make it acceptable and worthy of the official register of established sciences. Electricity, now, has its offices in town and endows university chairs. Galvanism went through the same ordeal. It first was made fun of and described as "childish," as attested by the five memoirs addressed to Spellanzani by Galvani; it was accepted only recently. Magnetism is only halfway in. The steamboat was "puerile" in 1816. Electric telegraph began by being inconsequential."[13]

The temporal pattern is very clear: what was, at one time, childish or of the nature of a practical joke is now legitimate. Progressive rationalization is the key. At the same time, Hugo knows of the inscription, read by Plutarch and Proclus on the pedestal of Isis' statue: "No mortal has ever lifted my veil." In other words, he is more or less aware of the real "occultist" tradition according to which the unveiling of Isis is an endless process and the only worthwhile revelation is the permanence of the veil itself. The nature of the occult is to be occulted, the fate of the seer is to be blinded, or, to put it in the words of Zacharias Werner, the freemason poet of eighteenth-century Germany:

Whoever wants to see must be blinded.

This tradition, known in the eighteenth century as the illuminist tradition was still very much alive a century later, even in France; and Ballanche, whose reputation was probably superior to his achievements, made the same sort of statement in his *Essais de Palingénésie sociale* ("Essays of Social Palingenesis"), when the narrator, Thamyris, succeeding the dying Orpheus, becomes in the same flash of lightning "initiated" and blind.

Although Hugo was not among the greatest admirers of Ballanche, he was very much part of this nonrationalist tradition, and his belief in "progress" did not seem to affect his equally strong belief in a pattern of revelation that could not be linked to a spiritual or intellectual progression towards a goal, but was an instant, blinding illumination, amounting to total rejection:

To see is to reject.[14]

Rhetorically, the concept of a vision that can only be defined negatively has far-reaching consequences: it makes Hugo the poet of preterition. The central section of "Magnitudo Parvi," the pivotal poem of *Les Contempla-*

tions, is made up of a negative enumeration, which is long and comprehensive, illustrating the line that equated seeing and rejecting. An initial proposition:

> He does not see . . .

is followed by a series of objects that cover more or less all the themes used by Hugo in his preceding poems, signifying, I believe, that preterition is the only *poetic* answer to the topos of the incapacity of language, according to which reality "cannot be penetrated by our vocabulary." When faced with the ineffable, Hugo will choose to fill silence ("Le silence universel") and infinite space with a wealth of negative attributes:

> No staircase, no bridge, no spiral, no ramp.[15]

But preterition is not Hugo's only weapon, and it is particularly striking that, at a time when he shows more and more interest in narrative forms (novels and epic poetry), he should choose to incorporate his conception of total *askesis* into a narrative framework. This is what happens in 1870, in a great, emblematic poem from *La Légende des Siècles*, "Supremacy." In it, an unknown light challenges the three major gods of Vedic mythology to show their power. The first two perform some extraordinary feats, and one wonders how the third one, Indra, is going to accomplish anything that would not be an anticlimax. He does so by demonstrating that he can embrace the whole universe in his gaze. Nothing, he claims, can hide from him. This is the time when the unknown light proves its "supremacy" by disappearing, occulting itself. The first title, crossed out by Hugo, was even more explicit: "To disappear is to show oneself" ("Disparaître, c'est se montrer"). Against the conception of Truth as a succession of revelations or unveilings, "Supremacy" establishes an entirely different, more paradoxical notion of truth as occultation.

Many in the "illuminist" tradition had sought refuge in a kind of Neoplatonic imagery, which helped bridge the gap between the two seemingly incompatible systems. The "cave" myth, for instance, provided a pattern of knowledge that allowed the seer to become blind to the world of phenomena while initiating him to the ideal (essential) world. Hugo is not totally insensitive to this model, and he often has recourse to a dichotomy between the material order (the material eye) and the spiritual one. He also uses the perennial metaphor of reading, whereby the visible universe is considered as a book, which can only be read by those who know the code, because they are poets or initiated. Expressing, that is, interpreting the mystery of the universe was indeed a Hugolian commonplace, the one that Baudelaire, for obvious reasons, chose to single out in his memorable article written for Crépet's anthology. It is, however, remarkable that Hugo should be incapable or unwilling to adopt a binary

structure that would have reduced the whole universe to two intercon-
nected levels and would have transformed writing into a paradigmatic
(metaphoric) activity. The truly emblematic figure of the occult is not,
for him, the Neoplatonic Isis (a typically paradigmatic figure) but the
Vergilian heroine Galatea. The metaphor of unveiling is replaced by the
metaphor of pursuit, "la poursuite de l'énigme."[16]

It might be in order to go back to the bizarre list that puts on the
same footing, among many other activities, spiritism and snake charmers,
and more particularly to a discreet use of an intertext. The presence of
Vergil, here, is both undeniable and capital. The cosmic Galatea ("prodigious multiple Being") runs away and disappears behind the willow trees,
but she wants to be seen, if only for a brief moment ("escapes almost
immediately our short terrestrial gaze"). One could, I suppose, take this
"occultation" as a negative, definitive answer to human questioning. This
is not, however, the Hugolian attitude: "Why not pursue her a little?"
Naturally Orpheus, the poet, will never be able to catch her, and there is
no hope for a happy ending, with a final, transgressive idyll between the
naked truth and the privileged seer. Naked truth is not an inviting image,
but a terrifying, negative one. Galatea, according to another fragment of
the same text, is "formidable," and this should be taken strictly in its
etymological sense. More important still, actual possession is impossible.
Enigma, personified, becomes in "Le Satyre" a naked figure "showing her
white shape in the bottomless depth."[17] Hugo's greatest poem, which was
left unfinished, probably because it was, by its very nature, unfinishable,
ends up[18] on an extraordinary note, when a masked spirit, the voice of
darkness, asks the transported seer (here, clearly, the poet) whether he
really wants to see God under His true form and whether he wants to
know what cannot be known. The answer, of course, is in the affirmative:

> Oui! criai-je. Et je sentis
> Que la création tremblait comme une toile;
> Alors, levant un bras et d'un pan de son voile,
> Couvrant tous les objets terrestres disparus,
> Il me toucha le front du doigt, et je mourus.[19]

This, however, is not the end of the route. At the bottom of the manuscript, another line was hastily written:

> Spectre, tu m'as trompé, je ne sais rien encore.[20]

Galatea, like Truth, is always beyond the point where we expect to find
her: "au-delà (beyond)."

Hugo as a Prophet

It seems more and more obvious that Hugo's world cannot be reduced to a network of metaphors (an allegory of truth) or to an antithesis
between the spiritual and the material. In other words, the occult is not,
in Hugo's poetic practice, a reduction of the unknown to the describable
but an endless activity, an unceasing pursuit. The corresponding rhetorical figure is not antithesis, in spite of what most of Hugo's readers have
been constantly repeating, but enumeration or, to be more precise,
accumulation. Our composite list of unexplained activities ended with a
sign, which is the very symbol of accumulation: "etc." Thousands of
words, hundreds of unconnected or repetitive fragments will be thrown
into the gaping hole. When it comes to *Dieu*, that is, to the pursuit of
the absolute, there is no real hope for a scientific integration into the
body of knowledge. The narration, which constituted the poem's framework, breaks down and is replaced by a problematic mass of verse, with
several possible layouts—none of them absolutely convincing—and quanti-
ties of fragments reiterating *ad nauseam* that God cannot be reached. In
rhetorical terms, the incompatibility between the proclaimed rational
belief in the future of scientific investigation and the true "illuminist"
tradition is translated into a conflict between the figures that entail an
open-ended construction (accumulation, digression, proliferation) and all
the techniques of closure, like tightly knit metaphors and antithetical
statements. True, Hugo is often trying hard to reduce all problems to a
carefully balanced, reassuring alternative: "Nothing between science and
ignorance." But this elegant solution, upholding the Aristotelian principle
of noncontradiction, does not seem able to stop the flow. Dual systems are
fragile parapets to put an end to the endless drift. Hugo has been either
praised or condemned for the extraordinary number of words he uses.
This, in itself, is part of the overall strategy that governs his poetic
practice. A single, untranslatable quotation will illustrate this point:
"Entrent en scène les psylles, les nages, les alungles, les démonocéphales,
les dives, les solipèdes, les aspîoles, les monocles, les vampires, les
hirudes, les dracogynes, les stryges, les masques, les salamandres, les
ungulèques, les serpentes, les garous, les voultes, les troglodytes, tout le
peuple hagard des noctambules, les uns sautant sur un seul pied, les autres
voyant d'un seul oeil, les autres, hommes à sabot de cheval, les autres,
couleuvres autant que femmes; et les phalles, invoqués des vierges stériles,
et les tarasques toutes couvertes de conferves, et les drées, dents
grinçantes dans une phosphorescence."[21] This is, of course, a passage
in which terror is tempered with humor, and the mere drifting of addition
by a complex system of structuration. The fact, however, remains that
accumulation is not a sign of the progress of knowledge, but the rhetorical
figure of what Hugo calls, "the loss of reality" ("la perte du réel").[22]

The most striking feature of this rhetorical shift from antithesis (or
metaphor) to enumeration is the emergence of a locution that almost

eradicates the type of antithetical disjunction that is usually considered as the very essence of Hugo's vision of the world. More and more, the disjunctive "either . . . or . . ." is replaced by "at the same time" or other expressions that consist of a nondisjunctive juxtaposition of incompatible notions. They may be, in their more condensed forms, oxymorons, but also simpler statements to the effect, for example, that loss and increase of reality are one and the same thing: "Supernatural as well as human."[23] Or: "Nature teaches and misleads us at the same time."[24] Or: "He was adored both under his true and false image."[25] The "universal analogy" dear to Baudelaire's heart is no longer an instrument of discovery, but an instrument of occultation. The myth of Galatea, as well as the shape of the sentence, or the book, or even the complete corpus are different aspects of the same allegory of desire (thirst for knowledge) and impossibility (occultation).

It may be interesting to note that most of these musings of Hugo were not published during his lifetime and became part of the nondescript mass of papers that he left to his heirs to sort out and publish.[26] Perhaps he did not want to appear so vulnerable. Perhaps he wanted to stretch the allegory of knowledge/nonknowledge to its limits—the actual publication, in book form, being a betrayal of Galatea's image. The book, like the philosopher's stone, can only be the horizon of knowledge, not an act of discovery. It may be significant also that these writings, which we have reason to believe Hugo deemed important, were written after the publication of Baudelaire's article, as if Hugo rejected the very terms of Baudelaire's brilliant analysis of his poetry. To the younger poet who praised him for being a great poet of analogies and who took the opportunity to express his own Neoplatonic doctrines, Hugo answers, privately, with a serious questioning of the magical, vaticinal function of poetry. He writes, so to speak, in the margin, the words that could, if published, shatter his own myth. Perhaps we should have been more attentive to this questioning. My feeling is that the myth, as transmitted to us, is almost Baudelaire's invention, an act of critical narcissism. The *letter* of the text, after all, always resisted the simplistic antithetical reordering of the world. Contradiction is the essence of Hugo's poetry, in an endless chain of words and an equally endless chain of aphorisms: "Ténèbres et rayons affirment à la fois" (Darkness and rays assert together).[27] And also: "Nous n'avons que le choix du noir" (Black is our only choice).[28] Who will deny that the old man who was so shamelessly institutionalized and misrepresented was one of the great prophets of things to come?

Notes

1. See my *Temps de la Contemplation* (Paris: Flammarion, 1969).
2. See "Le Message automatique," in *Point du Jour* (Paris: Gallimard, 1934), p. 237.
3. The detailed story of the episode and the text of the dialogue between the exiles and the "speaking tables," edited by J. and S. Gaudon, is to be found in the

complete edition of Hugo's works known as the *Edition chronologique*, 18 Vols., under the general editorship of Jean Massin (Paris: Club français du Livre, 1967-1970). See also *Ce que disent les tables parlantes*, edited by Jean Gaudon (Paris: Pauvert, 1963).

4. The word *medium*, in this particular acception, was apparently invented by Swedenborg and used in French by Allan Kardec for the first time in 1853.

5. See *Le Journal d'Adèle Hugo*, presented and annotated by Frances-Vernor Guille (Paris: Minard, 1971), Vol. 2, p. 279.

6. *Ibid.*, p. 283.

7. *Edition chronologique*, Vol. 9, p. 1293.

8. *Contemplation suprême*, in *Edition chronologique*, Vol. 12, pp. 115-116.

9. *William Shakespeare*, in *Edition chronologique*, Vol. 12, p. 171.

10. "Dieu dictait, j'écrivais" ("A celle qui est restée en France," the last poem of *Les Contemplations*.

11. *Contemplations*, Vol. 6, p. 23.

12. *Journal d'Adèle Hugo*, Feb. 7, 1854, quoted in *Edition chronologique*, Vol. 9, p. 1182.

13. *Contemplation suprême*, in *Edition chronologique*, Vol. 12, p. 117.

14. "Voir, c'est rejeter" ("Magnitudo Parvi," *Contemplations*, Vol. 3, p. 30.

15. "Point d'escalier, de pont, de spirale, de rampe" ("La Vision de Dante," in *La Légende des Siècles*, complementary series, poem written in 1853).

16. "Magnitudo Parvi" (*Contemplations*, Vol. 3, p. 30).

17. "Montrant sa forme blanche au fond de l'insondable" ("Le Satyre," in *La Légende des Siècles*, 1st series, poem written in 1859).

18. This controversial fragment was written in 1856, but there is no proof that Hugo meant it to be the final word of his poem. The subsequent additions to the poem and the rearrangement of the material precluded, in fact, this easy solution (and any other solution).

19. "Yes! said I. And I felt Creation shaking like a drape, and he lifted one arm, and covered all terrestrial things with a fold of his veil, and they disappeared, and he touched my forehead with one finger, and I died."

20. "Specter, you fooled me; I still know nothing."

21. *Promontorium Somnii*, in *Edition chronologique*, Vol. 12, pp. 471-472.

22. *Ibid.*, p. 452.

23. *Contemplation suprême*, in *Edition chronologique*, Vol. 12, p. 112.

24. *Philosophie. Commencement d'un livre*, in *Edition chronologique*, Vol. 12, p. 38.

25. *Ibid.*

26. Hugo's testament instructs his executors to publish every fragment written by him.

27. "Magnitudo Parvi" (*Contemplations*, Vol. III, p. 30).

28. *William Shakespeare*, in *Edition chronologique*, Vol. 12, p. 224.

PART 3

SUPERNATURAL
INTERPRETATIONS

7

Magic in the Writings and Life of Apuleius

CECIL PAIGE GOLANN

In the period between Alexander the Great and Constantine, the Orient made great inroads in the Graeco-Roman world in political forms, social organization, and religion, contributing incidentally to commerce, industry, law, and architecture as well. Gradually, the independent society of city-states was transformed into a theocratic, bureaucratic monarchy with a divine ruler and huge professional army. Astrology and magic inundated the West and even became allied with philosophy. Before this process was completed, Apuleius, a citizen of the North African town of Madaura, appeared in the second century A.D., enthusiastically embodying the tendencies of his age, with hardly a thought for the vanished political freedom and intellectual independence of the past and strongly foreshadowing the future. As philosopher and priest, rhetorician and satirist, he sheds great light on the major trends of the early empire, including the upsurge of magic.

The Enigma of Apuleius

Historically, Apuleius was the first important man of letters in North Africa in the Graeco-Roman period. He is most famous for his novel, the *Metamorphoses* (also called *The Golden Ass*), which describes a young man whose curiosity about magic, an evil and forbidden thing, has a tragic result—his transformation into a donkey.

The unprecedented predominance of the magic element in Apuleius' novel and its importance for him in his ideas on religion and philosophy have puzzled some modern scholars accustomed to the rational thought that typified classical Greece and Rome. In reading the *Metamorphoses*, one is struck by the fact that magic is one of the principal elements. Before Apuleius, as Tavenner pointed out,[1] magic was incidental in Latin authors. Apuleius was the first to make it a dominant feature of his work. Why is this so, and what does it signify?

One school of thought holds that Apuleius as an intelligent, educated upper-class man of the second century A.D. could *not* have believed in magic despite his preoccupation with it. But if he did *not* believe in magic, how are we to explain the *Metamorphoses*, his philosophical works, and some passages in the *Apology*, which was Apuleius' defense against the charge that he practiced magic?

Some Evidence of Apuleius' Belief in Magic

It is significant that the *Metamorphoses* opens with a discussion about the credibility of witchcraft between the hero, Lucius of Corinth, and two travelers whom he has joined. The purpose of this episode in my opinion is to convince the reader that magic and witchcraft are factual, not fictional. This is necessary not only to prepare the proper mental attitude for the tales of magic that follow but also to make the miracle of Isis, who restores Lucius to human shape at the end of the novel, seem possible. Book XI of the *Metamorphoses*, especially section 15, demonstrates that Apuleius believed Isis could perform such a miracle. By the same token Apuleius must also have believed it possible for a man to be changed into a beast because the whole effect of Isis' miracle depends on whether one can accept the initial transformation. One cannot believe in Isis' power to restore Lucius to human form without first believing in magic. If Apuleius did not believe in magic, as is often claimed, it is hard to see why he chose the story he did to glorify Isis in the *Metamorphoses*.

A parallel in the Christian religion to the episode in Book XI of the *Metamorphoses* illustrates that such miracles were given credence by the Christians of antiquity as well as by pagans. As E. H. Haight writes,

The Arabic Gospel of the Infancy, although its source is oriental, has a strange parallel to Apuleius' Lucius in the story of a man transformed into a mule who was restored by having the Christ child placed upon his back.[2]

We may note here that St. Augustine (354-430 A.D.), like Apuleius a native of North Africa, in discussing the *Metamorphoses*, wrote that he was not sure whether the events described in that novel were made up or had actually been experienced by Apuleius.[3] Such was the state of mind of a man of St. Augustine's stature in the late empire.

Another episode in the *Metamorphoses* shows the influence of Egyptian magic on Apuleius. In Book II, the hero, Lucius, attends a party. Conversing with the other guests, he says he fears the witches in Thessaly (II, 20). Immediately, a fellow guest, Thelyphron, echoes Lucius' sentiments and is prevailed upon to relate an eyewitness account of witches mutilating a corpse and of a necromancy performed by an Egyptian priest. By bringing a dead man back to life, the priest makes it possible for this dead man to reveal that he had been murdered by his wife (II, 21-30).

To surround this story with credibility, Apuleius has Thelyphron claim to have witnessed the marvel he related and offer as proof of the truth of his story the fact that he now has ears and a nose of wax as a result of his encounter with the witches. Apuleius, be it noted, treats the witches' magic as something sordid and criminal, but he describes the necromancy performed by the Egyptian priest with admiration and with a tone of reverence that is on a par with that used toward Isis in Book XI.

What is most interesting in this story is that in bringing the dead man back to life, the Egyptian priest used a well-known, traditional Egyptian magical rite, the ceremony of "opening the mouth," with which Apuleius was apparently familiar (see E. A. Wallis Budge, *Egyptian Magic* [London, 1899], p. 15). One gets the impression that Apuleius did not think that necromancy performed by an Egyptian priest was wicked despite the clear condemnation of such practices by the Roman law of his day.

A brief digression at this point is needed. As has been said, the hero of the novel is introduced as Lucius of Corinth (see *Metamorphoses* I, 22; II, 12), but in Book XI, 27, the young Greek is suddenly metamorphosed into "a poor man from Madaura" *(pauper Madaurensis)*; and, as an African from Madaura, he is initiated into the mystery cult of Osiris at Rome. Is Apuleius referring to himself in the phrase *pauper Madaurensis* in *Metamorphoses* XI, 27? (Madaura is believed to have been Apuleius' birthplace, partly because of this identification and partly because St. Augustine, in *Civitas Dei*, VIII, 14, refers to him as a Platonist philosopher from Madaura.) Was Apuleius so carried away when writing the scenes of the initiations that at one point he unconsciously described the hero as *Madaurensis* as if he were writing about himself? Such a theory is supported by passages from another of Apuleius' works, the *Apology*, that tell us that he was a devout member of a number of mystery cults. Moreover, his description of the Isis cult is reliable, authentic, and

reverent.[4] I believe that Apuleius identified himself with his main character because the recollection of his own religious experiences became so
vivid while he was working on Book XI that he unconsciously began to
write about himself—a Freudian error.

To recaptiulate at this point, the possibility of magic is the key to
the *Metamorphoses*. If magic is impossible, if a man cannot be changed
into a beast by a witch, the miracle of Isis in restoring Lucius to human
shape loses its force.

Today few educated people believe seriously in ghosts returning to
tell how they were murdered or in the cryptic prophecies of witches. Yet
Hamlet and *Macbeth* depend on just such beliefs. Shakespearean audiences
must have given credence to the ghost in *Hamlet* and the witches in
Macbeth, which today seem scarcely credible. I offer this as an analogy
with regard to the dispute about whether or not Apuleius, an intelligent
and educated man of antiquity, believed in magic.

Magic as Sinful

To return to the *Metamorphoses*, Lucius first sought amorous
pleasures and a knowledge of the black art to increase his own powers.
He was punished for these transgressions by being transformed into an
ass owing to an error during an experiment in magic practices. As a man
imprisoned in a beast's exterior, he underwent much suffering and was
tried by many ordeals. These experiences increased his sympathy for the
oppressed, the underprivileged, and the unjustly hurt on the one hand and
his hatred for the lascivious, the fraudulent, and the cruel on the other.
When he seemed to be on the brink of his greatest degradation, Isis
rescued him and raised him from the depths of despair and shame to the
heights of hope and salvation.

Despite Lucius' questionable behavior in the earlier books, he emerges
in Book XI as a totally changed and reformed character, desperately
sincere in his devotion to religion. Thus, I cannot agree with those who
interpret the *Metamorphoses* as merely a work of entertainment or
perhaps a piece of sophistical display. The novel surely has a serious
moral purpose, which the career of Apuleius as philosopher and priest
would bear out.

Some scholars are also puzzled by Apuleius' combining scenes of the
greatest depravity and the loftiest religious sentiments in his novel.[5] My
explanation is that Apuleius portrayed sin at its worst in order to make
more effective the contrastive scenes that followed of redemption and
piety. The *Metamorphoses* seems definitely to have had a religious intent,
and, to achieve this, Apuleius chose to give magic an important role.

There is a curious and relevant passage in *Metamorphoses*, XI, 15,
in which the priest of Isis tells the hero that he has suffered for his
improspera curiositas (untimely curiosity) and *serviles voluptates* (servile

pleasures), advising him to devote himself to Isis for the rest of his life. Curiosity and lust, then, are sins that bring down punishment. A person who is not under the protection of Isis is at the mercy of cruel Fortune. To find peace of mind and protection in his life and the life hereafter, one must join a mystery cult like that of Isis.

Curiosity, especially scientific curiosity, was respectable, even admired, in pre-Christian Greece and Rome. A change in the character of thought in the early empire is seen in Apuleius' representation of curiosity as sinful, not only in *Metamorphoses*, XI, 15, but also in his account in the *Metamorphoses* of the story of Cupid and Psyche (V, 6: *sacrilega curiositas* [sacrilegious curiosity]; VI, 20: *temeraria curiositas* [audacious curiosity]). Because of her curiosity, Psyche is deprived of Cupid for a long time and almost dies. Echoes of Apuleius' attitude toward curiosity are found in the writings of two other North Africans, both Christians; Tertullian (ca. 160-225 A.D.), who called human investigation *libido curiositatis* (unlawful desire of curiosity) in *De Praescriptione Haereticorum*, 14 ("On the Prescription of Heretics"), and St. Augustine, who uses the phrase *impia curiositate* (by impious curiosity) in *Civitas Dei*, IV, 314. This attitude toward intellectual curiosity, alien to the spirit of classical Greece and Rome, heralds a new outlook that comes in with Christianity and other Oriental religions. It is perhaps significant that the regarding of curiosity as sinful is common to three religious writers of the Roman Empire who came from North Africa.

The Greek Source of the *Metamorphoses*

A Greek work entitled *Lucius or the Ass*, with a plot similar to that of Apuleius' novel, has come down to us. It is thought to be an epitome of a lost Greek work entitled *Metamorphoses*. The relationship of the Lost Greek *Metamorphoses*, *Lucius or the Ass*, and Apuleius' *Metamorphoses* is still debated. For our purpose here, suffice it to say that in the Greek story Lucius is changed into a donkey by an error in magic rites and regains his human form when *accident* supplies him with the remedy. The whole story is told in a vein of mockery, and it really does not matter very much whether one believes the events took place or treats the whole tale as a joke. The possibility of magic *is* crucial to the purpose of the *Metamorphoses*, however, as I have attempted to demonstrate, for the main theme of Apuleius' novel is the ordeal of the metamorphosed Lucius till his sufferings win the mercy of Isis, who saves him. The book is serious, not frivolous like the Greek original, which *lacks* the miracle at the end (and many other episodes, such as the Thelyphron story in Book II, too). Just as educated people today do not believe in magic—or Isis either, for that matter—Apuleius probably *did* believe in magic as much as in the majesty and power of the divine Isis.

Apuleius' Trial for Magic

Apuleius had other connections with magic both in his writing and in his life. He was accused by the relatives of his wife, Pudentilla, of using magic to win her. He was tried for this capital crime (probably in 160/161 A.D.) and seems to have been acquitted. Though Apuleius was probably truthful in denying the use of magic to win his wife, we may infer from what he says in the *Apology* that he believed in magic, knew a lot about it, and may have practiced it on occasions other than this. In *Apology*, 25, for example, Apuleius argues that *magia* (magic) is really the lore of the Persian Magi, a noble priestly art, adding that if *magia* is only this, as Plato and other writers say it is, what harm and crime are there in it? But this is a specious argument, for the Magi gave magic a place in their theology.[6] Another charge against Apuleius in this trial was that he had had a skeleton made by a secret process for purposes of magic. He produced the statue in court so that all might see it was not a dread skeleton, as the prosecution had said, but a beautiful image of Mercury. However, Mercury was the Roman name of the Egyptian god Thoth-Hermes, best known as Hermes Trismegistus,[7] who was referred to in the magic papyri as the founder of magic. Apuleius scored a point when he proved that the statue he worshiped was *not* a skeleton, but perhaps he also left himself open to suspicion when the statue produced turned out to be one of Mercury, the god of magic.

Sorcery and Theurgy

Magic differs from religion in that its practitioners seek to compel supernatural powers to achieve their ends. By contrast, religion consists of propitiation, prayer, and sacrifice. In the early Roman Empire, magic was separated by some philosophers (the Neoplatonists, for example) into a lower magic (sorcery) and a higher magic (theurgy).

In a philosophical work, *De Deo Socratis* ("About the God of Socrates"), Apuleius deals with theurgy. He states that the gods can have no contact with human beings and are not subject to emotions. There exists, however, an intermediate order of beings between the gods and men called daimons. These daimons, like men and unlike the gods, are influenced by passions. It is these daimons, and not the gods, whom people worship in the cults because, as has been pointed out, man can have no contact with the gods and because the gods are never swayed by emotions. In fact, those portrayed as gods and endowed with emotions by the poets in their accounts of myths are really daimons and not gods for these same reasons.

In the *De Deo Socratis*, Apuleius uses demonology or the control of daimons to make it possible to believe in traditional mythology and a transcendent God at the same time. The use of propitiation of good daimons and of purifications, conjurations, and exorcisms against evil daimons was the basis of cult in the later empire. In other words, religion became the kind of magic called theurgy. (This, of course, was a philosophical, not a legal, distinction.)

In this sense of the word *magic*, it is highly probable that Apuleius practiced the art. As a philosopher, he held a number of ideas suggesting affinities with Neoplatonism, Neo-Pythagoreanism, and the Oriental mystery religions.[8] His emphasis on demonology (as in the *De Deo Socratis*) and his ecstatic religious devotion show little trace of Plato and have much more in common with Neoplatonist, Oriental, and perhaps even North African ideas. Egypt, the home of the Isis cult, is in North Africa.

Neoplatonism has been called Platonism "transformed almost beyond recognition . . . the great mystical philosophy of the third century,"[9] for although Plato believed in God and in the soul's immortality, he was not essentially a religious philosopher. But Apuleius anticipates Neoplatonism and differs from his master Plato by making religion the most important part of his philosophy.[10] Franz Cumont (op. cit.) discusses the large place given to demonology by the Neoplatonists and also the penetration of Persian demonology into Neoplatonism. Here we may recall my earlier reference to Apuleius' comment about the Magi in *Apology*, 25.

In short, Apuleius clearly believed in the existence of daimons (see his *Apology*, 43; *De Mundo*, 35 ["About the World"]; *De Dogmate Platonis*, I, 11-12 ["About the Doctrine of Plato"]), and in his elaborate demonological system he makes conventional religion a function of daimons rather than of gods. It is only a step from his emphasis on demonology to magical practices of a theurgic nature to control daimons.

A Possible Explanation

Apuleius is an indicator along the way of the change of classical thought. From being rationalistic, laical, and independent of faith, it succumbed to the sacerdotal culture of the Orient and Egypt with its caste of scholar-priests and its dogmatism, authority, and divine revelation. The Hellenistic ideal of the self-sufficient sage was replaced by the belief in ecstatic surrender to divine power for protection on earth and immortality in the hereafter. In short, mysticism was substituted for rationalism, and the highest good was sought, not during life, but after it.

Not only the ideas but also the style of Apuleius are at odds with traditional classicism. J. Wight Duff writes:

> Such is the general effect that the reader accustomed to normal Latin feels as if he had adventured into a strange land with a strange speech.[11]

Apuleius clearly in many respects presents problems that are difficult to resolve and explain.

It has been suggested that the difference between Apuleius and earlier Latin and Greek authors (for example, with regard to the magic element in his writings and life) can best be explained on the basis of his North African origins.[12] Though of native North African stock, Apuleius was Romanized like many of the local aristocracy and was well educated in Greek and Latin. However, this classical education was superimposed on a man of North African cultural background (where Phoenician and Egyptian influences, both replete with magic, were strong), and this cultural background shines through the superimposed Graeco-Roman veneer and perhaps accounts for many of the characteristics of Apuleius, such as his preoccupation with magic, his fanatical religious outlook, and his style, that seem so strange and perplexing when he is compared to pre-Christian Greek and Roman writers and philosophers.

Notes

1. Eugene Tavenner, *Studies in Magic from Latin Literature* (New York: Columbia Univ. Press, 1916), pp. 43-44.

2. E. H. Haight, *Apuleius and His Influence* (New York: Longmans, Green & Co., 1927), p. 95.

3. St. Augustine, *Civitas Dei (City of God)*, XVIII, 18.

4. See A. D. Nock, *Conversion* (London: Oxford Univ. Press, 1933).

5. See, for example, Samuel Dill, *Roman Society from Nero to Marcus Aurelius*, 2d ed. (London: Macmillan and Co., 1905), p. 389.

6. Franz Cumont, *Les Religions orientales dans le paganisme romain*, 4th ed. (Paris: Librairie orientaliste Paul Geuthner, 1929).

7. P. Vallette, *L'Apologie d'Apulée* (Paris: Klincksieck, 1908), p. 312, made the identification of Mercury with Thoth-Hermes.

8. Eduard Zeller, *Die Philosophie der Griechen*, 5th ed. (Leipzig: O. R. Reisland, 1923), Vol. 3, 2, pp. 225-226; J. W. Mackail, *Latin Literature* (New York: C. Scribner's Sons, 1907), p. 237.

9. H. R. Willoughby, *Pagan Regeneration* (Chicago: University of Chicago Press, 1929), p. 223.

10. Vallette, op. cit., pp. 218-220.

11. J. Wight Duff, *A Literary History of Rome in the Silver Age* (London: T. Unwin Fisher, Ltd., 1927), p. 652.

12. See Willi Wittmann, *Das Isisbuch des Apuleius* (Stuttgart: W. Kohlhammer, 1938), pp. 163-186.

Bloy and the Symbolism of History

JEAN-LOUP BOURGET

For some years now, there has been a renewed interest in Léon Bloy, which has been brought about to a large degree by the edition of his *Works* in 15 volumes (1964-1975) by Jacques Petit.[1] However, this rereading of Bloy is ambiguous and is at the expense of the ideas actually expressed. Bloy is the object of what may be called a formalist misrepresentation. Critics acclaim his style with enthusiasm because they feel a need to compensate for the embarrassment that the *substance of his thought* causes them. We are faced with both a paradox and an anachronism. Bloy is a symbolist, hence an author choosing a form that is not a mere garment but an intuition and an approximation of an invisible, ineffable, and unique idea. He defined himself as "the Pilgrim of the Absolute." The otherwise laudatory appraisal of Bloy by Roland Barthes contains a current misconception that I shall try to dispel:

> C'est sans doute cette volupté invincible du langage, attestée par une extraordinaire "richesse" d'expressions, qui frappe les choix idéologiques de Bloy d'une sorte d'irréalisme inconsé-

quent: que Bloy ait été furieusement catholique, qu'il ait
injurié pêle-mêle l'Eglise conformiste et moderniste, les
protestants, les francs-maçons, les Anglais et les démocrates,
que ce forcené de l'incongru se soit engoué pour Louis XVII ou
Mélanie (la bergère de la Salette), ce n'est là rien de plus
qu'une matière variable, récusable, qui n'abuse aucun lecteur
de Bloy; l'illusion, ce sont les contenus, les idées, les choix, les
croyances, les professions, les causes; la réalité, ce sont les mots,
l'érotique du langage, que cet écrivain pauvre, *de salaire nul*,
a pratiquée avec fureur et dont il nous fait aujourd'hui encore
partager l'emportement.[2]

(It is probably this invincible voluptuousness of language,
exemplified by an unusual "wealth" of expressions, that shows
up the inconsistency and the unreality of Bloy's ideological
choices. Bloy's impassioned Catholicism; the fact that he
insulted all at once the conformist and the modernist Church,
the Protestants, the Free-Masons, the English, and the Demo-
crats; the frenzied incongruity of his infatuation with Louis
XVII or with Mélanie (the shepherdess of la Salette)—all this
constitutes little more than a variable and untrustworthy
substance deluding none of Bloy's readers. Contents, ideas,
options, beliefs, professions of faith, causes create the illusion:
the reality is in the words, in the eroticism of language that this
impoverished, *unsalaried* writer used so passionately and that
still carry us away today.)

Notwithstanding Barthes, it would be easy to show that Bloy, the pamphleteer, did not choose his targets at random. Indeed, earlier in his text,
Barthes observes that Bloy "was almost never wrong." He congratulates
him for having taken aim at Bourget and for having "been one of the very
first" to recognize Lautréamont. My purpose, however, is not so much
elaborating on the traditional cliché of Bloy, the Catholic pamphleteer,
but rather examining his "infatuations," his historical heroes, and his very
concept of history. Several movements and themes essential to the late
nineteenth and early twentieth centuries will be illustrated: symbolism,
decadence, the occult, and the Catholic renaissance. Of course, Bloy
cannot be identified with or reduced to any one of these themes. For
instance, his idea of the absolute and his conviction that he belonged to
Catholic orthodoxy led him to vigorous, "con brio" condemnations and
satires not only of Joseph Serre's syncretic theosophy but also of "Sâr"
Joséphin Péladan's occultism and of Huysmans's Satanism in *Là-bas*.
Nevertheless, it is characteristic that he was associated with these two
authors for varying lengths of time and that he intermittently conceded
that they were very talented. In 1884 he expressed both the admiration
and the reservations that stemmed from his dogmatism: "of those writers

of my generation, Mr. Joséphin Péladan is ..., with the exception of Huysmans, the only writer whose intellectual boots I would not blush to scrape clean."[3]   Bloy, Huysmans, and Péladan presided in common over the "Funeral ceremonies of Naturalism."   It might also be mentioned that *Léon Bloy devant les cochons* (1894) was published by the occult book-store-owner and publisher Chamuel ("Librairie du Merveilleux").   Later on, Bloy offered Chamuel his pamphlet against Zola, *Je m'accuse*, but Chamuel refused it.

Not only did Bloy analyze his symbolic conception of history at great length and in a very theoretical way, he also illustrated this conception with specific examples.   *Le Désespéré*, a partially autobiographical novel, whose hero, Marchenoir, is also Bloy himself, contains a full statement of the author's principles.   Marchenoir wants to write a book on the symbolism of history.   In Marchenoir's words:

> Quel livre pourrait être le mien, pourtant, si j'enfantais ce que j'ai conçu! Mais quel accablant, quel formidable sujet! *Le Symbolisme de l'histoire*, c'est-à-dire l'hiérographie providentielle, enfin déchiffrée dans le plus intérieur arcane des faits et dans la kabale des dates, le sens *absolu* des signes chroniques, tels que Pharsale, Théodoric, Cromwell ou l'insurrection du 18 mars (1871 = la Commune), par exemple, et l'orthographe *conditionnelle* de leurs infinies combinaisons!   En d'autres termes, le calque linéaire du plan divin rendu aussi sensible que les délimitations géographiques d'un planisphère, avec tout un système corollaire de conjecturales aperceptions de l'avenir!!![4]

> What a book my book would be if I could deliver what I have conceived!   But what an overwhelming, what a formidable subject!   The *Symbolism of History*, in other words, the hierography of Providence, deciphered at last by the innermost keep of events and in the Cabbala of dates.   At least, the *absolute* meaning of chronicled signs, such as Pharsalis, Theodoric, Cromwell, and the uprising of March 18th (1871 = the Commune), for example, and the *conditional* spelling of their infinite combinations!   In other words, the linear trace of the divine outline made as tangible as the geographical delimitations of a planisphere, with an entire corollary system of conjectural apperceptions of the future!!!

The Metaphor of the Text

Basically, then, two metaphors are used for expressing the symbolism of history: the metaphor of the text and the metaphor of the chart.   In the case of the former, history is a sacred text. It is a Scripture in the Biblical sense, and "writing" history really means attempting an exegesis of history, deciphering and decoding its sacred and enigmatic text. Historical facts are mysteries and secrets; dates are the magical formulas of a Cabbala. "Chronicle signs," the signs of the times, are bearers of a hidden meaning that we can only glimpse. God alone has knowledge of the "absolute" meaning, and we must await the coming of the Holy Ghost, which will coincide with the end of time and, therefore, of history itself. Bloy reproached Péladan for his lack of familiarity with Sacred Scripture: "This Hebrew humanist was not even able to grasp the rudimentary Latin of the Vulgate."[5] Moreover, because Bloy had Joséphin Péladan read the relevant passage in *Isaiah* (39:1), he assumes that Péladan borrowed his name from "Merodach-Baladon, son of Baladon, King of Babylon." In addition (although Bloy himself hotly denies this), the importance that his personal theology attributes to the Holy Ghost and to the Paraclete inevitably suggested to some of his contemporaries the heresy of Vintras, Boullan's predecessor, and thus the Lyons mystic and occult groups.[6]

The Metaphor of the Chart

The second metaphor, the metaphor of the chart, belongs to the spatial realm: "the geographical boundaries of the planisphere." Here history is seen as an unknown terrain or sea that is to be explored. However confusedly, an endeavor must be made to draw its map. Finally, this "breaking" of the historical text, the "breaking" of the historical ground have as their corollary "a system of conjectural apperceptions of the future." This is a prophetic activity, doomed to the fumbling and uncertainty of a divinatory undertaking.

From the outset we are confronted with two paradoxes. On the one hand, rather than being a literary form of writing, history is a stumbling effort at reading a sacred Scripture. On the other hand, this reading of the past is essentially a search for the signs of the future. Bloy is then in a doubly false position. He seems to belie the "democratic" nineteenth century and its belief in progress. One need only read his pages on Michelet, for whom, in Bloy's eyes, everything is simple: Michelet prophesies "in full light" and not "darkly," in the words of Saint Paul.[7] At the same time, he differs from "reactionaries"—in the strict sense of the term— who simply invert faith in progress by preserving a nostalgia for a Golden Age situated in the past. It must be realized that here Bloy sets himself apart from his initial masters, Bonald, de Maistre, and Barbey d'Aurevilly. His passionate cult of Napoleon and the cruelty of his remarks about the Bourbons, from Louis XIV to the Count of Chambord, provide ample proof of this claim.

In keeping with these two metaphors, Marchenoir/Bloy sees himself as a decipherer, a decoder, and an explorer. "He dreamed of becoming the Champollion of history and of contemplating historical events as if they were divine hieroglyphics of a revelation through symbols, corroborating the first revelation."[8] "I am outward bound, like Columbus, about to explore the Shadowy Sea, certain that there is a world to be discovered, and fearful of stirring up, halfway, fifty idiot passions."[9]

The Historian as Miracle Worker

The sacred character of the historical text reveals itself further in a third metaphor—that of the miracle-working historian. Just as the authors of the books of the Bible were prophets possessing supernatural powers, so the modern historians should be magicians and miracle workers. Here again, Bloy is both close to, and far from, the occult. Close as to the spirit, far as to the form. He heaps violent satire on Péladan's sartorial and capillary affectations ("Zéphyrin Delumière" in La Femme pauvre) and criticizes his finicky style: "The role of apostle or diviner does not suit me at all, and I am more and more eager not to be presented as a miracle worker or a magician . . . why do you not write to me with simplicity? Why should you use sentences suitable for Péladan alone? . . ."[10] Here is what Bloy writes in his first published book, Le Révélateur du globe (1884), devoted to Christopher Columbus:

> Anyone can tell the story of Hannibal crossing the Alps; it is just a matter of using one's palette. But the conqueror had a soul and the God of conquerors had his designs: these are the supremely important things to know! The greatest books written by man are history books. We call them Holy Books and they were written by miracle workers. Sixty thousand atmospheres beneath them, historians whose inspiration is merely human, must in their own fashion, also be miracle workers.[11]

Quite literally, the historian resuscitates his past:

> You must lie, like the prophet, on the dead child, breast against breast and mouth against mouth, breathing into him your own life. Only then may learning intervene. Up to that point, documents and papers are Egyptian mummy wrappings that push the dead a little further into death.[12]

Notice the emphasis on the Egyptian metaphor and its ambiguity: deciphering of hieroglyphics in Champollion's manner. Resurrection is opposed to embalmment and to swaddling of the mummy just as the living spirit is opposed to the dead letter. By maintaining that history is a miraculous act of resurrection, Bloy converges with Michelet. The two writers differ as to the global concept of history's meaning. In addition, whereas Bloy considers the historian whose inspiration is merely human to be an inferior version of the inspired scribe, he defines the novelist in reference to the historian:

> . . . every novelist is an anxious, rebellious historian who dreams—if he has any genius—of becoming the chronicler not of the humanly real, but of the humanly *possible*. He is deluded into thinking that this activity is more profound than being the analyst of the Divinely *possible*, and it is the latter that is man's true reality.[13]

Bloy's Symbolic Conception of History

Bloy's symbolic conception of history may be summarized as follows: just as, according to Biblical exegesis, the Old Testament prefigures the New Testament either directly (Melchisedech as a Christ figure and Isaac's sacrifice as a prefiguration of the passion) or by antithesis (Eve, the cause of human downfall, takes on her true significance with the Immaculate Conception of the Virgin Mary), so history is a kind of New Old Testament. It heralds and prefigures the New New Testament, the definitive advent of the Holy Ghost. In an absolute sense, of course, everything has already been enacted. History and time are illusions. God views the whole of history simultaneously. In the sense of the "conditional," as Bloy calls it, the situation is different because of our marred vision: according to the Pauline formulation, we see everything "through a glass darkly." This is especially so because the protagonists themselves feel that they are free, whereas this apparent liberty manifests itself for the sole purpose of expressing, darkly, divine purposes. Hence the fundamental paradox of Catholicism . . . It claims to reconcile the omniscience and omnipotence of God with the individual's free will. Herein lies the source of an aesthetic effect and of a tragic pathos . . . of aesthetics and of literature because the "absolute cannot be transcribed."[14] The conditional can be transcribed insofar as it is defined as the object of imprecise writing; tragic pathos, because deciphering is a perilous task in which interpretation leaves a margin that cannot be explained so that we may hope against hope. Because the absolute is hidden from us, a rereading of the past and even a rewriting are still possible. Far from flattening history ("in the eternal plan, all men are contemporaries"[15]), Bloy's thirst for the absolute paradoxically heightens his feeling and taste for history and for literature: "We are literally caught in each fold of the multicolored apron of ancient history."[16]

Historical personalities and events constitute the text that is to be deciphered symbolically. They are reproductions of the New Testament, especially the Passion, and prefigurations of the final advent. History stammers out its own death:

THE OCCULT IN LANGUAGE AND LITERATURE

... the history of the world is a mysterious and prophetic pre-figuration of God's drama. It is, therefore, analogous to the corpus of prefigurative images making up Biblical revelation, impenetrably secret as far as the High Mass of Calvary. But the difference is that whereas the Jews prophesied the redemption of man, history's universal prophecy announces the *completion* of the redemption by the Holy Ghost's advent in triumph.[17]

Symbolic decoding will lean heavily on names and on emblems. Names are used because history is a code. The application of emblems is that "figuration" contains "figure." Just as the earth itself is the image of man and hence of God, so man is in God's "likeness." And for Bloy, geography is no less symbolical than history:

... every time an explorer, a navigator, whether a believer or a skeptic, whether humble or proud, traced unknown areas of the earth or of the sea on paper, he unwittingly described *Man*, who is the sovereign master, the paradigm, the mirror.[18]

Columbus, Joan of Arc, and Napoleon

Léon Bloy devoted two studies to Christopher Columbus: *Le Révé-lateur du globe* (1884), and *Christophe Colomb devant les taureaux* (1890). In fact, he called for the beatification of the discoverer of America, referring to him as the "bearer of Christ" and even as the "dove bearing Christ,"[19] "the *dove*, who toward evening, brings back the green olive-branch of remission from the Flood to the boatman of the symbolic Ark."[20] Columbus is also the new Christopher, the Christ-bearer prefig-ured by the saint of the legend: "the famous legend of the Syrian martyr could then be likened to an Old Testament that Columbus's evangelical story was to carry out."[21] Columbus, the bearer of Christ, is also Christ's precursor. He precedes Christ on his journey to America, announcing the universal, "global" reign of Christ (or of the Paraclete). Like the Precur-sor and like Christ himself, he is the victim of persecution. In a different context, we saw that Marchenoir identified with Columbus in the sense that a historian is also an explorer. The symmetry is clear: the explorer is an inspired writer because he traces the face of the New World on paper.

Elsewhere, Marchenoir identifies with a Byzantine emperor, the "dying emperor Andronikos," "this emperor of utter decadence."[22] And, like many of his contemporaries, Bloy was fascinated by the history of Constantinople and Byzantium, about which he wrote a book in 1906. Again, following a pattern familiar to writers about decadence, he ob-serves that a given Byzantine monarch prefigures a given personality of modern history: Basil II, "the slaughterer of the Bulgarians" (tenth century), is a harbinger of Charles XII of Sweden and, above all, of

Napoleon.[23] For example, Constantine IX (eleventh century) is an anticipation of Louis XV;[24] his adversary Tornikos, who is as stupid as "a
Bourbon of the last century,"[25] is meant to anticipate the Count of
Chambord. Indeed, Bloy speaks of the Bourbons at length in his first
literary work, *La Chevalière de la mort* (1877), a book dealing with
Marie-Antoinette. For example, the blade of the guillotine is compared
to Constantine's *labarum* (banner): both have changed the course of
history.[26]

It is not surprising that Bloy devoted much thought to the history of
France. He believed that France was a chosen country: the Jewish people
were chosen before the Redemption, and France was chosen afterwards.
He borrowed the idea and the phrasing itself from *Gesta Dei per Francos*
("The High Deeds of God Accomplished by the French"), the title of a
history of the First Crusade by Guibert de Nogent (twelfth century),
a title that J. Bongars used again in the seventeenth century.[27] In *Le
Fils de Louis XVI*, a work dedicated to Naundorff, who claimed he was
Louis XVII (his supporters had connections with Vintras, the heretic
leader), Bloy declares that "the history of France can be likened to a New
Testament sequel, a great parable that the four Evangelists omitted
because they were afraid to mention it."[28] While analysing the symbolism
of emblems, he notes the infrequent Scripture references to the *gallus*
(cock). At the same time, he also applies the Gospel's words about the
lilies of the field to the French monarchy: they grow "on the emblematic
blue field" of the arms and standard of the kingdom of France.[29] The
theme recurs in *Jeanne d'Arc et l'Allemagne*, written during the war
(1915). The history of France is described and deciphered as if it were a
breviary. *Matins* correspond to the Merovingians, the Carolingians, and
the Capetians; *Miserere* and *Lauds*, to Joan of Arc and Louis XI; the
Children's Canticle, to Napoleon; the small Hours, to Bloy's own time;
and soon perhaps Vespers, to the "Grand Soir."[30] This example reveals
the fundamental ambiguity of Bloy's vision. For him, the coming catastrophe, the "Fiery Deluge," is to be followed by the triumph of the
Paraclete. He speaks ironically about a possible bond between himself
and the anarchist theoreticians of the "Grand Soir," perceived as a spasm
of revolution heralding the establishment of social justice. Michel Tournier
has rightly observed that Vallès is "Bloy's fraternal enemy."[31] We must
bear in mind that when Bloy was writing his book about her, Joan of Arc
had been beatified, but not yet canonized. Whereas the Catholic church
gave satisfaction to Bloy on this point, the church failed to fulfill his
hopes for Christopher Columbus. In Joan, Bloy sees a reincarnation of
the Virgin ("La Pucelle"),[32] hence of Eve. Her sacrifice makes of her a
"refiguration" of Christ and also a prefiguration of Napoleon: "she was
related to *Fire* [...], just as, at a later date, Napoleon was identified
with Thunder."[33] The battle of Patay, on June 18, is the "superantic-
ipated anniversary of Waterloo."[34] It is interesting to Compare *Jeanne
d'Arc et l'Allemagne* with Huysmans's *Là-bas* (1891), and Bloy even refers

to its main character, Gilles de Rais, "who turned into a monster."[35] Péladan himself wrote a book called *Secret de Jeanne* in 1913. In his *Journal*, Bloy attacks the work because it denies the role played by the supernatural in Joan's mission and attributes it to the "occult powers" of a "real secret society," the *Franciscan International*.[36]

For Bloy, Napoleon is the most glorious precursor of the Holy Ghost. Indeed Louis XVII was its "most obscure image," and "Napoleon, the most dazzling."[37] Whereas Naundorff/Louis XVII, whose passage was totally unrecognized, prefigured the definitive advent, Napoleon announces its coming into glory. Because the evidence points to his being the last "prefigurant and precursor"—note how many exceptional men had intimated his coming—his position is a privileged one.[38] *L'Ame de Napoléon* is Bloy's best history book. Here Bloy is inspired by a genuine "enthusiasm" (in the etymological sense of the word) for his subject. And it is here that Bloy's ambivalent feelings about the end of history are most movingly apparent: "We are close to the eve of the world, my dear child; you will perhaps witness the divine and terrible things that the conqueror of kings seems to have prefigured so impressively."[39] Here, too, his ambivalent attitude to history is most clearly expressed, for he cannot help but question (even in the *Journal* that he keeps while thinking about writing the book) God's purpose. Wishing to alter the divine plan, he says: "Waterloo. When I write about Napoleon, I shall express my strange anguish each time Waterloo is mentioned by whomever it may be, and my own everlasting inability to accept this disaster."[40] Bloy thus deviates from orthodox Catholicism, although he would have denied it, and echoes another champion of universal symbolism, Saint-Pol-Roux. Just as for Saint-Pol-Roux, "tradition has its fruits in the past, but mark my words, its roots are in the future," believing, too, that Louis XVI derived his real significance from the French Revolution,[41] Bloy maintains that "one might—in all sanity—state that Louis XIV [. . .] was disrespectful toward Napoleon when he made his Duke of Anjou a king of Spain, after having scandalously *disobeyed* him, by signing the deplorable treaty of Ryswick."[42]

Long before Roland Barthes, a contemporary of Bloy, Remy de Gourmont, also refused to see in Bloy anything more than a stylist: "Mr. Bloy has a style of his own [. . .] All that he lacks to become a very great writer are two ideas, for he does have one already: the theological idea."[43] But Bloy also had a concept of the symbolism of history, an apocalyptic one. And, as we know, apocalypse means both the Revelation and global catastrophe: "I await the Cossacks and the Holy Ghost."

Translated by Eithne Bourget

Notes

1. All quotations refer to the edition in 15 volumes edited by Joseph Bollery and Jacques Petit (I-VI), completed by Jacques Petit (VI-X), and incorporating the edition of the *Journal* by Bollery (XI-XIV) (Paris: Mercure de France, 1964-1975).

2. "Bloy," in *Tableau de la littérature française: de Madame de Staël à Rimbaud* (various authors [Paris: Gallimard, 1974], p. 416. I have corrected the printer's error so that "Louis XVIII" reads "Louis XVII."

3. "Finis latinorum," review of *Vice Suprême*, XV, 194-196.

4. III, 88.

5. *Belluaires et Porchers*, II, 218.

6. "Le Mendiant ingrat," XI, 68-69.

7. Review of the *History of the French Revolution* by Carlyle, published in 1874, XV, 39. The quotation from St. Paul is from Letters to the Corinthians 12:12. In the same vein, in September 1914, referring to a prophecy about Antichrist that Péladan translated while assimilating Wilhelm II to Antichrist, Bloy remarks: "I am willing to accept the authenticity of this prophecy, but it has two faults: it is too precise, and, above all, it is Péladan who presents it" ("Au seuil de l'Apocalypse," XIV, 103).

8. *Le Désespéré*, III, 131.

9. Ibid., 133. The following chapter (XXXV) of *Le Désespéré* was published separately under the title "Du Symbolisme en histoire."

10. "Mon journal," XI, 236.

11. I, 176.

12. Loc. cit.

13. Ibid., 85. This illustrates the "autobiographical" character of Bloy's novels, *Le Désespéré* and *La Femme pauvre*.

14. *Le Désespéré*, III, 307.

15. *Le Révélateur du globe*, I, 55.

16. *Jeanne d'Arc et l'Allemagne*, IX, 179.

17. *Constantinople et Byzance*, V, 172.

18. *Christophe Colomb devant les taureaux*, I, 338.

19. *Le Révélateur du globe*, I, 93.

20. *Christophe Colomb devant les taureaux*, I, 329.

21. Ibid., 340.

22. *Le Désespéré*, III, 317, 318.

23. *Constantinople et Byzance*, V, 231.

24. Ibid., 261.

25. Ibid, 263.

26. V, 24; also p. 61.

27. The expression "Gesta Dei per Francos" often recurs in Bloy's work, for example, in *Le Révélateur du globe*, I, 66; *Le Fils de Louis XVI*, V, 96; *L'Ame de Napoléon*, V, 274.

28. V, 95.

29. Loc. cit.

30. IX, 161.

31. "L'homme de l'absolu," *Le Monde* (October 24, 1975), p. 26.

32. Violently anti-Protestant, Bloy had a cultlike devotion to the Virgin. A book by the occultist Grillot de Givry repels him because of its pedantic tone, but he continues to read it, for it "seems to be exclusively devoted to the glory of Mary"; Bloy wrote to the author to convey his admiration and also his reservations based on "the occultist formula that is [for him] almost indigestible—" ("Quatre ans de captivité à Cochons-sur-Marne," XII, 198-200).

33. IX, 163.

34. Ibid., 187.

35. Ibid., 201. A great deal could be said on the relations between Bloy and Huysmans. Bloy welcomes and encourages the break between Huysmans and Naturalism, exemplified by *A Rebours*. The first pages of *Là-bas* fill Bloy with enthusiasm, but he is soon disenchanted. Bloy accuses Huysmans of having used his own ideas (on the advent of the Holy Ghost especially) and of deforming them, of having fallen prey to the fascination exerted by the heretic leader Vintras and by the Satanist Boullan.

Cf. in Vol. IV, *Les Dernières colonnes de l'Eglise* and, in particular, *Sur la tombe de Huysmans.*

36. "Au seuil de l'Apocalypse," XIV, 29-30.
37. *Le Fils de Louis XVI,* V, 103.
38. *L'Ame de Napoléon,* V, 271.
39. Dedication of *L'Ame de Napoléon* to André Martineau, V, 269.
40. "Quatre ans de captivité à Cochons-sur-Marne," XII, 162.
41. *Le Trésor de l'Homme* (Limoges: Rougerie, 1970).
42. V, 293.
43. *Le IIe Livre des Masques* (Paris: Mercure de France, 1898).

 PART 4

ASCENT, DEATH,
DREAMS....

Mallarmé and the "Poison Tutélaire"

JAMES R. LAWLER

Il doit y avoir quelque chose d'occulte au fond de tous . . .

S. M.

As keenly as Valéry, Mallarmé was concerned to define the psychology of poetic effects. In this he was loyal to his encounter with Edgar Allan Poe and the importance of "The Poetic Principle." He elaborated his reflections, made them the theme of poems like "Mes bouquins refermés . . . ," and wittily treated them in certain of his essays. It is, however, in *Variations sur un sujet* and, particularly, "Le Mystère dans les lettres" of 1896, that his most incisive remarks are to be found. He was at pains to show that a refined literature provokes two different reactions in direct rapport with the fund of mystery in the reader himself. "There must be someting occult in the depths of all men, decidedly I believe there to be something recondite—signifying closed or hidden—that inhabits the crowd . . ."[1] To read a poem is to confront this original obscurity, which we might other-

wise ignore. For one category of readers, it results in prompt dismissal
of the poem as incomprehensible—"even if the guiltless writer should
declare that he is blowing his nose"; for the other—the small company of
poetry's connoisseurs—such obscurity holds no fears: deferred revelation
is their pleasure; dawning clarity, their incentive, as they penetrate the
"precious cloud floating above the intimate gulf of each thought," the
"labyrinth lit with flowers."[2] In either case, the mystery is the reader's
own, just as a musing woman invests her fan with inmost joys:

> Sens-tu le paradis farouche
> Ainsi qu'un rire enseveli
> Se couler du coin de ta bouche
> Au fond de l'unanime pli![3]

The poet's experience is not dissimilar. Before he writes, he must be
the reader who goes to the heart of the mystery of letters, where he
gravely finds his truth. Yet literature demands of him more than of the
common reader, for it becomes synonymous with a total gift of self. By
means of a predecessor whom he elects over all others, he deciphers the
text—both suffering and triumph—that projects his hidden drama of
desire.

The Occult Presence in Mallarmé

No aspect of Mallarmé is more striking than his progression in the
"occult": from poem to legend, and from legend to myth. The inner
logic of this development, and of his language itself, is tied to Baudelaire
and to *Les Fleurs du mal.*[4] When the twenty-three-year-old poet affirmed
his independence, he broke with "Angoisse" and "Renouveau," and with
the Baudelairean sonnet as well; yet at the very same time he conceived
the project of expressing in one long poem the mystery of a secret beauty,
whereby he drew closest to his master. His divergent evolution allowed
him to fashion an influence all too strong and to come to terms with the
object of his jealous glance.

A long line of Mallarmé scholars have by and large neglected this
question. Richard's comment of 1960 remains valid today: ". . . on the
deep relationship between the poetic worlds of Baudelaire and Mallarmé
we do not as yet have any critical synthesis"[5] —none, we may add, that
considers in detail the manoeuvers by which Mallarmé undertook the same
experiments, used the same words, and pursued a solitary research that
turned upon this crucial dialogue. Critics have limited the effects of the
influence—if influence they recognise—to the eve of the 1866 crisis, but
Mallarmé himself saw no final break. On the contrary, as he observed in
a letter of September 1867: "Vraiment, j'ai peur de commencer . . . par
où notre pauvre et sacré Baudelaire a fini" (Truly I am afraid of beginning

where our poor and sacred Baudelaire finished).[6]

What are the traits of this relationship? Evoked in allegorical form in Mallarmé's 1864 prose poem "Symphonie littéraire," they are already visible in the verse that dates from three years earlier. But "Symphonie littéraire" is distinct from the preceding poems because it sets itself apart from the language of *Les Fleurs du mal.* The vision is transmuted and the tone changed in a manner so much the more unusual in that the young poet was plainly able, if he had so wished, to adopt Baudelaire's voice. Thus, in "Symphonie littéraire," it is less the process of identification that touches us than the techniques of distancing: the scene has become rural and constituted of trees, fountains, flowers; the sunset overflows "avec un bruit lascif de baisers" (lascivious noise of kisses); consolation is "un hymne élancé mystiquement comme un lys" (a hymn mystically rising like a lily). The poem is arranged as a diptych balancing spleen and ideal, Satan and seraphim. But if this method is suitable for a representation of *Les Fleurs du mal,* the prose poem constantly veers towards abstraction. Baudelaire's bipolarity reappears, but the style controls too imperious a presence. The bonds are broken by antithesis so that Mallarmé can speak in his own name.

However, at the end of 1864 and over the next three years, the allegory deepened to become a general code—"vierge de tout, lieu, temps, et personnes sus" (virgin of everything, known place, time, and persons).[7] We are aware that this discovery came about by way of *Hérodiade,* which evolved from legend to myth. *"Je veux,"* he told Cazalis in October 1864, "pour la première fois—réussir. Je ne toucherais plus jamais à ma plume si j'étais terrassé" (I want, for the first time, to succeed. If I were struck down, I would never again touch my pen).[8] In the beginning, the important feature was not the subject, which he considered a mere pretext, but the treatment itself, aggressively opposed to pastiche and imitation. Mallarmé's ideal was to create a complex image—flower and blood, light and rain—like that which he had enunciated in an earlier poem:

> Cruelle, Hérodiade en fleur du jardin clair,
> Celle qu'un sang farouche et radieux arrose.[9]

Voluptuously, daringly, he elaborated his poem and took the sonorous name of Hérodiade as a kind of model. But in doing so, he found again the implacable beauty of *Les Fleurs du mal:* "ange inviole," "sphinx antique," "froide majesté de la femme stérile." In dynamic terms he developed the winter image of a queen whose innocence foreknows her future fall, but who yet moves in a sinless world. "En un mot, le sujet de mon oeuvre est la Beauté. . . (In one word, Beauty is the subject of my work. . .).[10] Hérodiade is whiteness threatened by blood, chastity disquieted by crime—the pure idea in cruel conflict with the real.

To recognize the true sense of his motif, Mallarmé needed two more years. He said then that *Hérodiade* was not solely a poem in honor of beauty nor the drama of the poetic word, but an intimate truth: "Hérodiade où je m'etais mis tout entier sans le savior"; "Je suis mort, et ressuscité avec la clef de pierreries de ma dernière cassette spirituelle. (Herodiade in which I had put all of myself without knowing it. I have died and am risen again with the jewelled key of my last spiritual casket).[11] The illumination he spoke of was that of the reciprocal relationship between "le Rien qui est la vérité" (Nothingness that is truth) and "le Glorieux Mensonge" (Glorious Lie),[12] emptiness and the poet's fiction, death and beauty. The drama of violation and expiation was already inscribed in *Les Fleurs du mal*, but it had not found its resolution; yet Mallarmé could now speak with calm confidence: master of himself because master of his myth and no longer a slave to spiritual agitation, he saw the *homo duplex* in a higher synthesis: "Oui, *je le sais*, nous ne sommes que de vaines formes de la matière, mais bien sublimes pour avoir inventé Dieu. . . ." (Yes, I know, we are but vain material forms but sublime for having invented God . . .).[13] He was convinced of subsuming the poetry that had gone before, of fulfilling the ambitions of other seekers of the ideal—among whom Baudelaire was the most anguished—in the élan of his lucid madness.

This was not the end point of his reflexions since, as his letters for the year 1867 show, he delved still further into the implications of the myth. In May he asserted an acute self-awareness: "Ma Pensée s'est pensée" (My Thought has thought itself). [14] He realized that he no longer informed his myth but that, on the contrary, the myth informed him, just as it contained the death of his St. John in order that poetry might declare itself: he himself was, so to speak, already dead, being nothing more than an "aptitude qu'a l'Univers spirituel à se voir et à se développer à travers ce qui fut moi" (an aptitude of the spiritual Universe to see itself and to develop through what was formerly me).[15] The Baptist dies after contemplating beauty; likewise, the myth incarnates humanity's evolution—Greek, Christian, post-Christian: the virgin Hérodiade, the rapist John, modern beauty, which the poet creates as if he were sculpting his own tomb. So poetry is a symbolic representation; no longer a flower of evil, it is the fiction that unfolds in the face of destiny. And yet a month after Baudelaire's death, Mallarmé saw that the necessity presiding over his poetic maturity was a filiation both tender and violent with Baudelaire—"notre pauvre et sacré Baudelaire."

The Significance of "Le Tombeau de Baudelaire"

I have, then, underlined this occult presence, whose virtue, to the end, inhabited Mallarmé's language, which became abstract so as to control it. He had to view Baudelaire from another level, possess the sexuality and death Baudelaire had articulated; he must of necessity go further into *Les Fleurs du mal* and not cast it aside. He took up once again themes familiar to Baudelaire—swan, hair, sunset, voyage—which he treated in apparent playfulness within a frame of his own. Each poem follows a curve in which the personal becomes impersonal: the swan attains a state of "magnificence," like a constellation, by its refusals; the hair no longer invites the imagination to exotic lands but defends time's diamond against doubt—"ainsi qu'une joyeuse et tutélaire torche"; the sunset, unconsumed, lingers in the "fulgurante console"; and the voyage is not a fatal course but the solemn act that changes loss to gain: "Nuit, désespoir et pierrerie," "Solitude, récif, étoile." In this fashion, the Baudelairean heritage was not nullified but, rather, elaborated. In it Mallarmé renounced the self, yielded the initiative to words, absorbed himself wholly in his death, as in the myth.

Nevertheless, we find no tributes or extended allusions to Baudelaire's work before the 1893 "Tombeau de Baudelaire" published in *La Plume*. This sonnet has not been among the most admired, and Claudel, for one, condemned it out of hand. Mallarmé, he said, "a abouti tristement à d'aussi mauvais 'chefs-d'oeuvre' que *Le Tombeau de Baudelaire*."[16] It has, then, few supporters; yet, remarkably, hardly a year goes by without the appearance of a new exegesis. The most recent to come to my notice is that of Deryk Mossop in an issue of *French Studies*.[17] Making ample use of previous interpretations, the writer concludes that Mallarmé adopted Baudelaire's words and images but made from his borrowings an unsatisfactory mixture. We note again the traditional criticisms: for D. J. Mossop, the "Tombeau" is composed "à la manière de Baudelaire" and therefore prescribes what we may term a "picturesque" reading. But it seems appropriate to read the poem in another perspective: Mallarmé, I think, has recourse less frontally to Baudelaire's imagery than to the structure of his own intimate myth, a language that in this sonnet is all the more touching in that it elicits its own point of origin. Thus the emblem of a hidden drama is proposed. The poet, moreover, well knew that his homage was oblique because he described it as "trop à côté, particulier et attaquable" (too divergent, private, and open to attack).[18] But he was nonetheless content with it and eager to observe that it was "ce qu'il me plaît." There can be no doubt: his remarks clearly denote that there had been a divergence from Baudelaire but that, by this detour, he found the means of asserting a central conception.

Thus the "Tombeau," breaking with *Les Fleurs du mal*, articulates the triumph of the ephemeral over time. None of Mallarmé's sonnets rises more swiftly to the mythical plane, sustained by the rare rhymes "Anubis" and "pubis" and by Egyptian, Greek, and Christian allusions. Across paradoxes and discontinuous metaphors a system of relationships is established at furthest remove from description. Here the links are dialectical, and the linguistic field constitutes a ritual.

> Le temple enseveli divulgue par la bouche
> Sépulcrale d'égout bavant boue et rubis

Abominablement quelque idole Anubis
Tout le museau flambé comme un aboi farouche

Ou que le gaz récent torde la mèche louche
Essuyeuse on le sait des opprobres subis
Il allume hagard un immortel pubis
Dont le vol selon le réverbère découche

Quel feuillage séché dans les cités sans soir
Votif pourra bénir comme elle se rasseoir
Contre le marbre vainement de Baudelaire

Au voile qui la ceint absente avec frissons
Celle son Ombre même un poison tutélaire
Toujours à respirer si nous en périssons.[19]

(The buried temple divulges by the mouth
Sepulchral of a sewer slobbering mud and ruby
Abominably some idol Anubis,
Its whole snout singed like a savage bark.

Or let the recent gas twist the oblique wick
Suffering we know from disgraces undergone
It illuminates untamed an immortal pubis
Whose flight in accord with the street-lamp uncouches. ·

What leafage dried in the nightless cities,
Votive, shall bless like it, like it resettle
In vain against the marble of Baudelaire

—Shudderingly absent from the veil that girds it—
His own true Shade, a tutelary poison,
Ever to be breathed though we should die of it.)

Mallarmé isolates the tragic vein of Baudelaire's work. We are face to face with eros and thanatos evoked in intermingled legendary and modern imagery and in the insistent sonorities. Of Mallarmé's sonnets on death, this is the most baroque in its formulation of poetry's scandal.

The language is organized with panache. In the first quatrain we read the paradox of a buried temple that serves to reveal. Death becomes immortal in the guise of a dolorous Anubis silently howling, as the synesthesia of the fourth line powerfully expresses. But these images are joined to those of an orifice—"divulgue," "bouche," "bavant," "museau," "abominablement" (which Littré derives from *ab-osmen*)—emphasizing the violence of the new language. Mallarmé's lines are a vehement prelude—overdense perhaps—which finds its complement in the second quatrain. A second unveiling takes place: "Il allume . . ." The "opprobres subis" echo "abominablement"; the twisted wick recalls the "museau flambé." The symbol of sexuality is proposed, as immortal as death, as agitated as a flight of birds frightened by the irrefutable dog Anubis.

We know that the encounter of death and sexuality is the nexus of *Hérodiade*. The queen sings to the dead Baptist in an admirable parenthesis: "le glaive qui trancha ta tête a déchiré mon voile" (the blade that beheaded you tore my veil).[20] Language is a double-edged sword that accomplishes a ritual death while at the same time illuminating the body of desire; the poet achieves, as we read in *Igitur*, the "preuves nuptiales de l'idée."[21] At the heart of anguish, transcendence occurs: the cursed cry of the first quatrain is resolved in a benediction; the agitation of the second ends in rest. The sonnet turns on the axis of the tenth line, which provides a symmetrical response:

Votif pourra *bénir* comme elle se *rasseoir.*

No leafery has a power of consolation comparable to that of the poet of *Les Fleurs du mal*, henceforth a shade both present and absent like a perfume, not vanquished but victor. Mallarmé rhymes "Baudelaire" with "tutélaire," proposes the image of protection. The contrast is thus complete between the density of the beginning and the lightness of the end, immanence and transcendence, anguish and salvation, by which the poet makes human destiny into a tragic and glorious symbol.

The "Tombeau" is seen to be a radical attempt to state Baudelaire's achievement in original terms, that is, according to the dialectic of *Hérodiade*, which overcomes anguish. Thought and design are admirable, although marred in some degree by the weakness of the second line and by the ellipses of the myth. But if the sonnet is without doubt not Mallarmé's best, it is one of the most important for the light it sheds on the poet's development. For here there is no question of "marivaudage avec l'absolu" (as Valéry said) but of a man who projects himself in the form of poetry by sacrifice and suffering. Baudelaire could indeed represent this idea in exemplary fashion; and what reader knew it better than Mallarmé, who had breathed *Les Fleurs du mal* to the utmost limit—to the point of symbolic extinction of himself?

Notes

1. Stéphane Mallarmé, *Œuvres complétes* (Paris: Gallimard, 1951), p. 383.
2. *Œuvres complètes*, p. 384.
3.   Do you feel the wild paradise
     Like some buried laughter
     Flow from the corner of your mouth
     Deep within the unanimous fold!
4. In one of the best studies we possess—doubtless the most precise since that of Jean-Pierre Richard—Sylviane Huot recently made an analysis of *Hérodiade*, its

genesis and growth *(Le Mythe d'Hérodiade.* Paris: Nizet, 1977). Her approach is tributary to the essays of Charles Mauron, but, far from restricting herself to psycho-criticism, she explores the various paths of possible influence (Heine, Gautier, Wilde) and, especially, the inner logic of Mallarmé's language. It will henceforth be difficult to avoid reference to this book, whose discretion is not the least of its virtues. One is, however, surprised that no mention is made of Baudelaire; Mme. Huot points to seminal readings, yet omits the impact of *Les Fleurs du mal* both before and after the "crisis" of 1866.

5. Jean-Pierre Richard, *L'Univers poétique de Stéphane Mallarmé* (Paris: Le Seuil, 1961), p. 75. Concerning Baudelaire's influence on the early poetry of Mallarmé see Lloyd James Austin, "Mallarmé disciple de Baudelaire: *Le Parnasse contemporain,"* *Revue d'histoire littéraire de la France,* 67 (1967), pp. 437-449.

6. Stéphane Mallarmé: *Correspondance* (Paris: Gallimard, 1959), Vol. 1,p. 259.

7. *Œuvres complétes,* p. 544.

8. *Correspondance,* Vol, 1, p. 137.

9. "Les Fleurs," *Œuvres complètes,* p. 34.

10. *Correspondance,* Vol. 1, p. 193.

11. Ibid., Vol. 1, p. 222.

12. Ibid., Vol. 1, p. 208.

13. Ibid., Vol. 1, p. 207.

14. Ibid., Vol. 1, p. 240.

15. Ibid., Vol. 1, p. 242.

16. Paul Claudel, *Œuvres en prose* (Paris: Gallimard, 1965), p. 1468.

17. "Stéphane Mallarmé: *"Le Tombeau de Charles Baudelaire,"* French Studies* (July 1977), pp. 287-298.

18. *Propos sur la poésie,* 2d ed. (Monaco: Editions du Rocher, 1953), p. 197. Concerning this sonnet, see Lloyd James Austin, *"Le Tombeau de Charles Baudelaire* by Stéphane Mallarmé: Satire or Homage," *Etudes baudelairiennes* (Neuchâtel: A la Baconnière, 1973), pp. 186-200.

19. *Œuvres complètes,* p. 70.

20. *Les Noces d'Hérodiade,* ed. Gardner Davies (Paris: Gallimard, 1959), p. 136.

21. *Œuvres complètes,* p. 387.

The Dangerous Game of Dreams: Jean Paul and the Surrealists

REINHARD KUHN

> . . . We are such stuff
> As dreams are made on, and our little life
> Is rounded with a sleep . . .
>
> Shakespeare, *The Tempest*

Ever since the appearance of Béguin's *Choix de rêves* (1931) with its revelatory preface, much has been made of the interrelationship between Jean Paul Richter's visionary *Traumdichtungen* and the oneiric writings of the surrealists. This is hardly surprising, for the dreams contained in this anthology seem to have been written expressly for André Breton and his followers. Although most of the critics have been reasonably cautious in their assessment of influence, Maurice Nadeau, in his classic *Histoire du surréalisme*, claimed that Jean Paul was indeed one of the masters of the surrealists (even though his name did not appear in Breton's several lists of recommended reading, which Nadeau appended to his thesis); and Walter Muschg, in his *Studien zur tragischen Literaturgeschichte* calls him "the father of surrealism." More responsible scholars like Claude Pichois[1]

and Robert Minder[2] were right in their restraint. It is an obvious fact
that Jean Paul had virtually no direct influence on the surrealists. Breton,
for one, does not include him either in his *Anthologie de l'humour noir* or,
even more astonishing, in his *Trajectoire du rêve*, nor does he even
mention his name in his official lists of the precursors of surrealism. In
fact, he only acknowledges his existence twice, and then merely in passing.
Aragon does refer to Jean Paul in a highly significant fashion, but only in
the postsurrealistic novel, *La Mise à mort*. In fact, the only major
French writer of the twentieth century whose work was distinctly shaped
by the works of Jean Paul and who had a first-hand knowledge of them
was Jean Giraudoux. The preciosity of style and the carefully structured
nature of the dream world in a novel like *Juliette au pays des hommes*
are very close in spirit to some of Jean Paul's most mannered writings,
and much more irritating.

Dreams

If there is no direct influence, there is certainly a deep affinity between Jean Paul and the surrealists. And even if the latter had never
studied his works, the informing spirit behind them might well have been
transmitted to them through the works of Gérard de Nerval. Despite
the allegorical elements one finds in such a famous dream as "The Speech
of the Dead Christ" and despite the carefully composed style and structure
of nearly all of the transcribed visions, the theory of dreams as formulated
by Jean Paul in his essays and that of the surrealists are fundamentally
the same. In his *Introduction to Aesthetics*, Jean Paul, well before Freud,
says that the source of all poetic inspiration lies in the subconscious,
which is indifferent to all questions of morality: "Das Mächtigste im
Dichter, welches seinen Werken die gute und die böse Seele einbläset,
ist gerade das Unbewusste" (The mightiest force of the poet, which both
the good and evil spirit inspire in his work, is actually the subconscious.).[3]
In an early article, "About Dreaming," Jean Paul claims that through
dreams the imagination, unfettered by "cold reason," manifests the free
workings of the imagination in what Breton would call a gratuitous game.
He goes on to say that, during sleep or during a trance, unsolicited images
appear before the spirit in an involuntary procession. In another essay
significantly entitled "Concerning the Natural Magic of the Power of the
Imagination," Jean Paul writes:

> Der Traum ist das Tempe-Thal und Mutterland der Phantasie:
> die Konzerte, die in diesem dämmernden Arkadien ertönen,
> die elysischen Felder, die es bedecken, die himmlischen
> Gestalten, die es bewohnen, leiden keine Vergleichung mit irgend
> etwas, das die Erde gibt [IV, 197].

> (The dream is the Vale of Tempe and motherland of fantasy;

the concerts that resound in this twilight Aracadia, the Elysian fields that bedeck it, the celestial figures that inhabit it suffer no comparison with anything whatsoever to be found on earth.)

In other words, there is a second marvelous reality, that of fantasy, to which one can only gain access through dreams. And, as Jean Paul explains in his "Dream within a Dream," from the vantage point of this other realm, "our world is a dream full of dreams." In other words, the world that is the stage for dreams is, when seen from within the dream, a dream itself. The distinctions between levels of reality become blurred, even irrelevant, as do those between the dreamer and the subject being dreamt.

Thomas Carlyle, who along with Mme. de Staël, was one of Jean Paul's greatest proselytizers, wrote concerning the dream sequences in his novels:

> ... with what strange prophetic power he [Jean Paul] rules over that chaos of spiritual Nature, bodying forth a whole world of Darkness, broken by pallid gleams or wild sparkles of light, and peopled with huge, shadowy, bewildered shapes, full of grandeur and meaning.[4]

To what extent Jean Paul actually did rule over the chaos of the spiritual world is subject to question, but otherwise this description is applicable not merely to the formally designated dream scenes but also to the novels of which they form an integral part. It is unfortunate that most critics have followed the lead of Béguin's *L'Ame romantique et le rêve* by considering the dreams in isolation[5] when they can only be understood within their context. It is true that easily identifiable links are often lacking between the dreams and the novels into which they are incorporated. Only rarely are they integrated into the plot of the story or into the psychological structure or development of the characters.[6] But if the border lines between different stages of reality are indistinct, it is hardly surprising that, on a far deeper level than plot or character, dream and fiction are one. This fusion is manifested in Jean Paul's language, which remains a constant in both realms, made up as it is of all varieties of word games, in which, as in the works of the surrealists, the puns, so natural to the German language, predominate. This unicity forged by style is indistinguishable from the ideal posited by Breton, who, in his "First Manifesto of Surrealism," envisages:

> ... la résolution de ces deux états, en apparence si contradictoires, que sont le rêve et la réalité, en une sorte de réalité absolue, de *surréalité*, si l'on peut ainsi dire.
>
> (... the resolution of these two apparently so contradictory

states, of dream and of reality, into a sort of absolute reality, of *surreality*, if one might say so.)

The novel is actually the inseparable substructure of the dream, or vice versa, and in their internal relationship they form an arcane whole. One example of this unity can be detected even in Jean Paul's first fragmentary novel, *The Invisible Lodge* (1793). Its protagonist, Gustav von Falkenberg, spends his first nine years underground, in the company only of his tutor and a dog, in a setting reminiscent of Plato's Allegory of the Cave. After this gestatory period, Gustav emerges as from a womb and is blinded by the rising sun; in his rapture he thinks that it is the moment of death and that the earth is heaven. This symbolic passage from darkness to light is repeated throughout the novel. In its most melodramatic form it is seen in the figure of Amandus, whose eyes had been plucked out by a crone, who then employed him to evoke pity in those from whom she begs. There is a revelatory passage to light when his sight is restored by Dr. Fenk. These episodes, which are repeated in various forms in the "real" world of the novel, find their counterparts in the oneiric portions of the work. Thus Gustav's first dream, a cosmic vision, represents a reversal of the movement of the overture and subsequent incidents. At first he sees a pearl string of brilliant suns encircling the earth. During the course of the dream, they sink and are replaced by shadows. As the last sun disappears, Gustav sheds his corporeal reality and knows the ecstasy of death. The emergence from darkness to light and its parallel in vision lost and restored, as well as the converse of this movement, are fundamental to all of the works of Jean Paul and find their most powerful expression in *Titan* (1800-1803). In the opening phase of this epic prose poem, Albano binds his eyes during the passage at dawn across the lake and has himself led to a vantage point on the Isola Bella. Only when the sun has risen does he tear off the scarf so that he can be struck by the immediacy of the dazzling light. And, as in *The Invisible Lodge* (and as in *Hesperus*, too, for that matter), there is a secondary character, Liana, who loses and regains her sight. Once again there is a dream in which this pattern is repeated. So obsessed is Jean Paul with the alternance between cecity and sight that in *Walt and Vult, or the Twins*[7] (1804-1805) he attempts to exorcize it through satire in the personage of the flutist Vult, who feigns blindness in order to attract attention to his concert. Jean Paul's treatment of this one theme is typical. The modes of discourse cover the gamut from the Gothic of *The Invisible Lodge*, the sublime of *Titan*, to the bitterly caricatural of *Walt and Vult*. Nonetheless, the diversity of expression is more apparent than real. Whatever the tone, the style is always one of convoluted preciosity.

This manneristic style so characteristic of the dreams that Jean Paul included in all of his equally manneristic novels could lead to certain suspicions concerning their authenticity. The same doubts could be raised about the sincerity of such polished and intellectually complex prose pieces as Aragon's *Paysan de Paris* or Robert Desnos's *La Liberté ou l'amour!.* In any case, the provenance of Jean Paul's visions is again remarkably similar to that of the surrealist aberrations. Jean Paul's original inspiration came from the waking reveries that he recorded in brief notations in his posthumously published biographical sketch, *Truth Extracted from Jean Paul's Life.* The otherworldly state conducive to the free play of the imagination was most frequently induced through artificial stimulants (notably coffee, alcohol, and music). The seminal sketches consisted usually of disjointed fragments and logically unrelated motifs and images. Curiously enough, the careful working out and elaboration of these bits and pieces into the unified whole of a composed dream do not detract from their oneiric quality, and the finished product has a more hallucinatory atmosphere than the authentic notations. The immediacy so cherished by the surrealists was preceded in the work of Jean Paul by a quality in no way inimical to it and one that might be called immobilized spontaneity. In their meticulous craftsmanship, which seems to freeze the dream into a timeless and immutable moment, these compositions remind one of Dali's so precisely delineated paintings, in which minute details stand out with an unreal clarity.

Aesthetics of Chance

The importance of dreams in the works of Jean Paul and the surrealists has blinded critics to other equally important similarities. Among these is the importance accorded to the element of chance. The random nature of art is an integral factor in Jean Paul's aesthetic, as it is in that of Breton or Queneau. This is illustrated in one of Jean Paul's briefest but most brilliant works, "The Army Chaplain Schmelzle's Voyage to Flätz with a Running Series of Notes" (1809), which consists of a number of interwoven texts. There is an explanatory preface by the supposedly real author; then there is an open letter in the form of an apologia from the army chaplain Schmelzle, who tries to exculpate himself from the charge of cowardice by describing a short but unsuccessful trip whose purpose was to solicit the post of Catechistic Professor; appended to this epistle there is a running commentary by an editor in the form of carefully numbered but nonsequential footnotes at the bottom of each page; finally, in the guise of an appendix, there is a short "Confession of the Devil." Most intriguing of all is the relationship of the notes to Schmelzle's letter. In his preface, Jean Paul explains that when he sent the manuscript to the printer, he had inadvertently included the notes in a separate package and, because he had thought of publishing them separately, he had neglected to put corresponding numbers in the body of the text. So the typesetter had simply inserted them at random, using only one guiding principle, namely, that of making certain that each page was provided with at least one note. And it would certainly be impossible for even the best intentioned and patient reader to reconstruct whatever the author's original text might have been, for the comments explain nothing and are mainly enigmatic aphorisms such as "100) Die Bücher liegen voll Phönixasche eines tausendjährigen Reichs und Paradieses; aber der Krieg weht, und viele Asche verstäubt" (VI, 14). (100. Books lie about full of the Phoenix ashes of a thousand-year kingdom and paradise; but war blows, and many ashes are covered with dust.) The printed text of this novella consists of a complex interplay between four voices: the *vox auctoris* of the preface, the voice of the fictitious critic responsible for the footnotes, the voice of Schmelzle as composer of the circular, and the voice of Satan. There is one undetermined element in this structure, which lends the whole work a feeling of instability. Because the footnotes are not affixed to any preordained positions in the letter, there is an infinite variability in the novella that makes it possible for the reader to reconstruct versions ad infinitum and thus to discover "a far greater subterranean treasure" (VI, 10) than even the author Jean Paul had found. Fundamentally, the procedure is the same as that employed by Queneau in the construction of his "Cent mille milliards de Poèmes."

The products of this method of composition are those fortuitous juxtapositions in which French poets since Lautréamont have taken such delight. The kaleidoscopic effect of chance encounters between totally disparate elements produces what is the essential element in the aesthetics of both Jean Paul and the surrealists: the marvelous. This is an element that is by no means limited to his dreamscapes. In *Titan,* for example, the depiction of the very real Isola Bella (which Jean Paul had never seen) is as enchanting as that of the purely imaginary Valley of the Flutes. Both the inner and the outer world of Jean Paul in their fairy-talelike atmosphere are illustrative of the principle that he announces in his *Introduction to Aesthetics:* "Alles wahre Wunderbare ist für sich poetisch" (V, 44) (All that is trully marvelous is in and for itself poetic). This proclamation anticipates Breton's assertion in his "First Manifesto of Surrealism" of the primacy of the marvelous:

> . . . le merveilleux est toujours beau, n'importe quel merveilleux est beau, il n'y a même que le merveilleux qui soit beau.

> . . . the marvelous is always beautiful, no matter what marvelous is beautiful; in fact, there is nothing but the marvelous that is beautiful.

Bourgeois Elements

Visionary dreams, random encounters, free word associations, all characterized by a perverse humor in which it becomes impossible to

"A dream of crime and expiation"

from *Last Drawings* by J. J. Granville (1803-1846)

distinguish between artifice and spontaneity, these are the elements with which one could begin to define both the art of Jean Paul and that of the surrealists. There is another, less apparent feature that explains the communality of the German preromantic and the surrealist spirit and simultaneously clarifies their mutual attraction to the occult world of dreams. Despite the radical nature of Jean Paul's enterprises (which consisted of nothing more nor less than a total revolution of the German language) and despite such heroic romances as *Hesperus* and *Titan*, Jean Paul was basically a bourgeois writer in the same sense as Vermeer was a bourgeois painter. After all, his first fictional work (and probably his most widely read) was a cheerful idyll, "Leben des vergnügten Schulmeisterleins Maria Wutz im Auenthal" (1793). The diminutive applied to the schoolmaster's title, the adjective *cheerful* used to describe him, his habitation in a valley, in fact, his name itself make of the very title of this work a definition in miniature of its bourgeois nature. And in this novella we find what is without question the ultimate expression of self-contentment: at the conclusion of every satisfying repast, the little schoolmaster pats his stomach and says with a sigh of happiness, "That did my Wutz good." And one of Jean Paul's last protagonists, Schmelzle, with his equally unheroic name, is an early incarnation of Walter Mitty. In between these two are the central figures of the other major novels: Siebenkäs is an impoverished country lawyer, Walt is brought up to be a notary public (although he would prefer to be a poet), and Nikolaus is the son of an apothecary. The ecstatic surrealist adventure, from Breton to Bachelard, was equally bourgeois in its nature. Both the founder of surrealism and its philosopher can sound self-satisfied and smug in their optimism, and quite typically both preferred streams to rivers or oceans.[8] They share Jean Paul's fondness for the miniature genre scene. The small interiors enclosing characters of no stature seem, nonetheless, to contain a mystery that undermines their reassuring solidity. This is certainly true of Picasso's delightful surrealist drama, *Le Désir attrappé par la queue*. One of the scenes depicts a perfectly ordinary hotel corridor, but the shoes, waiting in front of the doors to be polished, engage in a zany dialogue. It is certainly also the case in Aragon's extraordinary play *L'Armoire à glace un beau soir l'été*, whose setting is a vulgarly furnished living room decorated with cheap color prints and whose action consists of a mundane case of possible adultery. But when the suspected wife, in defiance of her husband, stands protectively in front of the wardrobe, which might contain a lover, she is represented as being crucified, and the closet she defends contains not the banal reality of a seducer but the marvelous visions of a dream. One senses not only delightful but also frightening forces at play that belie the pettiness of apparently self-enclosed lives. This is equally true of Jean Paul's novels. Hallucination, madness, and violent death lurk behind his tranquil interiors. Occasionally, these forces do erupt, as in the case of the cheerful materialist Schoppe in *Titan* whose involuntary contact with the occult drives him insane. The life that is rounded with a sleep is indeed a little one, but the dreams of which it is made can be monstrous or sublime.

The apparent contradiction between a transcendent vision and a bourgeois world view, which is the problem central to the education of Goethe's Wilhelm Meister, has preoccupied modern writers, many of whom have questioned the very propriety and seriousness of purpose of exploring a second reality. In Fogazzaro's *Piccolo mondo antico* Maria has recourse to an amateur in spiritualism in a desperate attempt to communicate with the child she had lost. As a consequence, she verges on a nervous breakdown. The disintegration of the carefully structured world of the sanatorium in Thomas Mann's *Magic Mountain* begins when the patients have recourse to turning tables in an effort to commune with departed spirits. The dangers of irresponsible dabbling with the occult are nowhere as clearly evidenced as in Jean Cocteau's *Les Enfants terribles*, in which the promiscuous experimentation of the children leads to madness, murder and suicide. Nowhere are these dangers handled so blithely as in Giraudoux's *Intermezzo*, in which Isabelle's flirtation with the occult, in the form of the ghost Arthur, leaves her unscathed and prepared for a bourgeois marriage. All of these authors seem to have been aware before its enunciation of Bachelard's warning that ". . . l'aspiration à l'inconnu, à l'imprévu, est extrêmement dangereux et néfaste" (. . . the aspiration toward the unknown, the unforeseeable, is extremely dangerous and ill-omened).[9] Neither Jean Paul nor the surrealists were unaware of this danger, even though they attempted to laugh it off. Indeed, Jean Paul's attitude toward the fantasy that he celebrated was an ambiguous one. In fact, in what is essentially a self-condemnation, he accuses those authors who are dominated by fantasy of being "poets of nihilism." (V, 31ff.).

A juxtaposition of the works of Jean Paul and the surrealists thus leads to a question that it is perhaps better to avoid. Are Jean Paul and Breton merely brilliant prestidigitators (like Cocteau, whom the surrealists detested precisely because they considered him an amateur), or do they belong to that select category of "horribles travailleurs" with whom Rimbaud sympathized? It would be easy to buttress unambiguous answers with simplistic evidence. The obvious artifices of Jean Paul's dreams, his exploitation of conventional pietistic metaphors, his intellec- tually referential style could all be used to demonstrate a superficiality that would be at odds with any meaningful spiritual endeavor. And his occasional references to the "Gauklerreich des Traums" (the juggler kingdom of dreams) indicate that he himself questions the high serious- ness of his enterprise. In similar fashion, it would be easy to dismiss Breton as a gifted charlatan. His all too often self-serving pronouncements are embarrassingly similar in tone to those of the advocates of the Reuni- fication Church or of transcendental meditation, and the "cadavre exquis" and similar activities are too closely akin to parlor games. On the other hand, one might argue that certain of Jean Paul's visions have such an immediate and compelling reality that their authenticity cannot be doubted. There is, for example, the concluding dream of the *Flegeljahre* in which the dreamer sees Chaos giving birth to the universe. The images have an unquestionable impact. For example:

> Dann sah ich ein weites leeres Meer, auf ihm schwamm blos das kleine graue fleckige Welt-ei und zuckte stark [II, 1061].

> (Then I saw a wide empty sea; on it there floated only the small, gray, spackled World-egg and twitched violently.)

Many of the passages of Breton's *Nada* are equally convincing. However, neither of these straightforward answers is satisfactory because each is based on the questionable assumption that Jean Paul and Breton are either exploiters or explorers. Such simple designations do not fit such complex poets.

A closer approximation to an accurate answer might be obtained if we think of the poetic enterprise of Jean Paul and the surrealists in terms of the Augustinian "medietatis experimentum" (trial of the middle), [10] the dangerous attempt to place the self in the center as a mediating agent or, perhaps, even as a medium. This point of view is exemplified in what is Jean Paul's most curious portrait of the artist, "The Life of Fibel" (1810). In some superficial respects, this work would hardly seem suitable for serious analysis of this sort. In one sense, it is a bourgeois idyll similar in tone to "Wutz." Those portions devoted to a depiction of Fibel's relationship with his mother and with Drotta, his fiancée and then bride, are the ultimate manifestations of this form of prose poetry. For example, when Drotta and Fibel are youngsters, they must walk in opposite directions. So that they will be able to find their way back to each other, they alternately sing stanzas from hymns, with the result that, although apart, they are as one, united by their voices and the spirit of simple piety. In another respect, this story also seems unsuitable for our purposes because it is manifestly a satire of the then very popular adulatory biographies of great writers and a product of what Jean Paul liked to call his "vinegar factory." The story, however, goes beyond mere mockery and calls into question the validity of the artistic enterprise itself. For Jean Paul has discovered that Fibel is the author of an anonymous primer,[11] which he analyzes as if it were a work of genius. He also sets out painstakingly to reconstitute the life of the fictitious writer. His sources are the original documents, which are now utilized as wrapping paper in various village stores and which the children gather for him. Fibel's masterpiece, which is reprinted in its entirety as an appendix to the story, is an illustrated ABC accompanied by absurdist verses replete with *non sequiturs.* For example, the last letter of the alphabet inspires, "Die Ziege Käse gibt drei Schock / Das Zahlbrett hält der Ziegenbock" (The nanny goat produces nine score cheeses / The toteboard is kept by the billy goat). But within the framework of this outrageous caricature, there are serious intimations. The inspiration for the magnum opus comes through a dream. Fibel is riding backwards on a crowing rooster when a voice from on high orders him to pluck out one of its tail feathers and to use it as a quill. It is with this instrument that Fibel can begin the arduous task of composition. This grotesque and at the same time provocative parable prefigures Cocteau's *Orpheus*, whose protagonist finds divine inspiration in the hoof-tapping of his horse. And just as Orpheus unwittingly incurs the wrath of Aglaonice by the verse dictated to him by his equine medium, so Fibel brings upon himself criticism for having impugned the reputation of the wife of Socrates with the poem devoted to the letter X: "Xantippe war 'ne arge Hur' / X mal X macht 100 nur" (Xanthippe was quite a whore / X times X makes only 100). In both the case of Orpheus and Fibel, the dangers of exploiting messages from the other world are emphasized. ". . . nous jouons très haut et sans filet de secours" (. . . we play very high up and without a safety net). These premonitory words are spoken in the Prologue by the author, who plays Orpheus, and could have been uttered by Fibel, although he certainly is no trapeze artist.

The *memorabilia* on which Jean Paul relies run out when the creator of the *ABC* is at the height of his fame. His official biographer, Peltz, who had produced the secondary sources that Jean Paul was using to write his version of the biography, had established an Academy whose function it was to do research on Fibel's life and works in order to celebrate him. Because of the dearth of material, Jean Paul threatens to cut off his study at this point. However, he does go on because fortuitously he encounters the very subject of his biography, whom he had presumed to be deceased. Fibel, with his 125 years, is now the oldest man on earth and completely unrecognizable. Just before he had reached the century mark, he had had a series of dreams from which he awoke transformed both physically and spiritually. He had grown a new set of white teeth and a mane of blond hair. Simultaneously, he had divested himself of the pride he used to take in his work and resigns himself to the realization that his widely used primer was an insufficient basis for his fame. He now spends his hours by singing simple church songs while accompanying himself on his hand organ. The rest of the time he occupies by reading an illustrated Bible and decorating the trees of his garden with colorful glass balls, in which he sees the world reflected and transmuted. The last we see of Fibel is in a glorious ascension, as the earthbound mystic seems to blend with a rainbow in the west and an aurora borealis in the east, which meet at their zenith.

Is this apotheosis in which the wedding between Occident and Orient is celebrated the sort of nonsense one finds in Hesse's *Siddhartha*, or is it the expression of a profound vision? With both Jean Paul and the surrealists we are far from the pop version of Eastern mysticism capitalized upon by writers as dissimilar as W. Somerset Maugham and Tom Robbins. Jean Paul, the beer-drinking devotee of reality, was haunted by a death-inspired vision that threatened to undermine the world he loved. When dream and reality merge, they cancel each other out, and the mediator between them is left in a void. As a youth, Jean Paul had been deeply impressed by the ascension of the brothers Montgolfier in 1783, and the figure of the balloonist as intrepid adventurer is central to his work. One of his most important creations is the "Luftschiffer Giannozzo," a forerunner of Mallarmé's "pitre châtié" and a precursor of Ionesco's "piéton de l'air," who undertakes the dangerous voyage into the ether where he finds a nothingness that makes the world he had left behind uninhabitable. Jean Paul and the surrealists are such balloonists, and their works are in part logbooks of their perilous excursions. These journals have also been tampered with. They are subterfuges, attempts to deny the validity of what had been discovered through artifice and humor. The bourgeois idyll is a construction designed to enclose and hide something too dangerous to be revealed directly.

With a persistence that betrays a deep fear, man has frequently attempted to belittle the import of dreams. Corneille's Polyeucte seems very sure of himself when he dismisses their significance:

> Je sais ce qu'est un songe, et le peu de croyance
> Qu'un homme doit donner à son extravagance,
> Qui d'un amas confus des vapeurs de la nuit
> Forme de vains objets que le réveil détruit.
>
> [I.i.5-9]

> (I know what a dream is and the little faith
> Man should attach to its extravagance,
> Which out of a confused accumulation of nocturnal vapors
> Creates vain objects which awakening destroys.)

But despite his tone of certitude, which seems more designed to convince himself than his interlocutor, Polyeucte is sufficiently impressed by Pauline's prophetic dream to hesitate in his resolution. This wavering when confronted with the unknown is the untenable stance momentarily adopted by Victor Hugo, whose intrepid explorations of the oneiric world also alternated with a familial lyricism based on quotidian reality. "La Pente de la rêverie," one of the key poems of *Les Feuilles d'automne*, opens with a somber warning:

> . . . Une pente insensible
> Va du monde réel à la sphère invisible,
> La spirale est profonde, et quand on y descend,
> Sans cesse se prolonge et va s'élargissant,
> Et pour avoir touché quelque énigme fatale,
> De ce voyage obscur souvent on revient pâle!
>
> [5-10]

> (. . . An imperceptible downgrade
> Leads from the real world to the invisible sphere,
> The spiral is profound, and during the course of a descent,
> Without cease it continues, longer and larger,
> And, because of having touched some fatal enigma,
> One often returns pale from this obscure voyage.)

Despite the manifest dangers of the visionary voyage, Hugo, in a blending of the vatic and the domestic typical of *Les Feuilles d'automne*, takes as his point of departure a reassuring scene. The poet opens the shutters of his home onto a brilliant spring day with the sun making the raindrops from a recent shower sparkle on the green lawn. It is from this tranquil setting that he plunges into a hallucinatory dream world. The poet re-emerges from "this hideous dream" and in the concluding verses describes the shattering effect that the voyage had produced:

> Soudain il s'en revint avec un cri terrible,
> Ebloui, haletant, stupide, épouvanté,
> Car il avait au fond trouvé l'éternité.

> Suddenly he came back with a terrible cry,
> Bedazzled, panting, stupefied, horrified,
> For in the depths he had found eternity.

Few writers are as fearless as Hugo (and subsequently Rimbaud). When faced with the dangers of dreams, most poets, in emulation of Polyeucte, shy away from the surreal world of visions by negating its reality. This is the strategy adopted by Jean Paul and the surrealists.

The most efficacious way of denying a menace is to play with it, which is precisely what Jean Paul and the surrealists did. But if the ludic element predominates, both dream and reality are reduced to a meaning-less game and we are left with Beckett's terrifying conclusion that ". . . all that wasn't anything but . . . play." Yet even games cannot last for ever, and, no matter how heroic the attempts to keep them going, sooner or later the vision of destruction reasserts itself. Jean Paul's most popular work, in fact, the best seller of its day, was the educational tract *Levana*, consciously written in the manner of Rousseau's *Emile*. There is nothing more reassuring than the good sentiments expressed in this often very practical guide to child rearing. But in the guise of a little appendix to this ponderous pedagogical tome there is an apocalyptic dream against which the whole structure of the book serves as but an ineffectual arma-ture. In this dream two children are sent from the realm of nothingness to be born again on earth. They arrive at the moment of the Last Judg-ment, and the scene that greets them is worthy in dramatic horror of Hieronymus Bosch's most violent versions of the Apocalypse. Its tone might have been characterized by Carlyle, who said of Jean Paul's dreams in his preface to his translation of two of the novellas: ". . . shadowy forms of meaning rise dimly from the bosom of the void Infinite."[12]   And so Jean Paul's dangerous dreams culminate in the universal destruction that the less consequent, less haunted surrealists like Breton and Aragon always succeeded in skirting but to which the more daring, like Jacques Vaché and René Crevel, succumbed. Balloonists can contemplate the earth from above or the void from below. Their vehicles can be deflated and destroyed in a fiery crash, or they can be cut loose from their moorings and become lost in the upper regions. Jean Paul and the surrealists knew all of these experiences.

Notes

1. *L'Image de Jean-Paul Richter dans les lettres françaises* (Paris: Corti, 1963). This is the most comprehensive study of the interrelationship between Jean Paul and French literature, but it is disappointingly sketchy for the twentieth century.
2. Two of his essays in *Dichter der Gessellschaft. Erfahrungen mit deutscher und französischer Literatur* (Frankfut a.M.: Insel Verlag, 1966) are among the best devoted to Jean Paul.
3. *Werke* (Munich: Carl Hanser Verlag, 1963), V, 40. All further references are to this edition. This and all subsequent translations are my own.
4. *German Romance* (London: Chapman and Hall, 1898) II, 121.
5 Notably Jacques Bousquet, *Les Thèmes du rêve dans la littérature romantique (France, Angleterre, Allemagne). Essai sur la naissance et l'évolution des images* (Paris: Didier, 1964) and Eva Anne Baratta in her otherwise comprehensive *Surrealistische Züge im Werke Jean Pauls* (Bonn: Bouvier Verlag Herbert Grundmann, 1972).
6. Cf. J. W. Sneed, *Jean Paul's Dreams* (London: Oxford Univ. Press, 1966), pp. 62 ff., who insists on this point. Jean Pierrot in *Le Rêve de Milton aux surréalistes* (Paris: Bordas, 1973), p. 67, fails to understand the true relationship between dream and text.
7. This is the usual rendition of the untranslatable title *Die Flegeljahre.*
8. Cf. Mary Ann Caws, *Surrealism and the Literary Imagination. A Study of Breton and Bachelard* (The Hague: Mouton & Co., 1966). This remains one of the finest and most provocative essays on surrealism, and the author's startling revelation of the bourgeois side of Breton is only one of her many original insights.
9. *La Psychanalyse du feu* (Paris: Gallimard, 1934), p. 199.
10. Cf. Walter Rehm, *Jean Paul—Dostoievski. Eine Studie zur dichterischen Gestaltung des Unglaubens* (Göttingen: Vandenhoeck & Ruprecht, 1962), for a profound analysis in this sense of "The Speech of the Dead Christ."
11. *Fibel* means "primer" in German.
12. Op. cit., 122.

Dark Framing and
the Analogical Ascent

MARY ANN CAWS

Do you see this world of arrows and letters?
... *In eo vivimus et movemur.*[1]

Perception plays good tricks, and language, too. Looked at straight on,
the occult nominally represents a mysterious unsayable and a dark un-
thinkable. Let me look here, however, at the verbal side of things: I want
to examine, as in a glass darkly, how the occulting of exterior vision—however it is stated, implicitly or explicitly—is connected to interior sight.
But I am claiming, and I want to be very clear about this, only a quite
modest view, itself half-obscured, of some relations of darkness to light.
This was originally suggested to me by the peculiar radiance of Borges's
late poems on his blindness and, in particular, by his "Una rosa y
Miltón," with its vision of that rose all the more luminous for its ac-
knowledged literal darkness.[2]

   But my concern is even more limited: it is the treatment of this play
of light and dark, always in deadly earnest, when it is a matter of ascent.
For in the image of the mountain develops a strange topography of

exterior and interior location, as if the vertical mapping were to place the stress in a singular fashion, itself, upon occasion, occulting the sight.

The Surrealist Frame

ombre de soleil . . .[3]

(shadow of sun . . .)

Surrealism's Second Manifesto demanded the true deep occultation of surrealism. That, of course, entailed the seeing clearly of one objective: to shut off the territory of the dangerous marvelous from the nonadept or, as it is phrased elsewhere, not to distribute the accursed bread to the birds. Now, keeping it for ourselves is not so very different from keeping it to ourselves; I have mused elsewhere in print about the problems of a manifesto or the open statement that demands, openly, a closing off.[4] But it is surely a wonderful find, quite like the eating and having of some cake truly and deeply dark or, to take a slightly more lyrical approach, the equivalent of the wonderful expression used by the surrealists for an exhibition of erotic art: "ombre de soleil," the shade of the sun. No better inscription could be found for the double framing of this essay, for I must speak here in chiaroscuro fashion rather than in the elegant extremes of manifestos and movements.

By way of secondary introduction, before an exploration of the kind to which the analogical metaphor is appropriate, we might glance at what surrealist thought has to contribute to another aspect of what will eventually turn out to be a double question, outer and inner: the capillary tissue enables, Breton points out, an exchange between world or between individual dream and exterior "real." René Nelli describes the surrealist quest as "the act according to which the real thinks itself out in us."[5] And, in fact, his meditation on the use of models itself serves as a model of the analogical ascent toward which a certain occult tendency might sway us: exterior perception as the study of the way things are related, on the road to our own *interior myths*.[6] It is, in reality, an interior myth of the mountain that lies at the center of the picture here: thus the importance of such exploration as Breton describes best:

> I claim . . . that only a deplorable timid and shortsighted view of things could accept the world's being changed once and for all so that one must not allow oneself—as if it would be some sort of profanation—any incursion into the immense lands that still remain to be explored.[7]

In a more militaristic vocabulary, *Brèche* (The title *Breach* given to one of the last surrealist journals) might also be taken as a clarifying concept for the advantages of the obscure. To make, as Philippe Audoin explains, a breach or opening in the wall of bourgeois habits, as one would lay siege to a town, is to intrude a patch of clarity into a dark wall—or then, I might add, a dark breach in a wall all too clear. One of Breton's works strongly influenced by the occult, in particular, by alchemy and the Tarot, *Arcane 17*,[8] is subtitled: *Enté d'ajours*, or pierced with holes: the openings to daylight here let in the *jour* (day) and remind us of that capillary tissue facilitating the exchange of in and out. That the image should be, on the one hand, passive and, on the other, active, is a further illustration of the necessarily ambivalent attitude for the contemplation of the analogous relation. The perspective to be taken on the quest—whether horizontal or vertical—is not meant to be a one-point renaissance perspective; surrealism demands quite another stance.

Quest and Mountain

The tradition of the hero who sets out to renew a devastated country or *Terre gaste* is rich, and rich, too, is the history of the eventual miring-down of the venturing ship or of the adventurers themselves in snow. Just to take three well-known cases in French literature, Apollinaire, Gide, and Desnos all use the *topos*, inclusive of the ventures turned aside and those proved vain, Gide's *Voyage d'Urien* or the Trip of Nothing ("du Rien") being the most clearly marked by its title. So far the ventures and the mockery of them have been located on the horizontal plane: breach and boat, wall and ice floe, like Mallarmé's swan stuck in ice.

But I want to change the plane at present, for the ventures of occultation and revelation to be discussed here are located on the vertical axis. Baudelaire's Correspondences, of course, include both the horizontal ones of synesthesia and the vertical ones of high and low; those to be considered here do not plunge so dramatically as his, and their height is not in any sense to be compared to a heaven or a hell of any traditional sort. The mountain here will include along its traveled slope the darkening of vision and exterior spectacle and the clarity of the inner sight. René Daumal's *Mont Analogue* is plainly analogical and not referential, symbolic and not locatable in any geographic place to be set upon an ordinary map. These texts will show in their rise and their cumulative difficulty the stress of ascent.

The accent of the texts chosen is strikingly different: Jacques Dupin's *Gravir* does not resemble René Daumal's *Mont Analogue*, but rather such texts as Jacques Garelli's *Prendre appui* and André du Bouchet's *Dans la chaleur vacante;* René Char's *La recherche de la base et du sommet* is yet another of the French mountain texts. These are subjective, even if, as in the case of Daumal, collectively experienced; and they draw upon the imagery of leader and follower, as Daumal's Sogol, the teacher whose name is an anagrammatic rendering of the Logos, already indicates the centrality of the poetic word. The mountain poem of Pablo Neruda, *The Heights of Machu Picchu*, moves from the individual toward a collective speech. From the emptiness of the wandering poet:

> Del aire al aire, como una red vacía,
> iba yo entre las calles y la atmósfera . . .[9] [MP, 2-3]

> (From air to air, like an empty net,
> dredging through streets and ambient atmosphere . . .)

it moves in a solitary ascension to a place once peopled, from the black cup of trembling and death up toward the chalice of a linguistic and racial communion of the people now gone, among the ruins marking a real place, a "permanence of stone."

Daumal's description is of a fictional pilgrimage, an inner meditation of the mind, mapped upon an imaginary mountain in order to show how map and mind work out their relation.[10] Neruda's is a pilgrimage in a poem upward to a place of the past, as the present is transfigured by imaginative memory; but once more, beyond the evident contrast of prose with poem in the case of Daumal or, as in the case of the French mountain-image poets, beyond the contrast of French and Latin-American imagination and style or of the visionary or the poetic with the committed, of invisible or unplaceable mountains with the visible heights of Machu Picchu and their legend, the analogical parallel can be drawn by the reader. That the reader's very passivity in the experience acts as a severe distancing from the text, as an enforced second-order experiencing of whatever the mountain-climbing poem conveys or *is*—this yet further complication is also an occulting of the original sign.

Mount Analogue

Mount Analogue: A Novel of Symbolically Authentic Non-Euclidean Adventures in Mountain Climbing—so reads the title of this odd and un-finished masterpiece of René Daumal as translated by Roger Shattuck: were it a spoof, it would be a splendid one. It is not a spoof but is rather in deadly, if mystical, earnest.

The Daumal tale is of an adept mountain-climbing instructor, whose practice and teaching keep in shape by a roof-and-rope ascent ordeal out of his own window, above the Passage des Patriarches. The expedition to be led has as its goal a so-far invisible mountain, whose base is acces-sible once one arrives but whose top is forever inaccessible, this mountain that might exist in any region; the lesson is the lesson of the occult par excellence, the lesson of alchemy, of theosophy, of symbolism: "The door to the invisible must be visible." The ship on which the adventurers sail is named *The Impossible*, just as Gide's *Urien* or his voyage "of nothing" marks a certain impossible with ironically perfect clarity: neither adventure could ever have been other than mental, a *fictional fictional.* The leader will break down into childlikeness—or attain that inner summit, depending on the point of view: "lest you become as a little child . . ."

But this wonderful tale will end with a comma only, and we have then Daumal's note of the final lesson of the tale: that the knowledge has to be passed on "to other seekers," that the resting places on the ascent have to be prepared for those coming after up the slope, and that the chain of learning and climbing must be maintained. Thus the individual, in this tale, too, is joined with the collective, as in Neruda's climb, although by different means and for different ends. Daumal's introduction to the venture is as essential to the framing of the whole voyage as, for instance, Valéry's "Introduction to the Method of Leonardo" is to an understanding of Valéry.

> I would have preferred to tell you the whole story right now. Since that would take too long, here is the beginning. Possibly it is deceptive to speak of the beginning and end of a story when we never grasp anything but the middle portions. At the heart of the events was an encounter, however, and every encounter is a relative beginning, and this encounter, especially, contains a whole story in itself.
>
> What I have to tell is so unusual that I must take certain precautions. To teach anatomy, conventional diagrams rather than photographs are used, and from every point of view these diagrams are different from the object of study, except that certain relationships—precisely those forming the *thing to be known*— are preserved. I have done the same thing here. [MA, 37]

Both encounter and diagram can be taken as a model for an occult rendering of an occult experience; the relationships may be sketched but must not be spelled out for the *suggestions* to remain resonant. A map made must be partial; a tale told must be fragmentary, for the truest rendering of *interior relations,* in an interior myth.

Here the relation of revelation to the occult framing is manifest. Whether the occulting be accomplished through fragmentation, incompletion, or the metaphors of blindness or darkness, the goal—the attaining of which is, ironically, often the acknowledgment that it cannot be attained—depends on the stumbling-blocks of the path for its height.

Climbing

Ascent is privileged in contemporary French poetry, as we have seen: the "Chant" or the "Canto" of David Mus's title is often equivalent to Jacques Dupin's *Gravir* [11] or *Climbing:* a song of height and stones, framed as this "Chant" is framed:

> A grandes enjambées, debout, demeurer: quelle pierre d'achop-
> pement.
> . . . .
> *voie de pierre pas de pierre*
> *pas de pierre paix de pierre*
> l'appel aux *marches*
> *de pierre* cris en vrac
> . . . .
> Ton objectif la borne, cette pierre que tu n'atteins[12]
>
> (In full strike to stand: this stumbling-block.
> . . . .
> *stone path stone pace*
> *stone pace stone peace*
> appeal to *stone*
> *steps* cries unsorted
> . . . .
> Your objective being such stone you don't reach.)

In Dupin's opening words, a free-verse introduction is given to the dense
prose poems of *Cendrier du voyage* ("Ashtray of Voyage"), and the lead
set by this "Frugal Path" ("Chemin Frugal") gives to the whole mounting
path a setting of thirst and difficulty, whose ambivalent structure is both
visible and unseen, searching and invisible. The flight upward itself is
multiple and single; the double body figured is both increased and annihi-
lated, the whole finding its resolution in the repetition of the first stanza
by the last, so that the opening frame to the climb is itself given a top and
bottom edge or foothold and also a block to rest upon or to stumble
upon:

> C'est le calme, le chemin frugal,
> Le malheur qui n'a plus de nom.
> C'est ma soif échancrée . . .
> . . . .
> Chassez-moi, suivez-moi,
> Mais innombrable et ressemblant,
> Tel que je serai.
> . . . .
> Chaque pas visible
> . . . .
> Chaque pas aveugle
> . . . .
> C'est le calme, le chemin frugal (etc.) [G, 9-10]

(This is the calm, the frugal path,
Unhappiness no longer named.
This is my thirst indented . . .

. . . .
Chase me, follow me,
But innumerable and similar,
Such as I shall be.

. . . .
Each visible step

. . . .
Each blind step

. . . .
This is the calm, the frugal path, [etc])

In the prose poems of *Ashtray of Voyage*, the climb is implicitly identified with the metaphor of struggle upon the surface of the book in which
the poems are inserted: these poems "la proie du vertige de la page"
("the prey of the page's dizziness"; G, 13); and in the *Basalt Suite* directly
following, an opening and overt expression of the allegiance to mountain
and to earth is a more energetic reminiscence, for the reader, of such
poems as Eluard's "Sans âge," that collective assault of a summit, which
itself begins: "Nous approchons" ("We approach . . .").

Grand Vent

Nous n'appartenons qu'au sentier de montagne
. . . .
Nous avons rapproché des sommets
La limite des terres arables.
. . . .
La chair endurera ce que l'oeil a souffert [G, 23]

(We belong only to the mountain trail
. . . .
We have brought nearer to the summits
The limit of tillable earth.
. . . .
The flesh will endure what the eye has suffered)

The nine poems of "Lichens," arranged along the trail and upon the
"abrupt slope" of the mountain in the blindingly white air, itself blind,
link quite clearly the metaphor of ascent to that of illumination and
locate the traveler within the play of shifting light and darkness.

La chaleur nous aveugle . . .
La nuit qui nous attend et qui nous comble, il

---

faut encore décevoir son attente pour qu'elle soit
la nuit.
. . . .
La lumière est simple. Et les collines proches.
Si par mégarde cette nuit je heurte votre porte,
n'ouvrez pas. N'ouvrez pas encore. Votre absence
de visage est ma seule obscurité. [G, 68-69]

(The heat blinds us . . .
The night awaiting us and fulfilling us, we must
disappoint once more its waiting for it to be night.
. . . .
Light is simple. And the hills, near. If by carelessness tonight
I stumble upon your door, don't open for me. Don't open yet.
Your absence of face is my single darkness.)

Climbing as erotic effort is at its height here, and action as well as
expression are to be situated on the promontory, "A l'aplomb," vertically, in the full light of a narrow space, and with no intention of descent.
At this peak of the work of *Climbing*, in its center, these illuminated
texts are bare of anything but rise:

Nul épi dans la lumière, nul escarpement dans l'étendue.
[G, 75]

(No stalk in the light, no steepness in the space.)

Suddenly, the occulting of vision appears inevitable: "Et le paysage
s'ordonne autour d'un mot lancé à la légère et qui reviendra chargé
d'ombre" (G, 87) (And the landscape arranges itself around a word lightly
uttered and which will return laden with shadow). Because, the light
upon the mountain seemed always to be stifling, at the sharpest of the
cutting edge, "Un voyage pur et transchant" (G, 99) (A pure and slicing
voyage), the sky menaces with its own obscuring of vision, its unreasoning
dark opposed to human reason:

Tu attends ta décollation
Par la hache de ténèbres
De ce ciel monotone et fou. [G, 99]

(You await your beheading
By the hatchet of shadows
Of this sky dull and crazed.)

The poet's language torn to shreds by the effort of the ascent yields, in
the final frame of one line, stressed by its italicization, the bare setting,

cold and dark, where only the shadow remains to guide the scythe and the cultivation of nourishment, spiritual and physical, The same tears that marked the beginning of the volume mark now its finality, and with the shadow, the question and the chill of the exhaustion of breath. The question is quiet, as the light goes out:

> *Arachnénne sollicitation qui menez de ténèbre en ténèbre*
> *ma faux jusqu'à l'orée du cri, ce noeud qui vante la*
> *récolte, dites-moi pour qui brilleront ma sueur et*
> *mes larmes, toute une nuit, sur cette gerbe hostile,*
> *près de la lampe refroidie.* [G, 105]

> *(Spiderly attraction guiding from shadow to shadow*
> *my scythe until the verge of the cry, that knot*
> *extolling the harvest, tell me for whom my sweat and*
> *tears will shine a whole night long, upon this hostile*
> *sheaf, near the lamp gone cold.)*

Because Dupin's is a private investigation of a climb and the strongest analogy is made with writing, the final interrogation by an extinguished lamp places retrospectively this light in its interior setting, along the slope of a mind.

The Heights of Machu Picchu

Neruda's ascent is altogether of a different sort. Dark has little place except as an implicit metaphor for death, thus, the dark cup to be drunk, trembling; the rise toward the light is identified with the rise toward the finding of a collective tongue, the vigor of the past civilizations infused into the present language of the contemporary poet.

"Como un ciego," like a blind man, the narrator wanders first along the streets, the opening already occulted then by dark and death: the emptiness of the net and the air already referred to leading, along with the sightlessness, to the strongest image in the whole poem, that cup in its blackness and its proffered knowledge of daily diminution, of collective and individual perishing, of the disappeareance of an entire race, as in the high ruins:

> entonces fuí por calle y calle y río y río,
> y ciudad y ciudad y cama y cana,
> y atravesé el desierto mi máscara salobre,
> y en las últimas cases humilladas, sin lámpara, sin fuego,
> sin pan, sin piedra, sin silencio, solo,
> rodé muriendo de mi propia muerte. [MP, 18]

(I came by other ways, through streets, river by river,
city by city, one bed after another,
forcing my brackish semblance through a wilderness
till in the last of hovels, lacking all light and fire,
bread, stone and silence, I paced at last alone,
dying of my own death.)

The twelve parts of this night or this day, arranged at first along the horizontal axis and then, in the center, climbing at the sixth part, match the wandering of a world and a poet. Once glimpsed upon the heights, this real lost city of the Incas holds illumination enough and the certainty of presence:

Alta ciudad de piedras escalares
. . . .
Alto arrecife de la aurora humana.
. . . .
Esta fué la morada, éste es el sitio . . . [MP, 26-27]

(Tall city of stepped stone,
. . . .
High reef of the human dawn.
. . . .
This was the habitation, this is the site . . .)

In this "permanencia de piedra y de palabra" (MP, 33) (permanence of stone and language), the black cup of death changes to a chalice upheld, made from these ruins and containing their life as their death. In the final, breathless pace of the poem, as line is situated along line in all the difficulty of breathing, the stone is repeated, harshly, and matched against the absence of man:

Lámpara de granito, pan de piedra.
Serpiente mineral, rosa de piedra.
Nave enterrada, manantial de piedra.
Caballo de la luna, luz de piedra. [MP, 46]

(Granite lamp, bread of stone.
Mineral snake, rose of stone.
Ship-burial, source of stone.
Horse in the moon, stone light.)

And "Piedra en la piedra, el hombre, dónde estuvo?" (MP, 56) (Stone within stone, and man, where was he?)

Finally, in the twelfth hour, the poet in all the "confuso esplendor" of the site takes on the past of his race and the future of its tongue and its dark and unseeing legend, giving to it all speech and life:

> Sube a nacer conmigo, hermano.
> . . . .
> Traed a la copa de esta nueva vida
> vuestros viejos dolores enterrados.
> . . . .
> Yo vengo a hablar por vuestra boca muerta.
> . . . .
> y dejadme llorar, horas, días, años,
> edades ciegas, siglos estelares,
> Dadme el silencio, el agua, la esperanza
> . . . .
> Hablad por mis palabras y mi sangre. [MP, 66-70]

> (Arise to birth with me, my brother.
> . . . .
> bring to the cup of this new life
> your ancient buried sorrows.
> . . . .
> I come to speak for your dead mouths.
> . . . .
> and leave me cry: hours, days and years,
> blind ages, stellar centuries.
> And give me silence, give me water, hope.
> . . . .
> Speak through my speech, and through my blood.)

The ascent here is, finally, from a past occulting of vision and speech to a revelation of the present word and living light.

Analogy

Of the three ascents, all analogical, one is unfinished and suggestive in its very incompletion, one conveys the struggle of a mind and a text, into its own possibilities, and the third is geographically and specifically situated toward the heights. All work with the occult and the revealing as necessary parts of their structure. Were the literary climb ever to be taken as a genre unto itself, with all its exterior and interior relations and rules and its contrasting forms of occulting and revealing, it might then be seen—somewhere toward its summit of difficulty—as inscribed under the shadow of an Analogous Mountain.

Notes

1. Paul Valéry, *Poems in the Rough*, trans. Hilary Corke (London: Routledge and Kegan Paul (Princeton: Princeton Univ. Press, 1969), p. 156.

2. Jorge Luis Borges, "Una Rosa y Miltón," in *Selected Poems*, ed. di Giovanni (New York: Delta, 1973), p. 144; "Elogio de la Sombra," in *In Praise of Darkness* (New York: Dutton, 1974), p. 124.

3. Philippe Audoin, *Les Surréalistes* (Paris: Seuil, coll. Ecrivains de toujours, 1974), p. 144.

4. "Notes on a Manifesto Style: 1921 Fifty Years Later," *Journal of General Education*, 27, No. 1 (Spring 1975): 88-90.

5. René Nelli, *Poésie ouverte, poésie fermée* (Paris: Cahiers du Sud, 1947), p. 26.

6. Ibid., p. 35.

7. *André Breton, Poètes d'aujourd'hui* (Paris: Seghers, 1950), p. 122.

8. André Breton, *Arcane, 17, enté d'ajours* (Paris: Sagittaire, 1947).

9. Pablo Neruda, *Alturas de Machu Picchu*, trans. by Nathaniel Tarn as *The Heights of Machu Picchu* (New York: Farrar Straus, 1966). Abbreviated in the text as MP.

10. René Daumal, *Mont Analogue* (Paris: Gallimard, 1952), trans. by Roger Shattuck as *Mount Analogue: A Novel of Symbolically Authentic Non-Euclidean Adventures in Mountain Climbing* (Baltimore: Penguin, 1974). Abbreviated in the text as MA.

11. Jacques Dupin, *Gravir* (Paris: Gallimard, 1963). Abbreviated in the text as G.

12. David Mus, "Chant," trans. as "Canto" by the poet; unpublished and referred to me by John Van Sickle, to whom I extend my warm appreciation.

PART 5

MAGIC WORD
PLAY

The "Neck Riddle" and Dramatic Form

B. H. FUSSELL

"I'll give you three guesses every night to guess my name, an' if you hain't guessed it afore the month's up, yew shall be mine." In this English version of "Rumpelstiltskin,"[1] the devil demands his due by striking a bargain: three nights, nine guesses. Although her life depends upon it, the girl who is spinning cannot possibly know the name of the "small little black thing with a long tail." The time, the action, the name are equally arbitrary, and it is only by luck that the girl learns his secret.

> Nimmy nimmy not,
> Yar name's Tom Tit Tot.

When the black thing heard that, the story teller says, "that shruck awful an' awa' that flew into the dark, an' she niver saw it noo more."

"Tom Tit Tot" is the simplest form of what folklorists call a "neck riddle."[2] *Riddle* and *read* derive from the same root, Old English *raeden;* and any riddle is an act of naming something hidden, of reading or interpreting a code, and by that means of discovering secret knowledge. Any

riddle is a verbal game of hide and seek. The "neck riddle" simply dramatizes the danger in naming, reading, and knowing; and it does so in three
ways. First, a condemned person, in order to save his or her own neck,
must answer a question: that is, he or she must name names. Further-
more, the question is asked by an enemy, a little black thing, a devil or
monster, in order to deceive the person who must answer. The riddle,
in other words, is a deliberate lie, in which the question "blocks" the
answer. Finally, the answer is a name that both solves the riddle and
resolves the crisis. However arbitrary the name and the question, speech
results in action.

The very term "neck riddle" suggests that it is a form of magic
naming and that it is already halfway to being a story or play. We
recognize in primitive charms that magic naming is a "dramatic" act
because it is an act of conjuring presences in order to exert power over
them: first to cast out evil and then to bring in good. In the story of
"Tom Tit Tot," the girl casts out "the little black thing" and brings in
the handsome prince; and because she cannot get one without the other,
a dramatic or narrative "plot" is born.

In "Tom Tit Tot" the form of the story is as simple as the silly
rhyme and silly name that resolve the riddle. As the couplet rhymes
simple sounds, "not" with "Tot," so the riddle "rhymes" simple identities,
a thing with a name. Unfortunately for the victim of a "neck riddle,"
the sillier the name, the greater the danger because of the impossibility of
discovering through reason what the victim must know to survive.
Ignorance is not bliss but terror. For the listener or audience, the greater
the victim's danger, the more pleasurable our suspense and excitement in
living vicariously a crisis that we know from the outset will end happily
however absurd the solution.

A more complex neck riddle is posed in the story of Pericles told by
Gower, in which answering a riddle proves to be as dangerous as not
answering. In Gower's ancient tale, Pericles will die unless he solves the
riddle embodied by the daughter of Antiochus. Shakespeare, or an
attendant playwright, expresses the riddle thus:

> I am no viper, yet I feed
> On mother's flesh, which did me breed.
> I sought a husband, in which labor
> I found that kindness in a father.
> He's father, son, and husband mild;
> I mother, wife, and yet his child.
> How they may be, and yet in two,
> As you will live, resolve it you.
>   [I. i. 65-72]

"As you will live . . ." The dilemma for Pericles is that if he interprets
truly, he will die because he will have uncovered falsehood in the incestu-

ous relation of father and daughter. The price of seeking what was hidden is summed up abruptly by the king:

> He hath found the meaning,
> For which we mean to have his head.
>   [I. i. 144-145]

Rhyming identities is a dangerous game, and to name names is not to cast out evil but to bring it in. In *Pericles*, the only recourse for the hero is in flight.

A riddle that combines the simple and complex forms of a neck riddle is posed in the story of Oedipus. Here the answer to the question posed by the sphinx is not an arbitrary and absurd proper name nor a specific person or thing but a generic name:

> What goes on four feet, on two feet and three
> But the more feet it goes on the weaker it be?

The answer rhymes the identities of "a man" with a shape-changing monster, a monster not unlike the woman-faced lion that has asked the question. In translating Sophocles' *Oedipus*, Anthony Burgess found that, as riddles go, this was a fairly easy one, and the puzzle was why the sphinx asked it. The catch for Oedipus is that "the riddle was not meant to be answered." The riddle was meant to deceive men like Oedipus into believing they have the power to cast out evil and bring in good by their own capacity for solving riddles. The riddle, of course, is a trap.

Oedipus, as a representative man who carries the stigma of his identity in his name, is called by his people,

> Solver of riddles,
> Slayer of monsters,
> Savior of the people.

But, as we know in advance, Oedipus, in averting one danger, will bring on another. In answering one riddle, he will uncover another. What Oedipus does not know and we do is that no matter what he does, he stands condemned, that any name he names will bring in evil, and that no flight is possible from the riddle of his own name and identity. "I will know who I am" is the dangerous action he pursues and, in pursuing, discovers that "savior of the people" rhymes with "father killer" and "mother fucker." In *Oedipus*, we discover that the tragedy of crime rhymes with the comedy of sex.

The peculiar shocks of *Oedipus* depend upon the audience's expectation fulfilled so overwhelmingly as to be almost funny because we know something the hero doesn't. While a neck riddle, like any riddle, works as a game of metaphor in which one term is hidden, at the same time the neck riddle ups the stakes by making the disguise as deceptive as possible and by giving out false clues. A play imitating this structure works as an extended metaphor by making the story, or sequence of events, conceal the meaning or context by which we can read those events, until the very end of the play. Sophocles structures the events of the Oedipus story on a riddle that the hero reads one way and the audience another. Because who he is disguises what he is and because it is his own experience that gives out false clues, Oedipus is compelled to read events as he does. Oedipus, in discovering what it is to be a man, discovers that the hidden term is fool-murderer-pervert. In other words, Oedipus unwittingly acts out the initiating riddle of the play that rhymed man with monster, and in the final naming of names, Oedipus unmasks that thing of darkness hidden within the best of men.

The Riddle as Trope

For Renaissance rhetoricians, a riddle was classified as an enigma related to the dark conceits of allegory, which George Puttenham termed a "Figure of False Semblant." Allegory and riddles are tropes that specifically exploit disguise of one thing by another and that hinge on the "turn" that gives a trope its name. As a figure of speech or thought, a trope originates in the physical action of "turning" and derives from the turns or *tropos* executed by the Greek Chorus in the circle of the theater to mark stages in the action and in the spoken verse. As both a figure of speech and a figure of action, a trope is "a turn away from ordinary meaning or a turn toward heightened meaning."

The *quem quaeritis* (Whom do you seek?) trope with which English drama began illustrates the way in which such a "turn" is indigenous not only to language but also to gesture and is made theatrical by exploiting the element of deceit. "Whom do you seek?" is the question of a neck riddle, posed in this instance by one priest to a trio of representative men condemned by their common mortality to death. In answering one riddle, "Jesus of Nazareth," the trio uncover another, a riddle of identity in which the hanged man hides a god. The trio of priests, disguised as Mary, Martha, and John, turn physically toward the altar and discover thereby a surprising "turn" of event. A rotting corpse has turned into a living spirit, and its cerements have turned into stage props. Through dramatic action, the lies of impersonation have uncovered a truth that can be known no other way.

The difference between simple and complex neck riddles helps illuminate Aristotle's distinction between simple and complex "plots,"[3] where the structure of the incidents is based on a "turn." In the simplest neck riddle, the turn of meaning and the resultant turn of fortune are brought about directly by magic naming. The *Comedy of Errors* executes such a turn when the abbess names herself "Emilia" and so resolves the

THE OCCULT IN LANGUAGE AND LITERATURE

riddle of two sets of rhyming twins, which saves the neck of her husband.

A more complicated turn of fortune occurs with a more complex form of riddle, where the distance between name and identity or between action and its meaning is increased. *Pericles* depends for its effects on the deliberate lie of a "miracle" in which dead bodies come to life. They do so by a magic naming, when Pericles commands Marina, "But tell me now/ My drowned queen's name." Marina's answer uncovers the living form of his dead daughter and at the same time uncovers "immortal Dian" in his dead Thaisa. The distance between name and person, symbolic of the distance between life and death, is so extreme that the gap can be bridged only by supernatural intervention. In *Pericles*, magic naming is no longer automatic but the result of a providence concealed by human suffering and endurance and experienced as an impossibility.

The neck riddle corresponding to the kind of complex plot Aristotle believed to be the most effective is one in which the condemned man, as in *Oedipus*, discovers that the magic name he looks for is his own and that to cast out evil he must cast out himself. Here, the distance between name and identity, or between story and meaning, is embodied within a central character. "Reversal of intention" and "recognition" coincide when three turns come together: a turn of fortune, a turn of meaning, and a turn from ignorance to knowledge on the part of the character who has deceived himself simply by being a man. In this structure magic naming takes on moral meaning because the arbitrary neck riddle is experienced as inevitable and even as just. Use a man after his desert, and who should 'scape whipping—or hanging? The trope of the neck riddle acted out in a play such as *Oedipus* turns street wisdom into nemesis and sick jokes into tragic irony.

The Riddle and Analogy

In the empty space where a play is enacted, Peter Brook finds that "every action happens in its own right and every action is an analogy of something else." When is a door not a door? When it's a jar. When is a good action not a good action? When it brings in the plague, undoes the doer, unleashes a monster. A riddle plays with the possibilities of analogy hidden in any word or action. What is black and white and red all over? A newspaper. Or a nun falling downstairs. Sick jokes often burlesque the riddle form they use in order to deny the platitude that some things are not laughing matters, that some things are sacred and exempt from analogy. But platitudes are not only dead metaphors; they are also dead actions, and the life of drama as of language depends upon reviving the dead by electric shock. Theater by definition works by analogy, and drama derives its energy and force from making impossible analogies, by making kings or presidents identical with monsters and fools, mothers with monsters, and perverts with saints.

Whether a turn is a comic one, as in vaudeville or farce, or a tragic one, as in melodrama and elegy, depends in large part on the kind of analogies the playwright makes. A comic turn is one that cuts man down to size by making him analogous to a lower or lesser form of existence, that makes him identical with his butt, his shoe or his cigar. It's a process of deanimation, as in Buster Keaton's dead pan. One of the most common devices of comic analogy is to identify a man with his name, as Wilde does in *The Importance of Being Earnest* or as the Marx Brothers do as a punning quatrain.

A tragic turn is one that enlarges man by making him analogous to forms of existence more powerful than himself, to things of darkness, demons, monsters, and creatures from outer space that are hidden from his ordinary experience. The question of a neck riddle implies a tragic turn because, in blocking the answer, it questions the possibility of making any analogy and yet demands the wizardry of a seer, to name the unknowable.

"What's in a name?" is a question Juliet asks and answers wrongly to her own tragic end. Because she is young, she is ignorant and believes mistakenly that "that which we call a rose by any other name would smell as sweet." A name like "stinkweed" would change the smell of a rose considerably, just as the names "Montague" and "Capulet" turn that which we call "love" into death in the action of the play. "Who's there?" is the opening neck riddle Bernardo poses in *Hamlet* and that Hamlet pursues to his death. Who's there upon the battlements, behind the arras, between incestuous sheets, beneath the grave? Is the ghost an analogue of the devil or a divine agent? Is his mother a queen or a whore? In plucking analogies from the full Chain of Being to answer the question, Hamlet is left with a "wounded name," which is not analogous to his story. He begs Horatio to save his name with the right analogue and so resolve the question of who, in truth, was there.

"Which of you shall we say doth love us most?" is the neck riddle posed by King Lear to his daughters. Lear does not know that asking the question will hang the daughter who loves him most because her love is beyond analogy. In Cordelia's answer, "Love, and be silent," she denies analogy and so foreswears the perversion of magic naming that Lear propounds. Lear finds his own analogue in both the chaos of the heavens and a mandrake root.

While a tragic turn finds its analogue in disruptive human identities, a tragicomic turn is the most interesting formally because it is a mixed metaphor that finds its analogues in dramatic form. Tragicomedy makes tragic turns analogous to comic ones and, further, discovers comedy to be the hidden term of tragedy, as tragedy is the artful disguise of comedy. We could say that tragicomedy applies Aristotle's "reversal of intention" and "recognition" to the form of drama itself.

"When is a tragedy a comedy?" is the unasked riddle that the title of *All's Well That Ends Well* answers. The plot of this odd tragicomedy turns upon a number of riddles but chiefly upon the bed trick in which Helena substitutes Diana for herself and rhymes their identities. The meaning of that event is hidden until Bertram, with his head in the noose, is asked by Diana to solve an impossible riddle:

> Dead though she be, she feels her young one kick.
> So there's my riddle: one that's dead is quick.
> And now behold my meaning.
> [V. iii. 302-304]

At that moment, Helena enters, alive and pregnant, and the king asks if what he sees is real or the work of an exorcist? Diana exposes the arbitrariness of the turn from tragedy to comedy by pointing to the impossible union of the quick and the dead in Helena and by unmasking one as a disguise of the other. She who before was a wife in name only, "The name and not the thing," is now "Both, both," by the action of the play. The completed context reverses the meaning of the enacted events in a way designed to shock.

What Samuel Johnson praised as true to life in Shakespeare's "mingled" drama, G. B. Shaw damned as a rape of British common sense. Both critics were right in that Shakespeare's plays belong to the theater of alchemy, in which shapes and emotions and lives hide in dark conceits and metamorphose into their opposites by means of theatrical analogy. His tragicomic mixtures make disguise and deception the subject as well as the means of drama. In his comedies and tragicomedies, some form of *deus ex machina* is more common than not as an artifice of theater that can make visible the miraculous working of metaphor. *Cymbeline* requires a Jupiter to resolve the riddle of Posthumus' name, and even then Jupiter's words are a riddle to Posthumus, "a senseless speaking, or a speaking such as sense cannot untie." Sense cannot untie the plot, only oracles can do that, oracles and prophecies fulfilled as a form of magic naming.

The Neck Riddle in Modern American Drama

The Renaissance metaphor of the play that equates the world with a stage frequently exploits the metaphor of the riddle that equates sense with senseless speaking. Both metaphors were "natural" to a time when science and philosophy were branches of occult learning, or magic, and when the turning of base metal into gold in alchemy provided a "trope" for other kinds of turnings, a trope for moral and spiritual transformations.

In our own more secular time, it is more surprising to find the persistence of these forms in drama as "realistically" oriented as American drama of the mid-twentieth century. Characteristic plays of such dramatists as O'Neill, Williams, Miller, and Albee continue to exhibit elements of the neck riddle and of magic naming at the same time that the action of their plays denies the possibility of magic.

O'Neill's *Long Day's Journey into Night* is structured on a question raised and left unanswered by the pathetic figure of Mary Tyrone: "What is it I'm looking for? I know it's something I lost." Meaning, context, purpose—all are lost, not just for Mary but for her family. All the Tyrones stand condemned because they no longer even know what they are looking for; they only know what they've lost. No naming of monsters will save their necks because to conjure presences from the past is to conjure names that torment but do not affect actions. Naming a name cannot "turn" the action around because there is no place to turn toward or from. There are no analogies to be made and no invisible powers to invoke that will change the meaning of their identities. What displaces the "turn," either of fortune or of ignorance, is a character's stubborn assertion of a proper noun, a particular name. In the final moment of the play, Mary remembers that something once happened. "I fell in love with James Tyrone and was so happy for a time."

The naming of names is an overt motif in Williams's A *Streetcar Named Desire.*" Blanche says, "They told me to take a streetcar named Desire and then transfer to one called Cemeteries and ride six blocks and get off at—Elysian Fields." Blanche's naming of the streetcars names the three parts of the action: the pursuit of happiness, dissolution, and insanity. Instead of a "turn" in the action, there is progression from sexual games to rape as a kind of death and to insanity as a kind of escape. Blanche is like Mary Tyrone in that her power to conjure names from the past into the present is an aborted power. Blanche tries to cast out the ugly sound of "Mrs. Stanley Kowalski" and to bring in "Stella! Stella for Star!" But this is fake conjuring because the magic doesn't work. Blanche does not seek answers; she wants to put a stop to questions, to turn off all the lights. "I don't want realism," she cries. "I want magic." Magic is not available, neither for her nor Stella nor Stanley. All remain trapped between death and desire, ignorant of the springs of their own action. And yet they assert their humanity, not by knowing, but by a helpless naming, as when Stella begs her sister's forgiveness by calling, "Blanche! Blanche! Blanche!"

Arthur Miller explained that the first title he chose for *Death of a Salesman* was "The Inside of His Head" because he wanted to create a form that would show "the process of Willy Loman's way of mind." Miller's phrase is inept but revealing, for Willy is not an emblem of man thinking but of man feeling. Not gifted with a strong capacity for thought, Willy, nevertheless, persists in questioning and in asking always the wrong questions. "What's the answer?" he asks Ben. "How did you do it?" Willy is condemned from the beginning because he does not know what questions to ask and can understand miracles only literally, in terms of money. For Willy, Ben is a figure of magic because he walked into the jungle when he was 21 and walked out rich.

Biff, not Willy, is the truth-searcher, and it is Biff who "turns" away from his father when he discovers that knowledge turns truth into lies and his father into a fake. But Biff, like Juliet, is mistaken in the deceptive simplicity of names and their meanings. Again, there is no turn in the action but a progression from despair to suicide on the part of Willy as he fails to answer the riddle of his failure. He can, however, assert the meaning of his existence by naming his name. His assertion lends him a kind of dignity and reveals in him a humane instinct that is deeper than Biff's discovery that a man's words and acts may differ. "I am not a dime a dozen! I am Willy Loman and you are Biff Loman." Stripped of analogy, of history, of social or cultural context, Willy is still Willy and Biff is still Biff.

Albee's *Who's Afraid of Virginia Woolf* is more complex in its action because there is a turning from comedy to tragedy in the playwright's more sophisticated exploitation of the way in which words relate to actions. George and Martha stage the events of the play they perform by posing neck riddles for each other. The question stated in the title of the play suggests the parodic form of the games they share and the dangers in playing them. Along with the outsiders, Honey and Nick, the audience discovers that the successive games of Humiliate the Host, Hump the Hostess, and Get the Guests are all designed to conceal their secret game, that of *not* naming a name. The three sections of the play, Fun and Games, Walpurgisnacht, and Exorcism, suggest that the turn from comedy to tragedy is a magical one in which exorcism is possible. By naming their fictional son to outsiders, Martha has "killed" their child, and so George "kills" Martha. Language again has real powers, and naming has magic but only black magic. Exorcism can cast out, for a moment, the demons of hate and self-hate, but it cannot bring in the good. Dignity comes to George and Martha only in their recognition of a mutual state of damnation. "Who's afraid?" Martha asks at the end. "I am, George, I am."

In each of these very American plays, proper names are repeated as if by simple reiteration one could conjure lost associations and recover lost meanings. But what is hidden remains hidden. Identities remain puzzling because they do not give up their secrets through analogies or miracles or transformations. Conjuring images or moments from the past does not illuminate the present but confirms the isolation of each of the characters, who are each imprisoned by deceptive memories that make a mockery of the present. Time and its changes do not redeem but destroy, and man can only suffer.

The fact that a play can be experienced only in the immediate present and by means of an elaborate fakery is both the glory and the curse of dramatic form. It plays havoc with the constructions of time and language by which we attempt to order our experience. But must a play mean what it says? The statement made by the sequence of events may be reversed entirely by the context created by the completed play.

Words may be divorced from action; both words and action, from meaning.

That divorce Beckett theatricalizes in the space empty of theatrical properties and the language empty of meaning in *Waiting for Godot*. The only stage property is a tree suitable for a man to hang himself from had he a rope strong enough for hanging. Didi and Gogo act out the bare elements of the neck riddle as they wait condemned to ask rhetorical questions and repeat senseless answers. In *Godot*, time is the monster that cannot be exorcised by naming because nothing can change by word or deed. There are endless nights and endless guesses, but no Tom Tit Tot or Godot to save their necks. There is no turning there. There is only a sense of something lost.

Notes

1. See Katharine Briggs, *An Encyclopedia of Fairies* (New York: Pantheon Books, 1976), pp. 404-409.

2. For an excellent analysis of riddles and their relation to charms, see Andrew Welsh, *Roots of Lyric: Primitive Poetry and Modern Poetics* (Princeton: Princeton University Press, 1978).

3. Aristotle uses "plot" to mean both story and context together, whereas we tend to distinguish "plot" from "action" as the two terms of dramatic structure that refer to opposite time schemes, the one sequential, the other concurrent.

13

Occulted Discourse and Threatening Nonsense in Joe Orton's *Entertaining Mr. Sloane*

MAURICE CHARNEY

In its root sense, the occult is that which is hidden, concealed, or covered over in order to protect arcane truths from the eyes of the uninitiated. In other words, there is a sharp contrast between the manifest and the latent meanings. *Contrast* may be too mild a word because the most likely form of relation between surface and implied meanings is one of contradiction. The stated meaning is bland, polite, innocuous, even vacuous, in order to conceal a violent, chaotic, and painful truth. To formulate this double effect in a different way, we may say that the language is deliberately and systematically occulted in order to sustain a continuous irony between what is said and what is meant. In popular parlance, language as an expressive vehicle is rendered meaningless, banal, and jejune so that the real tenor and purpose of that language may be safely protected. Harsh truths are insulated by the trite formulas of social discourse. The characters speak an amusing and titillating babble of stock phrases, trite moralizing (often of a proverbial turn), and prepackaged emotional clichés drawn from the crockpot of daytime television serials. When this style is cultivated self-consciously by the author, the effect is that of collage, because the author is aiming at an occult contrast between the nonsense that is revealed and the deeper meanings that lie hidden. In this limited sense, the author is using a secret language for his surface discourse.

We are speaking of a general tendency in contemporary literature to appropriate nonliterary materials and to employ them in disguised and ironic ways. No modern playwright uses this occulted discourse (or threatening nonsense) more brilliantly than Joe Orton, the English drama- tist whose very brief career ended so tragically and so luridly in 1967, bludgeoned to death with a hammer by his homosexual roommate—a histrionic ending in the style of his own plays. Orton has remained so much in the shadow of Harold Pinter that it is worth making distinctions between Pinter's more civilized and traditional "comedy of menace" and Orton's more anarchic, more savage, more genuinely chaotic and turbulent farces of daily life and its empty deceptions. Orton ruthlessly cuts away Pinter's significances, so that "menace" would seem a preten- tious term for what Orton is doing. Orton's short radio play, *The Ruffian on the Stair* (1963), begins with the following very un-Pin- teresque dialogue:

> JOYCE. Have you got an appointment today?
> MIKE. I'm to be at King's Cross station at eleven. I'm
>   meeting a man in the toilet.
> JOYCE. You always go to such interesting places.[1]

Orton's sense of language as farcical exhibitionism undercuts and neutral- izes any feeling of menace, although the play is obviously indebted to Pinter in its dramatic assumptions. Orton doesn't write comedies of menace, but rather comedies of need and greed, where the only truths behind a facade of epigrammatic and pointless discourse are those generated by the blind instincts of self-preservation and self-aggrandize- ment. In this sense, unthinking egoism and self-expression are the only realities in Orton's world.

Entertaining Mr. Sloane (1963) is so distressingly autobiographical that it offers the most explicit illustrations of Orton's occulted discourse. We know from John Lahr's recent biography, *Prick Up Your Ears* (1978), that the old and more or less useless dadda, Kemp, is modeled on Orton's own father, that the sentimentally lascivious housewife Kath draws largely on Orton's mother, and that the idle, violent, and bisexual drifter, Sloane, has many qualities of the playwright himself. The play is suffused with a sense of grandiloquence, a heightened style that is the language of a preposterous self-love. In other words, the style is continuously inflated as the tired platitudes of middle-class respectability are trolled out to decorate the naked lust, greed, and aggression of the characters. The thin and shabby veneer of civilization very imperfectly hides the monstrous truths on which the action is based.

The central event of the play is that Sloane brutally kills Ed's and Kath's old father, who happens to know about an earlier murder that Sloane had committed. The homosexual brother, Ed, and the whorish-motherly Kath both desperately need Sloane as confidant and lover, so that Sloane's murder of their father has absolutely no moral resonance. There is no real question of turning Sloane over to the police—only a question of Ed's and Kath's bargaining with each other to "find a basis for agreement" (p. 134). The negotiations are conducted under a barrage of meaningless assertions about law, order, and decency. As a street-wise kid, Sloane is fully aware that Ed and Kath are only spouting worn-out formulas that have no relevance to the present situation. Their mechanical moralizing will cosset and flatter their own respectable consciences while Sloane can choose the best deal that will keep him out of prison. He can rely on Ed's and Kath's rampant sexuality to protect him.

In the following dialogue, the language is only a bubble and froth of words meant to embellish the harsh, implicit truths that cannot be spoken:

> ED. You're completely without morals, boy. I hadn't realized how depraved you were. You murder my father. Now you ask me to help you evade Justice. Is that where my liberal principles have brought me?
> SLOANE. You've got no principles.
> ED. No principles? Oh, you really have upset me now. Why am I interested in your welfare? Why did I give you a job? Why do thinking men everywhere show young boys the strait and narrow? Flash cheque-books when delinquency is mentioned? Support the Scout-movement? Principles, boy, bleeding principles. And don't you dare say otherwise or you'll land in serious trouble. [p. 134]

The proliferation of "Principles . . . bleeding principles" is positively oppressive, as well as the pervasive persistence of moral formulas. Is Ed a representative of "thinking men everywhere," with or without their flashing checkbooks? It is all strictly language as display, and Sloane's penitence is equally hollow and sardonic: "I'm very bad. Only you can help me on the road to a useful life" (p. 135). Sloane is mimicking the empty slogans of welfare-state paternalism. The whole play, in fact, sounds like a parody of media doublespeak, especially in its painfully moralistic phrases. The language is authentic babble without any relation to truth. As Orton wrote in his diary, "The whole trouble with Western society today is the lack of anything worth concealing."[2]

Although Orton's work was undoubtedly shaped by early Pinter, especially *The Birthday Party* (1958), *Entertaining Mr. Sloane*, written two years before Pinter's *The Homecoming* (1965), clearly influenced that play. Pinter's Ruth develops the mother-whore stereotype of Orton's

Kath, and, more pointedly, Pinter's overbearing hustler, Lenny, has a type resemblance to Orton's hollowly successful and vaguely criminal Ed. Both are full of insufferable pretensions to middle-class manners and style. Both Lenny and Ed speak a language that is peculiarly synthetic and literary—a language of disguise that is entirely stripped of any affect, emotion, or human resonance. Thus, when Ed learns that his sister is having sexual relations with Sloane and is, in fact, pregnant, he reacts with a cool and vituperative eloquence:

> What a little whoreson you are you little whoreson. You are a little whoreson and no mistake. I'm put out my boy. Choked. *(Pause.)* What attracted you? Did she give trading stamps? You're like all these layabouts. Kiddies with no fixed abode. [p. 119]

The stilted diction, including the archaic "whoreson," and the posed emotions—"Choked"—contain the violence. It is all very stagey and histrionic, but threatening nevertheless. Ed is speaking for his own pleasure rather than from any need to communicate with Mr. Sloane. The message is there for Sloane in Ed's icy detachment.

The formulaic quality of the speech in *Entertaining Mr. Sloane* emphasizes the isolation of the characters from each other. Everyone seems to be talking to himself or herself, except perhaps for the old father, Kemp, who has a dangerous secret to communicate about Sloane's past and who winds up dead for his troubles. Orton seems to deny any possibility of communication, so that language is almost by definition occult, because it serves chiefly as a way of concealing meaning. Once this assumption is accepted, it becomes easier to feel the strength of Orton's sardonic playfulness. In connection with the staging of *What the Butler Saw* (1967), we know that Orton typed up a list of phrases that could be used ad libitum by the cast for comic putdowns: "You revolting fur-covered bitch!"; "You shoulder-length prick!"; "He likes women—you know strip clubs, menstruation, mothers-in-law"; and the Wildean epigram: "A word not in current use except in the vernacular."[3] Orton could afford to be in love with language for its own sake, because the words are so separated from any determinative meaning.

Some of Sloane's speeches are detachable arias, little pop culture vignettes of hard-boiled sentimentality, such as his extravagant narration to Kemp of the circumstances leading to his first murder:

> It's like this see. One day I leave the Home. Stroll along. Sky blue. Fresh air. They'd found me a likeable permanent situation. Canteen facilities. Fortnight's paid holiday. Overtime? Time and a half after midnight. A staff dance each year. What more could one wish to devote one's life to? I certainly loved that place. The air round Twickenham was like wine. Then one

day I take a trip to the old man's grave. Hic Jacets in profusion. Ashes to Ashes. Alas the fleeting. The sun was declining. A few press-ups on a tomb belonging to a family name of Cavaneagh, and I left the graveyard. [pp. 124-125]

This is fashioned in the mock-pastoral, mock-poetic mode, with air "like wine," bits and pieces of tombstone inscriptions, a part-line from "The Rose of Tralee" ("The sun was declining"), and satire on the work ethic in the style of Orton's bitter play, *The Good and Faithful Servant* (1964). Sloane is exuberant as he leads up to his encounter with the pornographic photographer who likes "certain interesting features I had that he wanted the exclusive right of preserving" (p. 125). The blatant sexuality is always guarded and disguised—not part of a system of pleasure or hedonism, but only an expression of need and greed, the overpowering desire to use and possess another person.

Sloane's style collects fragments and puts them together in a pattern that has no relation at all to any meaningful context of ordinary discourse. The fragments are displaced and juxtaposed so that they have what Orton called a "collage quality."[4] His room with Kenneth Halliwell was an enormous collage of pasted-up images, and they both were sent to prison in 1962 for their extraordinary collage effects in at least 72 books from the public libraries of Islington and Hampstead. Their most offensive collage was apparently the tiny monkey's head pasted in the middle of a rose on the cover of *Collins Guide to Roses*. This violated the deepest verities of English domestic life. In the bewildering welter of media inputs and pop culture imagery, Orton took seriously his role as collagist. "Shakespeare and the Elizabethans did the same thing. I mean you have absolute realism and then you get high poetry, it's just language. I think you should use the language of your age and every bit of it. They always go on about poetic drama and they think you have to sort of go off in some high-flown fantasy, but it isn't poetic, it's everything, it's the language in use at the time."[5] But Sloane's eloquence and Orton's eloquence are extremely self-conscious. The comparison to Shakespeare and the Elizabethans is apt because Orton wrote with such bravado. In its exuberant flamboyance, his style is certainly closer to Marlowe's than to Shakespeare's.

Orton delights in collecting sentimental clichés for the part of Kath, the fading, mock-voluptuous mother-whore, who seduces Sloane and mothers him without any feeling of contradiction. Kath is the consumerist par excellence of the ladies' magazines, and she lives in a world of tawdry, commercialized romance. Her knickknacks define both her respectability and her illusions about the existence of a larger world outside her house built in the middle of a garbage dump. Her "sophisticated" conversation with Sloane is all mindless twaddle, civilized foreplay leading up to the sex act:

KATH. Isn't this room gorgeous?

SLOANE. Yes.

KATH. That vase over there come from Bombay. Do you have any interest in that part of the world?

SLOANE. I like Dieppe.

KATH. Ah . . . it's all the same. I don't suppose they know the difference themselves. [p. 93]

Kath's Bombay and Sloane's Dieppe are both equivalent cities of the mind—only high-sounding words for places that have no reality. Kath's discourse has no relation to her transparent negligee, with which she is teasing Sloane: "I blame it on the manufacturers. They make garments so thin nowadays you'd think they intend to provoke a rape" (p. 93). By the time she is rolling on top of Sloane, he has become her baby: "What a big heavy baby you are. Such a big heavy baby" (p. 95). Kath dresses up her naked need for Sloane's body in various middle-class clichés, but the language moves on an entirely separate plane from the realities of seduction.

When Sloane threatens to leave the pregnant Kath after the murder of Kemp, Kath trolls out all the warmed-over tag lines of soap opera: "I've a bun in the oven," "Mr. Sloane was nice to me," "He's free with me," "Can't manage without a woman" (pp. 139, 141). Kath is the archetype of all injured women, both long-suffering and unappreciated mother and jilted lover who has no regrets. She speaks in the parodic formulas of domestic tragedy. "Who tucks him up at night? And he likes my cooking. He won't deny that" (p. 140). "I gave him three meals a day. Porridge for breakfast. Meat and two veg for dinner. A fry for tea. And cheese for supper. What more could he want?" (p. 141). A lascivious Mrs. Portnoy, who has managed to preserve the integrity of English family life. What more indeed could one possibly want? We know that Orton had very ambiguous feelings about his cold, sexless, very respectable, but nevertheless seductive mother. Kath projects a powerful incest fantasy of an omnipotent mother who is sexual and nurturing at the same time, but whose overwhelming love must ultimately be rejected by her guilty, adolescent son.

Orton dramatizes his own sexual ambiguity in the struggle between Kath and Ed for the possession of Sloane's body. The play has a surprising bisexual conclusion, but the language throughout is intensely misogynistic. Ed has a whole series of apothegms for putting women in their place: "Women are like banks, boy, breaking and entering is a serious business. Give me your word you're not vaginalatrous?" (p. 88). *Vaginalatrous* is an Orton coinage on analogy with *idolatrous;* it indicates a perverse attachment. To Ed, women are essentially frivolous vamps intent on deceiving men: "The way these birds treat decent fellows. I hope you never get serious with one. What a life. Backache, headache or her mum told her never to when there's an 'R' in the month" (p. 113). This is an

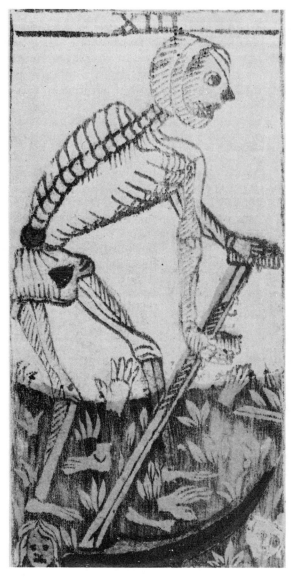

Tarot card XIII showing death. Attributed to Amphous and Arnous (1801) who are said to have adapted it from a 1760 pack by Nicolas Conver

old vaudeville formula that seems to turn on disgust at menstruation. When Ed is grappling with Kath for Sloane in the last act, he is not above insulting her physically, as if she represented all women: "Flabby mouth. Wrinkled neck. Puffy hands." "Sagging tits." "Sawdust up to the navel" (pp. 142-143). Her genitalia are scored off in a parody of Dante: "You showed him the gate of Hell every night. He abandoned Hope when he entered there" (p. 143). It's interesting how scrupulously Orton avoids any direct references to sexuality; they are always covert, circumlocutious, bitchy, and metaphorical. Female sexuality is a theme too forbidding and too disgusting to be directly represented. As a sexual being, Kath can only be shown histrionically. In an exaggerated gesture, she offers Sloane her hand: "Kiss my hand, dear, in the manner of the theater," and Ed's final insult is to Kath as an actress, falsely evoking theatrical sentiment: "What a cruel performance you're giving. Like an old tart grinding to her climax" (p. 143). The old tart, of course, mocks both sexuality and the theater. Ed's language of vituperation seems the most expressive idiom in the play, but he himself assumes a position of moral and social superiority to Kath that is based only on vigorous but hollow assertion. No moral positions are possible in this play. Everyone is wholly occupied by the struggle for survival.

Entertaining Mr. Sloane is hardly occult in any of the popular meanings of that term, yet there is a pervasive irony by which the surface action of the play is radically different from what is really happening. On the one side we see a parody of middle-class English values, full of vain moralizing and empty social gestures. On the other are power and greed nakedly striving to fulfill themselves without regard to human values. Behind the comedy of manners facade, aggressive lust dominates the play. In other Orton plays, such as *Loot* and *What the Butler Saw*, farce transforms the grossness and greed of the characters, so that the comic energies do not seem so raw as they do in *Entertaining Mr. Sloane*. The nonsense in this play is still very threatening; it has not been neutralized by farce. We still feel the tremendous effort at concealment by which the deeper meanings have been occulted and trivialized, so that turbulence and chaos are only very imperfectly mastered. Although Orton's whole career as a playwright occupies only about five years (from 1963 to his death in 1967), it is becoming apparent that he belongs in the classic tradition of English comedy that includes such writers as Swift, Wycherley, and Wilde. In his own disguised and farcical way, Orton sought to make contact with bitter truths. Beneath the occulted and at times nonsensical collage of pop culture dialogue, Orton tried for an emotional effect like Swift's savage indignation. Some lines from *Head to Toe* (1971), Orton's only published novel, state his comic credo with remarkable lucidity: "Cleanse my heart, give me the ability to rage correctly."[6]

Notes

1. All quotations from Orton are from *The Complete Plays* (New York: Grove Press, 1977), and the page numbers are included in the text.

2. Quoted from John Lahr, *Prick Up Your Ears: The Biography of Joe Orton* (New York: Knopf, 1978), p. 131. The chronology of Orton's works is from Lahr, especially pp. 291-293.

3. Quoted from Lahr, op. cit., p. 258.

4. Quoted from Lahr, op. cit., p. 154.

5. Quoted from Lahr, op. cit., p. 154.

6. Quoted from Lahr, op. cit., p. 122.

Note: This paper was presented at the ninth annual convention of the Popular Culture Association (April 1979) in the section "Varieties of Violence in Humor."

14

Numerology:
The Butorian Imagination

JENNIFER WAELTI-WALTERS

Michel Butor's use of alchemy in his texts has recently become the subject of critical commentary.[1] *Portrait de l'artiste en jeune singe* and "L'Alchimie et son langage" *(Répertoire)*[2] have been cited as keys to reading Butor's work, providing as they do reference to the importance of multiplicity of meaning, correspondences, close reading, and interpretation of language and symbols, as well as to the importance of quotation. Nor have the didactic and initiatory aspects of alchemy and its elitest hermetism been ignored in the discussion. All of this is certainly interesting, but it seems to me, on further reflection, that Butor's use of alchemy in *Portrait de l'artiste* is a symptom and not a cause; a manifestation designed to draw us into a symbolic and associative way of thinking and then to turn that mode of thought toward the book itself, which, while borrowing certain alchemical techniques and certainly aiming at its transformational goal, is directing the reader's imagination into formal exercises in numerological and serial composition.

The discovery of alchemy, initiation into its teaching, and the resulting personal development are stages in the author's life that produce the natural divisions in the book. *Portrait* is divided into three parts, each of

which has two titles printed in different types; those in roman letters—
Prélude, Voyage, Envoi—explain the structure of the book and what it
offers to the reader. Those in capital—LE DOCTEUR H, LE SAINT-
EMPIRE, L'AUTRE VOYAGE—indicate the theme that is essential to the
comprehension of the section. The sections describe the author's past,
present, and future.

Inside this triple division are others whose titles are used for their
evocative power. The "Prélude" is divided into five chapters: the "Voyage," into fifteen; and the "Envoi" is a blank that the future should fill.
It has a title but nothing else and hence confronts the reader as a unity, a
void pregnant with possibility. There are three sections, five and fifteen
chapters. The number of sections and chapters is not a matter of chance.
These numbers are important in numerology and cabbalistic studies. The
theory on which the scientific discoveries of Jabir, alchemist at the court
of Haroun-al-Raschid, were based was created by means of a square of
primary numbers. Five was in the center, and the other figures were
arranged in such a way that the sum of every line was fifteen. Fifteen thus
became a natural number that consequently played a part in all combina-
tions and movements of the natural elements.

The three dominates all alchemical experiments, representing in the
Christian era the Holy Trinity in various guises. Of these, the most
important are the sun, moon, and Mercury; the white and red stones and
the elixir, body, soul, and spirit. In addition, the geometrical symbol for
life in primary matter is ✡ . The first triangle ▽ represents water,
from which everything was made. The other triangle △ is fire, the
traditional manifestation of the holy spirit. Fulcanelli explains the
concept in *Les Demeures Philosophales*,[3] a book that plays a major role
in *Portrait* and stresses the interrelation of the alchemical quest and
Christian aspiration.

All symbolic objects are grouped in threes in the fifteen chapters of
"Voyage," and frequently a single example of the same thing, French
instead of German, will be found as a guide in the "Prélude." There are
three German castles where Butor studies alchemy, but his initial interest
was created in a French one. He has to learn three foreign languages:
Latin, Old High German, and modern German, but he first reads the
subject in French. In castle *H* he finds the works of three German alche-
mists—Basilus Valentinus, Jacob Boehme, and Athanasius Kircher—but
he has previously discovered that of the Frenchman Nicholas Flamel.
He meets Dr. H[4] in France, and he is the Hungarian who interests Butor
in the Holy Roman Empire with its threefold geographical division into
Germany, Australia, and Hungary, and also arranges the young man's
stay in Germany.

Among the authors whose books are quoted in *Portrait*, the alche-
mists are German, Franz Werfel and Alfred Kubin; the science-fiction,
fantasy writers are Austrian; and Jules Verne sets his tale in Hungary.
Hungary is central to the historical and symbolic development, the point

of contact with the Middle Eastern triplicity of Egypt, the Ottoman Empire (Jabir and Haroun-al-Raschid), and Palestine. These are represented by *Joseph in Egypt* and the *1001 Nights*. The books quoted can also be classified according to period: Medieval-Renaissance, eighteenth century, and modern. The visual arts are also threefold: engraving, painting, and sculpture. As a means of making this grouping even more obvious, three kinds of type are used for the chapter headings: roman type indicates life in France, Gothic script shows life in Germany, and copperplate is for dreams .

After three, the number most important to the structure of *Portrait* is seven—the number of days of the week of the Creation. Butor quotes from the description given by Jacob Boehme in his *Mysterium Magnum*.[5] Each of the odd-numbered chapters of "Voyage" mentions one day. Butor stays seven weeks in the castle; he dreams seven dreams; the count teaches him seven ways of playing patience. There are seven stages in the initiation of an alchemist, seven chemical reactions during the transmutation of lead to gold, seven planets as symbols of the primary elements of the natural world. Boehme lists them all.

Seven has always been a magic number, but in *Portrait de l'artiste en jeune singe* (a seven-word title), it stands for the infinite possibility present at the end of Creation week. Each of the German chapters describes one day of the week, but of a different week; hence Butor has to leave on a Monday because the seven weeks of his stay passed concurrently with the seven days described. A double time scheme is produced that incorporates the unique into the universal, personal into general in such a way that ordinary persons can take their place in the cosmos, as the quotations from Boehme's explanation of the Creation constantly indicate.

Here time is number; creation is number producing a particular yet universalizing mode of thinking, of which alchemy is but one manifestation. Behind the alchemical progress reflected in *Portrait de l'artiste* lies a numerological schema of the universe, covering the Great Chain of Being from end to end, the cosmos from the orbiting planets to the humblest rock on Earth. And thus Butor's text is, in fact, based on a rhetoric of numbers developed from Pythagorean, Gnostic, and early Christian writing and widely used in all medieval learning to relate all things by analogy within one all-encompassing universal system.

One visible pattern of such an interlocking universe is made by the list of chapter headings of the central section of *Portrait*, in which a young man's life develops step by step (Ch. 1, 3, 5, 7, 11, 13, 15) entwined with the general statement of spiritual development and search for God, of which alchemy is a symbol.[6] The chapter headings are:

1. L'aller (setting out)
2. *L'homme de grande vieillesse* (the very old man)
3. La bibliothèque (the library)

4. *L'étudiante* (the girl student)
5. Minérologie (minerology)
6. *Le forestier* (the forester)
7. Le chemin de ronde (the battlements)
8. *La métamorphose* (metamorphosis)
9. Mundus Subterraneus (subterranean world)
10. *Les patiences* (the patience games)
11. Orbites (orbits)
12. *Le tournoi* (the tournament)
13. Le Musée Allemand (the German museum)
14. *Le bannissement* (banishment)
15. L'Adieu (the farewell)

The even numbers follow the sequence of the seven stages of alchemy but indicate dream also—a mirror of the young Butor's unconscious mind and measure of his own initiation into understanding; thus they maintain the link with the symbolic, interpretive, initiatory aspects of medieval number philosophy and incorporate it into Butor's private world. The odd numbers refer to the daily life of the young Butor and have, until now, been pushed aside as relatively unimportant. However, in retrospect, I realize that each chapter title (except numbers 1 and 15, which are transitional pivots in the system) indicates one of the categories of objects that recur listed within the text: book, types of rock, towers containing collections made by previous inhabitants of the castle, natural elements, planets; finally, in "The German Museum," a list of categories to be found is provided.

These lists function not only as a link to the Great Chain of Being but also, given their proximity to quotations from the *1001 Nights*, as an encouragement to the reader to dream for himself of the infinite treasures to be discovered in the world around us and in the wider scheme. Within the text they appear as leitmotivs or, better yet, scales in different keys, providing the notes from which the composer of the dream chapters may choose to create his piece each evening. As there are eight of these chapters, the last taking up the theme of the first, the musical analogy would seem to be acceptable, especially when we remember that *Portrait de l'artiste en jeune singe* (seven words) is subtitled "capriccio."

Alchemy is number; alchemy is re-creation of the universe; the universe is number. It was seen to consist of arithmetical series and ratio creating form or geometry. Thus music, when recognised as number, also became a definition and description of the universe in a manner similar to that of alchemy. Hence it is logical that musical and alchemical series, side by side, should reveal two faces of Butor's world.

In revealing this parallel function, the alchemy has served its purpose however, for it is numerical and musical structures together with lists and series that have dominated Butor's writing from the beginning. If we take a few very brief examples, we find that *Passage de Milan*[7] is set out like an orchestral score with each apartment representing one family of instruments. *L'Emploi du Temps* is constructed in canon form,[8] and *Degrés*[9] seems to be an early attempt at serial composition, for the characters are grouped and Vernier tries to write a description in which all the members of each group appear in strict order whenever one of them is needed in the story. Also each of the novels has a formal structure built, like the first numerical codes, on time divisions: 12 hours for *Passage de Milan;* 12 months and 7 days for *L'Emploi du Temps;* the train timetable for *La Modification* and the school timetable for *Degrés.* A more elaborate structure would be that of *Description de San Marco,* in which Stravinsky's *Canticum Sacrum in honorem Sancti Marci Nominis,* itself modeled on the form of the basilica, provides a subtext for Butor's book.[10] Similarly, the thematic motifs present in *L'Emploi du Temps* and *La Modification* (the parks in Bleston, the stations on the line to Rome) develop very clearly into the lists and series in *Mobile.*[11] André Helbo[12] categorizes them into three groups in his interesting analysis of the text: (1) Simple alphabetical listings of objects in a given category: ice-cream flavors; (2) semantic groups: fragments of a given narrative distributed throughout parts of the book. (3) Recurrent series with repeats and variations: cars, shirt colors, lakes, mountains. Three kinds of series were used both to create a representation of certain aspects of the United States and also to stimulate the readers' imagination in a way similar to that of the lists of categories in *Portrait de l'artiste.* The reader is challenged to create for himself a greater, more all-encompassing picture. It is as if he were being offered—as indeed he is—the first few elements in an arithmetical or musical progression, and is being asked to complete the series. Through a study of the parks, the form becomes apparent—individual units combine to produce figures and then forms whether we are dealing with Pythagorean mathematics, music, or literature. And such correspondences dominate Butor's writing from *Mobile* to *Portrait de l'artiste.*

That such correspondences do not appear by accident in his work is made abundantly apparent by Butor in the books published immediately after *Portrait de l'artiste en jeune singe* (1967), namely, *La Rose des Vents: 32 rhumbs pour Charles Fourier* (1970) and *Dialogue avec 33 variations de Ludwig van Beethoven sur une valse de Diabelli* (1971).[13] Each of the texts is an elaboration of a complex, precisely ordered universe—those of Charles Fourier and Beethoven—and the texts are linked one to the other by the similarity of their number systems. As Butor remarks in the *Dialogue,* each is built on a base of 32 divided into four movements. Concerning Beethoven, he continues:

> Il y avait en effet les 32 variations en ut mineur sans numéro d'opus, il y a les 32 sonates que Beethoven considérait comme un ensemble organique et dont il voulait faire une révision générale en leur donnant à toutes un nom; il y a nos 33 variations sur la valse de Diabelli, c'est-à-dire 32 plus une introduc-

tion, le thème, et un final, le menuet varié. Nous savons par les cahiers d'esquisse qu'à une certaine époque il avait eu l'idée de commencer sa série par la phrase qui ouvre la grande fugue (32); c'est donc, si étrange que cela puisse nous paraître à première vue ou audition, qu'il la considérait à certains égards comme symétrique de la marche Jupiter (1). Le menuet, varié d'une façon toute particulière, serait l'équivalent de la reprise de l'aria qui termine les *Variations Goldberg*.

L'exécution complète de celles-ci comporte aussi 32 numéros; aria, 30 variations, aria, ce qui correspond aux 32 mesures complètes de cet aria; l'ensemble est d'ailleurs nettement divisé en deux ailes par le fait que la 16e variation y est nommée *ouverture.* [pp. 36-37]

(There were indeed the 32 variations in C minor which have no opus number; there are the 32 sonatas that Beethoven considered to be an organic ensemble and of which he wanted to make a general revision, giving them all a name; there are our 33 variations on the Diabelli Waltz, that is 32 plus an introduction, the theme, and a finale, the varied minuet. We know from the notebooks that at a certain period he had had the idea of beginning his series with the phrase that opens the great fugue (32); so, however strange that may seem to us at first sight or hearing, he considered it in some ways symmetrical to the Jupiter march (1). The minuet, varied in a singular manner, would be the equivalent of the repeat of the aria that ends the *Goldberg Variations*.

The complete performance of these has 32 numbers also: aria, 30 variations, aria, which corresponds to the 32 complete measures of this aria; besides the whole thing is clearly divided into two wings by the fact that the sixteenth variation in it is called *overture.*)

And from that symbolic pattern and number lore, he extrapolates for each an entire macrocosm and microcosm in which cosmic cycles and human life-styles are tied together as they were in number philosophy.

In both cases, Butor creates parallel and interchangeable series of musical terms, planets, ages of history, seasons, times of day, description of public and private life, all built on a sequence of two major and two minor scales, for which the sun serves as pivot.

Henri Pousseur has published a comprehensive commentary on the creation of *Dialogue*,[14] from which we can establish the lists in Table 1. From *La Rose des Vents*, we get a set of very similar but more detailed equivalences. The main elements of the first octave are shown in Table 2.

Each age also has its dominant sense, color, and so on. This octave is followed by its parallel on a higher scale, which continues from Hyper-

Table 1

Planet	Age	Life-style	People	Place	Season	Qualifier
Jupiter	Bronze	Elegant life	nobles	palace	Winter	tonic
Morning Star	Copper	Bourgeoisie	students	faubourgs	Spring (thaw)	dominant sous-foyer
Earth	Stone	Country life	peasants	fields		enseign
Mars*	Iron	Military life	soldiers	woods		dominant
Moon*	Silver	Political life	representatives	ruins	Summer	tonic
Uranus	Uranium	Bohemian	fairies	theaters		fanion
Mercury	Mercury	Deliverance	scholars	vineyards	November	standard
Saturn	Lead	Profound life	musicians	caves		

*Jupiter overthrown by Saturn.

Table 2

Planet	Age	Passion	Life-style	People	Season	Time	Wind
Venus	Eden	love	perfection	Babies (0-4)	Winter solstice	birth night	N (Aquilon)
Phoebina	Savagery	friendship	Authoritarian	Cherubins (4-6½)	January	disturbed night	N (Bise)
Ceres	Patriarchy	family	Private property	Seraphins (6½-9)		night of a bad moon	Mistral
Earth	Barbary	ambition	slavery	School boys (9-12)	February	dark night	Major hurricanes
Juno	Civilization	intrigue	our era	high school boys (12-15½)		feverish night	Winter Monsoon
Pallas	Guarantism	alternates	right to work			day break	Aeolian
Mercury	Seriosophy	composite	pre-Eden	Youths (15½-19)		dawn	E
Encelade	Harmony	love	perfection	Adolescents (19-24)		sunrise	Harmattan

eden to Hyperharmony, bringing the men to their natural term of 100 years old, the winds to south, and so on. The central pivot is provided by the summer solstice, noon, and a period of androgyny, after which everything shifts into the feminine, the minor key, and reverse order, descending from Hyperharmony minor to Eden minor and the death of the planet at midnight at the winter solstice.

As in *Portrait de l'artiste*, the lists established are juxtaposed by a technique designed to create the maximum amount of correspondence and symbolic resonance between groups. In each case, the readers' imagination is stimulated by the richness, texture, and extent of the system evoked by the words in front of them—a system by means of which the entire cosmos seems to dance within the readers' grasp, tempting them to think, in concert with Fourier, that they have finally understood it all:

> Dieu sait qu'un habitant de ce globe a saisi le calcul du mouvement. *[Rose des vents*, p. 33]

> (God knows that an inhabitant of this globe has grasped the method for calculating movement.)

If the history of the symbols does not captivate the readers, then the harmony of the pattern, the beauty of the logic should attract them as a piece of music does—by its numbers and proportions.

The originator of each system works from a number series based on the musical scale of eight notes, in which the eighth is a repeat of the first. Beethoven used it four times to give 32 variations plus a reprise. Fourier's mathematics begin simply too:

> Fourier nous déclare que le premier tome du *Traité de l'Unité universelle* est organisé en série de 32 termes plus le *pivot* (Ce qu'il appelle selon les textes: série mesurée de 2e ou de 3e puissance), ces 32 termes comprenant 2 octaves de 12 demi-tones chacun: les 24 chapitres, plus 4 *sous-pivots* et 4 transitions qu'il nous détaille . . . [p. 13]

> (Fourier tells us that the first volume of the *Treatise of Universal Unity* is organised in series of 32 terms plus the *pivot* (what he calls according to the texts: measured series of the 2d or 3d power), these 32 terms comprise two octaves of 12 semi-tones each: the 24 chapters, plus four *subpivots* and four *transitions* that he details . . .)

The mathematics quickly become much more complicated. Starting with a fairly restricted scale of 32 keys for each tonality, the following numerical progression is produced as Fourier's system completes its four cycles:

Do: 12
Do dièse: 24,
Ré: 32,
Ré dièse: 66,
Mi: 134,
Fa: 134,
Fa dièse: 810,
Sol: 1 622,
Sol dièse: 3 246,
La: 6 494,
La dièse: 12 990,
Si: 25 982,
Do: 77 948

> A partir du *ré*, la relation numérique entre les différentes
> touches est fort simple: 66 = (32 x 2) + 2, 1234 = (66 x 2) + 2,
> etc. Entre 2 touches blanches du piano, *mi* et *fa*, *si* et *do*, la
> relation serait: 404 = (134 x 3) + 2 ou 77948 (25982 x 3) + 2.
> [pp. 152-153]

C: 12,
C sharp: 24,
D: 32,
D sharp: 66,
E: 134
F: 404
F sharp: 810
G: 1 622,
G sharp: 3 246,
A: 6 424,
A sharp: 12 990
B: 25 982
C: 77 948

> (From *D* on, the numerical relation between the different
> keys is very simple: 66 = (32 x 2) + 2, 134 = (66 x 2) + 2,
> and so on. Between two white keys on the piano, *E* and *F*, *B*
> and *C*, the relation would be 404 = (134 x 3) + 2 or 77,948 =
> (25, 982 x 3) + 2.)

Despite the fact that Fourier's calculations are based on a scale of
eight notes (this *C* = 12 being irregular *C* should be 6½, and *C* sharp, 15),
Butor insists on several occasions that Fourier is really using a dodecaphonic scale:

En enlevant de chaque aile transitions et sous-pivots, nous découvrons une gamme de 12 touches correspondant aux 12 demi-tons de l'octave en musique. [p. 22]

(By removing transitions and subpivots from each wing, we find a scale of 12 keys corresponding to the 12 semitones of the octave in music.)

And by adding his 16 interventions (8 x 2) to Beethoven's variation (8 x 4) + 1, he transforms the latter into 48 + 1, that is, into four scales of 12, also, in which either the seventeenth variation combines with the sixteenth to form the double doors of the sun or the thirty-third is considered a repeat of the opening theme.

The entire plan of the work is shown in Diagram 1.

This pervasive transformation from the octave to the dodecaphonic scale is very interesting because the second time Butor describes it in *La Rose des Vents*, the description is very similar to that of the technique of serial music itself, in which the original twelve-tone row may be used in four forms: original, retrograde, inversion, and retrograde inversion. Butor writes:

Les 2 octaves à 12 demi-tons des séries à 32 termes se modulent en majeur (5 + 7) et mineur (4 + 8); mais elles peuvent être parcourues en sens direct ou en sens inverse (ce qui donnera 7 + 5 et 8 + 4). Chaque octave est donc susceptible de 4 aspects. [p. 94]

(The two octaves of 12 semi-tones of the series of 32 terms are modulated in the major (5 + 7) and minor (4 + 8); but they can be played forward or in reverse order (which will give 7 + 5 and 8 + 4). Each octave has, therefore, four possible aspects.)

Indeed, when we consider both *Dialogue* and *La Rose des Vents* in this light, reflecting on the lists established earlier in this paper, it would seem that Butor himself is writing serially, establishing for each text a series of rows, which are then used in order, as a composer might use a tone row, rhythm row, and so on, in conjunction to create a piece of music.

In other words, Butor is constantly working on a numerological model whether he is actually manipulating numbers (and hence the values attached to them, as he does in *Portrait, Dialogue,* and *La Rose des Vents,)* or whether he uses words alone: referential series in mathematical progressions. It has been a quarter of a century since he created the structure of *Passage de Milan* with its 12 hours, 7 modifying to 8 floors and families mainly in groups of 3, and yet the significant numbers and the way in which they are used reappear constantly in Butor's writing.

"Cyclades and Sporades" from *Antisèche* by Butor and Stavitsky

The theme
1. Major march or Jupiter

Intervention I

Intervention II

The winter ball
2. introduction: frost
3. prelude to the waltz: through the windows of the room, one sees a snowy landscape at night.
4. the court waltz

Intervention III

5. the burst of spray or morning star

Intervention IV

The lovers' walk
6. introduction: the thawing wind
7. prelude to the waltz: the troubled heart
8. the tender waltz

Intervention V

9. Minor march or the Earth

Intervention VI

The country fête
10. introduction: two children running in the rain, Paul and Virginia.
11. prelude to the waltz: the couples are formed
12. the round waltz

Intervention VII

13. Military march or Mars

Intervention VIII

The storm
14. introduction: the clouds gather
15. prelude to the hammer: dwarf march
The doors of the sun or the defeat of Jupiter by Saturn
16. the hammer

17. the anvil

Intervention IX

18. prelude to the fantasia: the rainbow

Intervention X

19. fantasia of rays

Intervention XI

20. the moon

Intervention XII

Divertissement of a summer afternoon
21. overture: Oberon and Titania
22. prelude to the fantasia: Leporello-Bottom
23. Puck's fantasia

Intervention XIII

24. the little fugue of Uranus

Intervention XIV

The vine-growers' fête
25. the copper waltz
26. prelude to the fantasia: the grape harvest
27. the vat fantasia

Intervention XV

28. Phantom march or Mercury

Intervention XVI

November meditation
29. the phantom waltz
30. dreaming prelude to the fantasia
31. fantasia pathétique
32. the great fugue or Saturn
33. variation minuet

Diagram 1

If we take as one final example *Troisième dessous*[15] ("Third Level Down"), published in 1977 and third in a series of anthologies of fictional dreams, we find that four of the five dreams interconnect around a central pivot, just as the books on Fourier and Beethoven do. Dream 1 shares elements with dream 4; dream 2 with dream 5. Hence we find the four forms of row we are coming to know in Butor's writing. Looking closely at dream 5, we find that it shares with the rest of the volume an alphabetical series of nationalities, now drawing to its close: the Yugoslav, the Vietnamese, the Zambian; of *Departements* and their monuments (Orne-et-Marne); a retrograde series of countries: New Canada, New Ceylon, New Africa (South); a number of shared literary allusions, quotations, and characters, including a large number of variations on passages drawn from *Portrait de l'artiste* itself. These elements form sequences running horizontally through the book. There are other sets of references running vertically through the three books of *Matière de Rêves*.[16] This fifth dream draws on the fifth dream in each of the previous volumes to create another set of resonances, as the fourth uses the fourths, and so on. And as well as those sets, each dream contains a further row of references leading out into work Butor has done with another artist; in this instance the artist is Bernard Saby and the work *L'oreille de la lune*.[17] Finally, this dream contains a sequence that is of interest to us because it offers in symbolic form (Butor writes of "lichenology") a description of Butor's technique. First:

> J'essayais d'organiser mes lichens par des symétries, puis par des homologies. C'est-à-dire que je faisais jouer une espèce avec une autre semblable mais plus grande ou plus petite. A partir du moment ou l'oeil identifiait une série croissante ou décroissante automatiquement celle-ci se disposait dans l'espace. [p. 199]

> (I tried to organise my lichens symmetrically and then homologically; that is, I created a play between one species and another of the same kind but bigger or smaller. From the moment the eye identified an increasing or decreasing series, this series automatically became spatial.)

Then as a variation on a theme and finally and more precisely:

> —C'est que je cherchais à établir des échanges non seulement entre l'avant et l'arrière, la figure et le fond, le creux et le plein, mais aussi entre la forme et la matière; car ce qu'on appelle les matières en lichénologie est toujours constitué d'organisations de microformes, de formes beaucoup plus petites que celles qui vont se détacher. Ainsi les matières qui apparaissent dans une telle espèce sont pour ainsi dire déduites

des formes organisatrices; dans d'autres ce sera plutôt le mouvement inverse. [p. 227]

—I wanted to establish exchanges not only between the front and back, the figure and ground, hollow and raised, but also between form and matter; for what is called matter in lichenology is always made up of organisations of microforms, forms much smaller than those that will stand out. Hence the matter that appears in a certain species is deduced, one might say, from the organising forms; in others, it is rather the opposite movement.)

L'idéal serait pour moi d'introduire une continuité absolument d'un bout à l'autre de l'univers lichénologique . . . [p. 228]

(For me the ideal would be to introduce a continuity totally from one end to the other of the lichenological universe . . .)

Here we see the medieval desire to understand the design of the entire universe that I postulated at the beginning of this paper. Butor has this all-encompassing imagination and wants to share it with his readers. This he tried to accomplish by giving us continued practice in association, stretching our imagination to incorporate more and more elements provided by the varied series within his books. Indeed, Butor substantiates my claim firmly by stating at the end of the dream:

La lichénologie est ainsi un exercise méthodique d l'imagination. [p. 246]

(Lichenology is thus a methodical exercising of the imagination.)

Hence by means of the quotations from *Portrait* in *Troisième dessous*, we return to the original book, and from the beginning of *Portrait*, I quote this passage from an old book on alchemy:[18]

[Artephius] il explique en ce traité tout l'art [l'alchimie] en paroles très-claires, interpretant tant qu'il peut les ambages et sophisme des autres. Toutefois afin que les impies, ignorans & meschans ne peussent aisément trouver le moyen de nuire aux bons en apprenant cette science, il a un peu voilé le principal de l'art, par une artificieuse méthode . . . [p. 29]

(. . . in this treatise, he [Artephius] explains all the art [alchemy] in very clear words, interpreting as much as he can the

"The resonance of dreams"
from Butor and Stavitsky's *Antisèche*

circumlocutions and sophisms of the others. Still, so that the impious, ignorant, and wicked cannot easily find the way to harm the good by learning this science, he has veiled the most important part of the art a little by an artful method . . .)

It seems to me appropriate that we should apply this quotation to Butor, extending the hermetic analogy from alchemy through numerology, serial music, and "lichenology" to writing as an initiatory exercise destined to illuminate our imagination and understanding.[19] And, therefore, I should like to end with the words of the alchemical treatise once more:

Il serait superflu de parler dauantage de nostre autheur . . .
Regarde donc, si (peut estre), cestui-ci n'a point mieux entendu

la façon de l'vsage de cette pierre, que les autres. Toutefois tout tel qu'il est, vse-en, et de nos labeurs à la gloire de Dieu et vtilité du Royaume de France. A Dieu. [pp. 29-30]

(It would be superfluous to speak more of our author . . . Look then, whether (perhaps) he has not understood the way of using this stone better than the others. Yet, such as it is, use it and our labours to the glory of God and service of the Realm of France. A Dieu.)

Notes

1. See, for example, J. Waelti-Walters, *Alchimie et littérature: à propos de Portrait de l'artiste en jeune singe* (Paris, Denoël, 1975), and *Michel Butor, 1954-74: His View of the World and a Panorama of his Work* (Victoria, B.C.: Sono Nis Press, 1977), M. Spencer, *Michel Butor* (New York: Twayne 1974); T. D. O'Donnell: "Michel Butor and the Tradition of Alchemy," MLA Conference, New York, 1974.

2. *Portrait de l'artiste en jeune singe* (Paris: Gallimard, 1967); "L'alchimie et son langage," *Répertoire* (Paris: Editions de Minuit, 1960), pp. 12-19.

3. Fulcanelli, *Les Demeures Philosophales* (rpt. Paris: J. J. Pauvert, 1965), Vol. 1, p. 201.

4. Henry Hunwald, author of the Preface to Alexander von Bernus's *Alchemy and Medicine* (1904).

5. J. Boehme, *Mysterium Magnum*, trans. J. Ellistone and J. Sparrow M. Simmons for H. Blunden (London, 1654).

6. For elucidation of this, see either J. Waelti-Walters, *Michel Butor*, pp. 124-127, or *Alchimie et littérature*, pp. 34-40.

7. *Passage de Milan* (Paris: Editions de Minuit, 1954).

8. *L'Emploi du Temps* (Paris: Editions de Minuit, 1956); D. and J. Y. Bosseur, "Michel Butor et la musique," *Musique en jeu*, No. 4 (Paris: Editions du Seuil, 1971), p. 65.

9. *Degrés* (Paris: Gallimard, 1960).

10. *Description de San Marco* (Paris: Gallimard, 1963); J. Waelti-Walters, "The Architectural and Musical Influences on the Structure of M. Butor's *Description de San Marco*," *Revue de littérature comparée* (in press).

11. *Mobile, étude pour une représentation des Etats-Unis* (Paris: Gallimard, 1962).

12. André Helbo, *Michel Butor vers une littérature du signe* (Brussels: Editions complexe, 1975), pp. 42-92, especially p. 70.

13. *La Rose des vents: 33 rhumbs pour Charles Fourier* (Paris: Gallimard, 1970); *Dialogue avec 33 variations de Ludwig van Beethoven sur une valse de Diabelli* (Paris: Gallimard, 1971).

14. Henri Pousseur, "Ecoute d'un dialogue," *Musique en jeu*, No. 4 (Paris: Seuil, 1971), pp. 73-81.

15. *Troisième dessous, Matière de rêves III* (Paris: Gallimard, 1977).

16. *Matière de rêves* (Paris: Gallimard, 1975); *Deuxième sous-sol, Matière de rêves II* (Paris: Gallimard, 1976).

17. M. Butor and B. Saby, *L'oreille de la lune* (Boulogne-sur-Seine: Robert Blanchet, 1973).

18. *Philosophie Naturelle de Trois Anciens Philosophes Renommez, Artephius, Flamel & Synesius*, Traitant de l'Art occulte et de la Transmutation métallique. DERNIERE EDITION augmentée d'un petit Traité du Mercure, & de la Pierre des Philosophes de G. Ripleus, nouvellement traduit en François. A PARIS Chez LAURENT D'HOURY, sur les Quay des Augustins, à l'Image St Jean, MDCLXXXII. Avec Privilège du Roy.

19. For a discussion of creativity and serial music, see Henri Pousseur, "The Question of Order in New Music," *Perspectives in New Music*, 5 (Fall-Winter 1966), pp 93-111.

Thanks to Sono Nis Press for permission to quote pp. 120-121 and 122-123 from my *Michel Butor*.

PART 6

TEXTS
AND
DOCUMENTS

Stanisław Przybyzewski's Visitors

TRANSLATED BY
DANIEL GEROULD
JADWIGA KOSICKA

A Dramatic Epilogue in One Act

Dedicated to Konrad Rakowski

Characters

Adam	First Old Man
Bela (his wife)	Second Old Man
Pola (his sister)	Leader of the Dance
Visitor	Visitors
Stranger	

(The music played in the mansion throughout the drama is Saint-Saëns's *Danse Macabre.*)

The park. A moonlit night. In the background, the mansion ablaze with lights. Couples, laughing and chattering, pass back and forth through the park—now going into, now coming out of, the mansion. Two OLD MEN *appear on stage and sit down on a bench.*

FIRST OLD MAN. How changeable everything is in this world! I remember this mansion in the days when the old count was still alive. You wouldn't believe what vivacious, joyful balls used to take place here . . . But since these newcomers bought the mansion, everything has changed. I am still attached to it, simply from force of habit, but I no longer feel at ease here any more.

SECOND OLD MAN. But where did they come from?

FIRST OLD MAN. No one knows. No sooner had the count's heirs put the mansion up for sale than they appeared—God knows from where— and bought it. That's all.

SECOND OLD MAN. There is some mystery concealed in that mansion.

FIRST OLD MAN. *(lost in thought)* How joyful it used to be here! I remember the good times I had here 30 years ago—oh, it was a different house then from what it is now . . . so different, so very different . . .

SECOND OLD MAN. Because a clear conscience, peace, and happiness prevailed here then.

FIRST OLD MAN. And now?

SECOND OLD MAN. There is some mystery lurking at the bottom of it. Some terrible mystery. I am not deceived by appearances or by these incessant balls and all that artificial gaiety . . .

FIRST OLD MAN. What could be hidden at the bottom of it? Some sort of mysterious crime? Is that it?

SECOND OLD MAN. How should I know? Crime—hmm—everything is a crime. Man has been created for the engendering of crime.

FIRST OLD MAN. True, true, everything may prove to be a crime.

SECOND OLD MAN. Including life itself, since everyone lives at some one else's expense.

FIRST OLD MAN. *(lost in thought)* You marry a woman, yet you never know whether she loves you or not.

SECOND OLD MAN. A child is born, but you are incapable of bringing it up . . .

FIRST OLD MAN. Say you strangle a repulsive old miser, whose money you could use to make the whole world happy . . .

SECOND OLD MAN. Suppose you violate a law which in itself is some sort of crime . . .

FIRST OLD MAN. Oh, that's true! Everything may prove to be a crime . . .

(After a pause.)

SECOND OLD MAN. Let's not blame human beings—they have been created for the engendering of crime, and everything may prove to be a crime . . . Oh! Humans are so wretched, so wretched . . .

FIRST OLD MAN. And as for the new owners, they seem to be joyous, and yet such strange anxiety peers out from the depths of their eyes . . .

SECOND OLD MAN. Ha! Because such strange, strange visitors have filled their house. Especially the one who follows Adam step by step; wherever Adam goes, he's by his side . . . like an inseparable shadow . . .

FIRST OLD MAN. I feel strangely uneasy. I feel as though a terrible disaster were hanging over this house.

(A moment of silence.)

SECOND OLD MAN. Only let's not blame human beings. Sometimes humans are so wretched—although they may not even have committed any crime. Nature can be strangely malicious. It punishes for sins that it has itself implanted in the human heart.

FIRST OLD MAN. True, true! A moment of insane happiness takes its revenge in strange ways . . .

SECOND OLD MAN. Sometimes a man does not even know that he has committed a crime. All at once a little gash appears in his heart . . . it grows bigger and bigger with frightful speed . . . and suddenly he sees it all clearly, but only when he's already in the clutches of madness . . . And sometimes, even in a moment of happiness, a sudden recollection— a slight pang of conscience—makes itself felt . . . and this self-reproach brings on thousands of others, which grow more and more insistent . . . investigations and inquests follow . . . the most insignificant detail, the slightest wrong swells to monstrous proportions—and lo and behold! Your house becomes filled with strange visitors.

FIRST OLD MAN. True, true, the internal order of things decrees that sort of mysterious, veiled justice . . .

SECOND OLD MAN. It was not created by human beings—men know only punishment, but justice is done by the heart itself . . .

FIRST OLD MAN. By the heart itself . . . he, he . . . for its own evil promptings and enticements . . .

SECOND OLD MAN. *(laughing quietly)* True, true, true . . .

(Music is heard from the mansion. Couples gather; they all assemble on the terrace of the mansion.)

LEADER OF THE DANCE. *(clapping his hands)* Ladies and gentlemen— the dance is about to begin!

FIRST OLD MAN. *(to the second)* Let us go, too. So that I can recall those beautiful bygone days when joy and conviviality reigned here . . .

SECOND OLD MAN. And a clear conscience . . .

(They go out.)

ADAM. *(comes down the steps from the terrace of the mansion, deeply engrossed in thought. He stops for a moment and shakes his head. After a pause)* A terrible visitor has taken up residence in this house . . . *(lost in thought)* . . . a terrible, terrible visitor . . .

POLA. *(comes down the steps from the terrace, goes over to Adam, and takes him by the hand)* Adam! Adam! My poor brother—I must leave this house of yours . . .

ADAM. *(terrified)* What? What? You wish to leave this house of mine?

POLA. There is no place for me here—that visitor of yours is driving me out . . .

ADAM. What? There's no place? No place for you? No, that cannot be! I shall build new mansions for you, made of marble—or crystal, if you like, or red porphyry and green syenite—I shall construct entire towns for you . . . entire towns . . . I shall raise up a whole new world for you—only stay here, stay here with me . . .

POLA. Oh, even if you built up the entire earth for my sake, there would still be no place for me. Your visitor will drive me out from everywhere . . . I no longer am of any use to you . . . This house of yours is a house of misery and fear, a house of bad conscience . . .

ADAM. Pola!

POLA. What does it matter, what does it matter—I know that something terrible has happened in this house, but I won't ask you anything; I do not wish to pick your soul to pieces—oh, God, why did you have to move into this house, Adam? What was it that brought you here?

ADAM. Love.

POLA. But you have committed a crime . . .

ADAM. What? What's that you're saying?

POLA. *(with a faint smile)* I sensed it all from the start, and I curse this house that has killed your soul.

(A moment of silence.)

POLA. Yes! I am no longer of any use to you. Adam, do you remember our great happiness, that peaceful, quiet happiness before you moved into this house? That time on the cliffs overlooking the ocean by the shore? The sea was as soft and smooth as the palm of a beloved woman; the unearthly melody of dusk and the dying purple of the sky suffused the entire world—and the ocean disappeared, and the whole world drifted by and vanished from our sight . . .

ADAM. *(suddenly)* Oh, how happy I was then!

POLA. Do you remember only last year, before you moved into this ill-fated house, do you remember those white nights by the North Sea? The sun, which had just set, hid for a moment behind the sea—only to rise again at the very next instant—and long golden rays of light, which in a moment were about to flood the world with white radiance, pierced the vast crimson majesty covering the sky. Do you remember how ecstatically you drank in those strange wonders?

ADAM. I remember! I remember it only too clearly—perhaps if I had forgotten it all . . .

POLA. Then? Then?

ADAM. Then I might have been able to rid myself of this frightful visitor . . .

(Silence)

POLA. Where did you meet him?

ADAM. Where did I meet him? Where did I meet him? Ha! On the path

of life, my dearest sister. When I lost my footing and heedlessly, reck-
lessly plunged headlong into this, this . . . disaster—he, he—it was supposed to be happiness . . . whoever loses his footing . . . you know . . .
ends up with such visitors in his house . . .

POLA. Adam! What have you done?

ADAM. *(looks at her with a faint smile, evasively)* Where did I meet
him? Well, you see, it was in a big city that he first attached himself to
me. I was returning to my hotel late one night, and the way led
through a dark and strangely gloomy park. And suddenly, out of
nowhere as though he had sprung up from the earth, a man appeared
before me and looked at me with the sort of glance, with exactly the
sort of glance that penetrates all the pores of your body, makes your
heart contract, and causes cold shudders to run up and down your
spine and chest. I stood there shivering and shaking, but our eyes
were already interlocked. I could not tear my gaze away from his, our
eyes were glued together . . . These were his only words: "From now on
we shall remain together for the rest of our lives."

POLA. What crime have you committed, Adam?

ADAM. What human being is there who has never committed a crime?
Not even a small one? And besides, what does it mean, big or small,
when it comes to crime? The biggest crime may have such insignificant
consequences that it turns out to be small, and vice versa . . . And what
about you? At times don't you feel dread and anxiety that you may
have unconsciously committed a crime, without even realizing it?
Don't you feel dread and anxiety?

POLA. Not enough to make me run away from myself.

ADAM. You are fortunate!

POLA. You see, my life is quiet, peaceful, stable . . .

ADAM. Stable . . . yes . . . the way our life together used to be only a
year ago.

POLA. Only a year ago.

ADAM. And are you happy with your husband?

POLA. I'm at peace, at peace. If that can be called happiness . . . *(lost in
thought)* But why did you let . . . a visitor like that into your house?

ADAM. I had to, I had to! Just tell me: is there any house where such a
gentleman has not paid a visit?

POLA. Frightful, frightful! *(After a pause, she points to the mansion,
from which louder and louder music can be heard.)* And what about
that? Doesn't it benumb you?

ADAM. What does it matter, what does it matter—at times I long to
stupefy myself, but my visitor does not allow me to forget—that *(points
to the mansion)*—that was for her, for my wife; a woman can be
benumbed by something like that, but *I* never can . . .

POLA. Adam, I must leave you, a house of that sort is like the plague . . .
The virus of unhappiness will stick to my clothes, and I'll carry it home.

ADAM. Yes, go away, go away—but with you goes my last bit of peace and consolation. *(Suddenly, in despair)* Oh, if only it were possible to forget, if only it were possible to forget!

POLA. *(profoundly discouraged, in a hollow tone of voice)* Oh, if only it were possible to forget . . . *(after a moment)* But couldn't you leave this house?

ADAM. And where could I run away to? Run away from oneself? Impossible!

    (BELA *comes down the steps from the terrace.)*

BELA. Adam! Adam!

ADAM. What is it? Here I am.

BELA. *(comes over to them)* You are not behaving well. Why do you ask visitors to come here if you constantly keep running away? At every moment I have to look for you in all the nooks and corners. *(Irritated)* And besides, you have invited strange, strange visitors.

ADAM. *(lost in thought)* Yes, terrible visitors have taken up residence in our house.

BELA. Why did you invite them?

ADAM. *(significantly)* But we both invited them, didn't we? Yes, both of us brought them into our house.

BELA. What do you mean? Both of us? What's that you're saying?

ADAM. What does it matter, what does it matter—it's only that Pola told me she's leaving us and going home.

BELA. What's that? Pola, are you leaving us? Adam, don't let her go! What will happen to us? Pola, take mercy on us; do you know what emptiness you'll leave behind you?

POLA. Alas, I know, but I have to go now, I have to—here, here, in this house of yours, I feel uneasy, and it is so quiet in my house, so sad, but peaceful, so very peaceful . . .

    (The VISITOR *unexpectedly appears.)*

VISITOR. *(politely)* But my dear hosts, the visitors are looking for you . . . They want to drink your health. Adam, why are you so out of sorts? And you, Madame, look somewhat downcast too.

ADAM. *(nervously, to BELA)* Go back to the ballroom, and tell them that I shall be with them soon. I have a headache. I want to walk through the park for a little while more . . .

POLA. *(hostilely to the VISITOR)* Let us leave him alone for a moment—come with me . . .

VISITOR. *(politely)* Oh, no, I'll have a little talk with him. I can usually calm him down.

BELA. Let's go, Pola, let's go—do you hear? They're dancing, they're dancing . . .

    (They leave. ADAM *and the* VISITOR *remain alone together.)*

ADAM. *(looking at the VISITOR with hatred)* Well? Won't you leave me alone for a second? Won't you give me even a moment's peace?

VISITOR. You know that I am your inseparable companion. Do you remember that night in the darkened park?—I told you then that we'd remain together forever. It's not a pleasant task, but I have to stay with you. It is my destiny—You see, I am your shadow. Understand?

ADAM. *(profoundly discouraged)* And you will never leave me?

VISITOR. Never.

ADAM. *(forcefully)* And what if I throw you out of my heart, if I find enough strength and courage to defend myself from you, if I become so strong that I am able to tell you, "Get out!" What if I find someone or something to fill my soul and you have to stop dogging my footsteps and keep silent forever . . .

VISITOR. Hmm, perhaps someone else would be able to do that—but not you!

ADAM. And what if my reason gains the upper hand and I tell myself: what I have done, I had to do, it was the only way? . . .

VISITOR. To happiness?

ADAM. What difference does it make? To the precipice, to the abyss, to endless despair—but only that it had to happen.

VISITOR. Reason is strangely unreasonable in such cases.

ADAM. But suppose that I succeed?

VISITOR. Then I shall cast my shadow upon the wall. It will spread its frightful wings above you—wherever you go, those ghastly black wings—no! rather frightful arms, the fingers outspread and menacing, like Satan's claws, about to catch you—wherever you go, you'll always see those frightful, insidious claws lying in wait—for the moment those arms are outstretched, waiting to strike, like . . . yes . . . like a panther ready to jump: in another second they'll squeeze you in their fiendish grip, right here! Around your throat—they'll enlace you in a fiendish embrace and choke you tighter and tighter . . .

ADAM. Until, until?

VISITOR. Until they suffocate you. *(laughing)* You're mine! Mine! Mine!

ADAM. *(jumps up)* But why am I yours?

VISITOR. *(laughing in his face)* Oh, how you'd like to silence it all and smother it somewhere in your heart! How can you ask me why you are mine? You are the one who knows the answer to that question best of all.

ADAM. And what if those arms never come down from the wall?

VISITOR. Hmm, then it will be still worse for you. I told you that those arms seem ready to spring like a panther lying in wait—he, he—in fact, those arms will slowly become transformed into a Satanic beast of prey—you will have it constantly before your very eyes—and at each and every moment you will feel that this beast of prey is about to jump at you, wrapping its front legs around your neck, and sinking its hind legs into your thighs, its jaws buried deep in your breast: it starts tearing apart and pulling to pieces, it cracks your ribs and gnaws through to your heart—he, he, he—until it finally rips out your heart, your poor miserable heart dripping with blood . . .

ADAM. Stop, stop . . .

VISITOR. You know, in ancient Mexico among the Aztecs there was a custom for a human heart, freshly cut out of a man's breast, to be sacrificed to the Mother Sun . . .

ADAM. And to what Sun is my heart to be sacrificed?

VISITOR. Justice.

ADAM. Human justice?

VISITOR. There is neither human nor divine justice. There is only a certain order of things that decrees that everything has to be the way it is and not some other way—whoever violates this law has his heart condemned to death . . .

ADAM. Are you implacable?

VISITOR. I am a frightful visitor . . . Do you hear? A frightful visitor . . .
      (Louder and louder music can be heard.)

ADAM. Oh, that music, that accursed music . . .

VISITOR. Doesn't it benumb you? Doesn't it stupefy you? Just try, try—dance, get drunk, deaden your feelings with pleasure, music, dancing . . . Why are you running away from all that? Why do you constantly hide in the park and make it so difficult to find you?

ADAM. I cannot listen to that music. I cannot watch that dancing! It bites—it stings—it burns! Oh, those shadows, those sleeping shadows on the wall! I have always seen them. I have always been frightened by them. Every object would grow into that beast which has been ripping my heart out with its fangs and tearing and biting . . .

VISITOR. Ha, ha, ha . . . (leans over and whispers into ADAM's ear) It bites? He? It stings?

ADAM. (remains silent, in a daze)

VISITOR. Ha, ha—some kind of rats, eh? Rats? So it nibbles away with its tiny little razor-thin teeth, and it gnaws and slashes and crunches—is that it? Like a mole that uses its little paws to dig into hard bedrock, into parched ground—some sort of hardened shell—it had only seemed to be rock—and you know, with those little paws it loosens the soil, digs down slowly, ever so slowly, but deeper and deeper with such furious obstinacy. And then the mole can no longer be seen, all that remains visible is a small pile of earth—oh, no! rather a tiny grave, which grows and grows—growing higher and higher the deeper the mole digs down—until all of a sudden a burial mound has been raised up; and at last it stops growing . . .

ADAM. What does it mean?

VISITOR. That the mole has done his job.

ADAM. And that grave?

VISITOR. At the crossroads.

ADAM. For murderers? Is that it?

VISITOR. Or for a suicide—he, he—why didn't you think of that before? . . . That's how you could have freed yourself from me . . . And it is so easy after all. We treat death far too seriously . . . And it could be arranged so discreetly, without any fuss or needless gossip. You want to avoid certain unpleasant things. You don't want it talked about . . . there is a solution for that too: right behind the park there's a lake—you go out rowing in a small boat, suddenly a storm comes up, or suppose the boat is half rotten, and—you sink down to the bottom just like that . . . An unfortunate accident . . . You'll be buried in sanctified ground . . . he, he . . . or say you're coming back from hunting: you've slung your rifle carelessly, you bump into a door—the gun goes off— well! it's an accident again . . . Or you go up into the mountains—now, this is the surest way of all—your foot slips on some moss, or a stone gives way . . . They say it's a pleasant death: you go flying, flying through the air; in just one second you experience the most beautiful moments of your life . . .

ADAM. So only death can deliver me from you?

VISITOR. *(coldly)* Only death!

ADAM. So only by death can I redeem myself?

VISITOR. Only by death!

ADAM. You are frightful.

VISITOR. Death is not as frightful. Death is kind . . . Why can't I be as kind as death?

    (Voices are heard from the terrace; laughter and the hum of conversation.)

LEADER OF THE DANCE. Adam! Adam! Won't you come join us now? We're drinking your health!

ADAM. I'm coming, I'm coming! *(He goes off to the mansion.)*

VISITOR. Remember! That is the only way to get free of me.

    (A long pause.)

STRANGER. *(appears from the other side; he stares at the windows of the mansion, then turns to the VISITOR; suddenly)* Now is this the house in which those strange and mysterious things took place?

VISITOR. Yes, this is the place.

STRANGER. *(after a short pause)* A ball, music, dancing . . . hmm . . . it fails to benumb, it cannot deaden . . . It won't drive ghosts away, it intoxicates for an instant, and then the heart, momentarily inebriated, takes double vengeance for allowing itself to become intoxicated. For the human heart is frightful and vindictive. It won't give you any peace, it won't ever give you any peace . . . *(after a pause)* Can I come in here? I am strangely drawn to where it's bright and cheerful. I am somehow irresistibly drawn.

VISITOR. Why shouldn't you come in? One visitor more—what difference doesn't it make? In any case, soon this house will be filled with visitors whom the host himself has never met—and even now isn't he already entertaining strange visitors!

STRANGER. Strange visitors? *(looks around, lost in thought)* Oh, if only I could come in!

VISITOR. But the host has been waiting for you for such a long time.

His destiny is to have this house of his filled with stranger and stranger visitors.

STRANGER. Perhaps I am mistaken. Perhaps this house really is a place of peace and happiness, and you see, I have this unfortunate habit of coming in at moments of happiness and joy . . . But I cannot stand loneliness: it's as though I were being pursued by furies—I run through the streets, I wander aimlessly; frightful anxiety drives me, lashes me with a frenzied whip . . . and at such moments I'll crouch at rich men's gates—where the windows are brightly lighted, and there's the sound of music, and joyful laughter and the hum of voices, and all of a sudden I have the impression that I'm lost in a swamp—in total darkness—I don't know which way to turn—until all at once there appears a dancing flame, a will-o'-the-wisp! Oh, I'm saved. It will guide me. It will show me the right direction—and I go on and on, I sink in deeper, but keep going I must . . . Don't throw me out now—don't! You cannot throw me out—look! I'm decently dressed, I won't be out of place—all I want to do is watch the dancing, drink in the music, and dazzle my eyes with the light . . . oh! it won't deaden or benumb, but it will bring a moment of forgetfulness—and in the houses of the rich one is still safe, relatively safe. You see, I am like a cunning animal, the humans hunt me down and have brought me to bay; obsessed by conscience, their hearts refuse to lie, and their minds have gone astray . . .

VISITOR. You are not mistaken this time—you will be most comfortable here. These are people who suffer terribly, but do not know how to benumb themselves . . .

STRANGER. Is that so? Then I'll come in. I love people who suffer—I love them . . . and . . . and in the houses of the rich, one is safe, relatively safe . . . *(goes slowly to the mansion).*

(The stage remains empty for a moment. Loud music. The VISITOR stares at the mansion, without moving. Suddenly the music stops, and after a moment, ADAM comes out, swaying unsteadily on his feet, and goes over to the Visitor.)

ADAM. Was it you who let him in?

VISITOR. He came in all by himself.

ADAM. Why did you let him in? Now I cannot cross the threshold of this house ever again.

VISITOR. No, not ever again.

ADAM. Is there no way out?

VISITOR. No way out.

ADAM. Not even for her?

VISITOR. For who?

ADAM. For my wife.

VISITOR. She will soon be here.

ADAM. Where is Pola?—I've been looking for her, I've been looking for her everywhere. Pola! Pola!

VISITOR. She has hidden in the most inaccessible recesses of your mansion. Usually so peaceful and quiet, she is now full of fears. Because you have strange and frightful visitors.

ADAM. How frightful!

VISITOR. Remember what I told you. It's easy to have an accident. A boat can sink by accident—your foot may slip in the mountains—there are thousands of possibilities . . . *(after a moment)* Besides, you humans are strange. You take life so frightfully seriously. What for? It's the merest scrap of happiness, that ridiculous phantom which conceals the abyss of life for one moment, only to disclose a still deeper and more frightful chasm at the next . . . These moments of intoxication, the delusion that one lives for some purpose and because of some goal—and that one has aims in life—he, he—how ridiculous you all are— poor worms, balls in the hands of fate and destiny, controlled by the great veiled mysteries—and you still imagine you are at the helm . . . But I won't ever leave you, I cannot ever leave you . . . Look, your wife is coming this way . . . She too has been driven out of the house by that Stranger . . . Now I can leave you for a moment to your own reflections —in the great, decisive moments of life, I usually leave people to themselves . . . *(lost in thought for a moment)* or perhaps I'll wait for you; I'll take a walk in the park . . . Humans are so strangely fainthearted at moments like this: all of a sudden life seems to them to be so strangely beautiful and appealing . . . I'll wait . . . No one has ever deceived me so far, no one has ever escaped me . . . *(withdraws, meeting BELA on the way—they stare at each other for a moment).*

BELA. You are frightful! You are accursed!

VISITOR. Not me, but life itself is frightful and accursed! *(disappears into the park)*

BELA. *(to ADAM)* Adam! Adam! Adam! Pola has already left—now everything is finished. I have lost all my strength—I cannot endure this torment any longer . . . Madness has crossed our threshold. Wild abandon, music, intoxication are of no help any more . . .

ADAM. So Pola has left?

BELA. She has run away from this house . . .

ADAM. From this house of bad conscience . . .

BELA. She ran away as I was trying to benumb myself in the dance.

ADAM. *(forcefully)* Now there is no way out.

BELA. *(springs back)* Let's run away.

ADAM. Where?

BELA. *Anywhere*—even to the ends of the earth.

ADAM. Pola told me that even if I built up the entire earth with the most costly mansions, there would still be no place for her . . .

BELA. Oh, we'll forget, we'll forget—look! my arms are strong as steel—I shall take you away in them; I'll cuddle and console you. I'll hug you so tight that we'll forget everything in that pleasure.

ADAM. No, no! That frightful, frightful visitor won't give us any peace.

BELA. Then what is left for us? What is left?

ADAM. What is left? We'll go rowing on the lake—the boat is rotten—the lake is deep . . .

BELA. Adam!

ADAM. Or we'll go up into the mountains—we'll climb to the heights, to the most dangerous peaks—my foot will slip, I'll pull you down with me and—and—we shall be free.

BELA. There is no other way out!

ADAM. There is no other way! *(Sobbing loudly, BELA throws her arms around his neck.)*

   (POLA runs in, looking around fearfully in all directions.)

ADAM and BELA. *(joyously)* Pola! Pola!

POLA. Calm down—calm down . . .

BELA. *(throwing her arms around her neck)* Now you'll stay with us—I won't let you go.

POLA. *(incoherently)* I will not stay—I cannot stay. There is no happiness in my home, but I have peace—here you have the plague—it will cling to my dress, and I shall bring it home to my husband. I shall infect my children with the poison . . .

BELA. Stay here with us! Stay here! . . .

POLA. No, no—I ran away, I hid, but they chased me, they're doing frightful things in there—do you hear? The music has stopped—the lights are going out—look! Do you see? The mansion is dark.

   (The mansion disappears into the darkness—there is only the moonlit night.)

POLA. I ran to you. I had to see you once more. Oh, Oh! What have you done? What crime have you committed?

ADAM. *(harshly)* What crime? No crime at all! Millions do the same and are happy . . .

POLA. Then what is this frightful penance for?

ADAM. What for? What for? *(suddenly to BELA)* Why didn't you redeem me—why didn't you give me a single moment of happiness?

BELA. Because you didn't want me to—you wouldn't let me. You hid from me, you drove me off, you taunted me with your sneers, you pushed me away—while all the time I longed for you, I desired you . . . All you thought about was to benumb yourself, grow stupefied, become intoxicated, while our house kept filling up with more and more visitors.

ADAM. With strange visitors . . . Ha! Even the walls were covered with lurking black shadows—the black beast that was ready to spring at my throat. You see, I kept hearing screams and wailing, such frightful, heartrending cries—like the weeping of a child to whom a great, great wrong has been done simply because he was good and loving . . . ha, ha . . . *(suddenly to POLA)* Go, go! This is a house of bad conscience. It is contagious.

POLA. *(tries to throw her arms around his neck)*

ADAM. *(pushes her away)* The plague is in this house—look! What a frightful house! Go!

POLA. Oh, God—there's no way out—and I loved you both so much, I thought I could help you . . . (starts to leave).

ADAM. Too late, Pola, too late . . .

(ADAM and BELA remain alone for a few moments.)

ADAM. (lost in thought) So I'll go up into the mountains—up where the moss will slip under my feet, where a stone will give way by accident . . .

BELA. I'm afraid. I'm so young—and still so strong. I'm afraid!

ADAM. Then I shall go alone.

BELA. No, no, no! I'll go wherever you want, but I'm afraid—I'm still so young . . .

ADAM. I too am young. . . .

BELA. I'll envelop you with such passionate love. I'll comfort and console you—look, I'm strong. I must go with you, but wait a bit; try once again; don't push me away from you—let's throw ourselves into the whirl of life, we'll drink it all in and revel in it . . .

ADAM. You won't chase the shadows from the walls; you won't find the mole in the ground . . .

(The VISITOR slowly approaches.)

BELA. What do you want? What do you want? Accursed creature! You are frightful!

VISITOR. It is only life that is frightful. How utterly ridiculous for people to be so attached to life! Death is kind and restful . . . And all this? This scrap of inane happiness, this illusion, this Satanic mirage! This intoxication with one's own strength and goals, this conviction that one is great and has so much to accomplish: all that is folly, the lure with which life catches humans. Death, death, it's the only way— to spit right in life's face and say, "You won't delude me!" And go meet death with great dignity and contempt!

ADAM. (to BELA) Come, come! Are you going to come with me?

BELA. I'm so afraid, I'm so afraid!

ADAM. (softly to the VISITOR) Woman is always afraid . . . (dementedly) he, he . . . Then I'll go alone . . . there's no help for it . . . you stay—you still have life before you—You are still young and strong . . .

BELA. Adam! Adam! (remains as though nailed to the spot)

ADAM. (starts to leave, turns and looks at her, but says nothing.)

VISITOR. I'll go with you. It will be easier for you that way. But now it's time, it's time . . .

CURTAIN

About the Authors

HASKEL M. BLOCK is professor of comparative literature at the State University of New York at Binghamton. He has written extensively on the symbolist movement and on modern drama. His books include *Masters of Modern Drama*, with Robert G. Shedd (1962), and *Mallarmé and the Symbolist Drama* (1963).

JEAN-LOUP BOURGET has taught French at Trinity College, Dublin; the University of Glasgow; and Trinity College, University of Toronto. He was French cultural attaché in London and in Chicago and at present holds the same position in New York. The author of a volume of poetry, he has also published numerous articles on the history of the American cinema, the fine arts, and nineteenth-century French literature.

FRANK PAUL BOWMAN is professor of French at the University of Pennsylvania. A recipient of Guggenheim and NEH fellowships, he has written several books and many articles on French romanticism and on autobiography.

MARY ANN CAWS is executive officer of the Comparative Literature Program at the Graduate Center, CUNY; editor of *Dada/Surrealism*; and the director of *Le Siècle éclaté*, a French journal on the avant-garde. Her publications include *Surrealism and the Literary Imagination, The Inner Theatre of Recent French Poetry*, and many other works on contemporary poetics, as well as translations of Tristan Tzara and René Char.

MAURICE CHARNEY, professor of English at Rutgers University, is the author of *Comedy: High and Low, How to Read Shakespeare, Style in "Hamlet,"* and *Shakespeare's Roman Plays*. He is the editor of numerous plays of Shakespeare and was special editor of *Comedy: New Perspectives (New York Literary Forum*, volume 1), and has published various articles.

B. H. FUSSELL, who teaches courses on movies and the drama at The New School for Social Research, has written on figures as diverse as T. S. Eliot, M. F. K. Fisher, and Margaret Dumont. As a free-lance writer, she has published articles on food, travel, movies, and drama in *The New York Times, Holiday, 1,000 Eyes*, and *The Hudson* and *Sewanee Reviews*.

JEAN GAUDON is currently professor of French at Yale University. He is author of several books on Victor Hugo, has edited works of Hugo and Paul Verlaine, and has written several novels and a volume of prose poems.

DANIEL GEROULD is a playwright, translator, and critic who teaches theater and comparative literature at the Graduate Center of the City of New York. His critical study *Witkacy* will be published in 1980, and a new volume of translations, *The Beelzebub Sonata*, will soon appear in the *Performing Arts Journal Playscript Series*.

CECIL PAIGE GOLANN received her Ph. D. in Greek and Latin from Columbia University in 1952 and spent the following year in Italy on a Fulbright grant. Since then she has taught English and the Classics at Hunter College, CUNY, worked as an editorial researcher for NBC-TV, and served on the editorial staff of Macmillan Publishing Company, Inc. At present she is a free-lance writer and editor.

JADWIGA KOSICKA is a translator and historian, formerly with the Polish Academy of Sciences in Warsaw, who writes about European intellectual history. Her translation of Bolesław Miciński's *Portrait of Kant* appears in the current issue of *The Polish Review*, and she is now preparing a volume of plays about the Warsaw Ghetto Uprising.

REINHARD KUHN is professor of French and comparative literature at Brown University. His publications include *The Demon of Noontide: Ennui in Western Literature, The Return to Reality: A Study of Francis Viele-Griffin, Panorama du théâtre nouveau, L'Esprit nouveau de la littérature française,* and the translations *New Ways of Ontology* and *Dying We Live.*

JAMES R. LAWLER is professor of French at the University of Chicago. He has written many distinguished books about Paul Valéry, René Char, and the language of French symbolism.

HERMINE RIFFATERRE has taught for many years at Barnard College. She is now associate editor of *Teaching Language through Literature*, a pedagogical journal. She is the author of *L'Orphisme dans la poésie romantique* as well as articles on French romanticism. In collaboration with Mary Ann Caws, she is preparing a book on the prose poem.

ANYA TAYLOR is an associate professor of English at John Jay College of Criminal Justice, CUNY. She is author of *Magic and English Romanticism*(1979) and edited "Romanticism and the Occult," the spring 1977 special issue of *The Wordsworth Circle*.

JENNIFER WAELTI-WALTERS is associate professor of French and chairperson of the department at the University of Victoria, British Columbia. Her publications include *Alchimie et littérature* (on Butor's *Portrait de l'artiste en jeune singe), Michel Butor, J. M. G. Clézio,* and papers on other twentieth-century writers. Currently, she is working on metamorphosis in French literature since 1945.

Bibliography

Arnold, Paul. *Esotérisme de Shakespeare.* Paris: Mercure de France, 1955.

Azcuy, Eduardo A. *El ocultismo y la creación poética.* Buenos Aires: Editorial Sudamericana, 1966.

Banta, Martha. *Henry James and the Occult.* Bloomington: Indiana Univ. Press, 1972.

Barclay, Glen St. John. *Anatomy of Horror. The Masters of Occult Fiction.* London: Weidenfeld & Nicholson, 1978.

Bays, Gwendolyn. *The Orphic Vision. Seer Poets from Novalis to Rimbaud.* Lincoln: Univ. of Nebraska Press, 1964.

Béguin, Albert. *L'Ame romantique et le rêve.* (1939) Rpt. Paris: Corti, 1947.

Bénichou, Paul. *Le Temps des prophètes. Doctrines de l'âge romantique.* Paris: Gallimard, 1977.

Brémond, Henri. *Histoire littéraire du sentiment religieux en France . . .* 11 vols. Rpt. Paris: Collin, 1967-68.

Breton, André; *Arcane 17. Enté d'Ajours.* Rpt. Paris: Pauvert, 1971.

Budge, Ernest A. T. Wallis. *Egyptian Magic* (1899). Rpt. NY: Dover, 1971.

Cattaui, Georges. *Orphisme et prophétie chez les poètes français (1850-1950).* Paris: Plon, 1965.

Cellier, Léon. *Parcours initiatiques.* Paris: P. U. G., 1978.

Cumont, Franz. *The Oriental Religions in Roman Paganism* (1929). Rpt. NY: Dover, 1956.

Doutté, Edmond. *Magie et religion dans l'Afrique du Nord.* Algiers: Joudan, 1908.

Eliade, Mircea. *Shamanism: Archaic Techniques of Ecstasy.* Trans. by W. R. Trask. Princeton: Princeton Univ. Press, 1960.

Elliott, Robert C. *The Power of Satire: Magic, Ritual, Art.* Princeton: Princeton Univ. Press, 1960.

Festugière, André. *La Révélation d'Hermès Trismégiste.* 4 vols. Paris: Lecoffre, 1944–1954.

Foley, Augusta E. *Occult Arts and Doctrine in the Theater of Juan Ruiz de Alarcón.* Geneva: Droz, 1972.

Fossey, Charles. *La Magie Assyrienne.* Paris: E. Leroux, 1902.

Frazer, James G. *The Golden Bough.* 12 vols. Rpt. NY: Macmillan, 1935.

Fulcanelli. *Les Demeures philosophales.* 2 vols. Rpt. Paris: Pauvert, 1965.

Garry, Thomas G. *Egypt: The Home of the Occult Sciences.* London: Bale & Danielsson, 1931.

Gaudon, Jean. *Le Temps de la contemplation.* Paris: Flammarion, 1969.

Girard, René. *Des Choses cachées depuis la fondation du monde.* Paris: Grasset, 1978.

Glover, Terrot R. *The Conflict of Religions in the Early Roman Empire.* Rpt. Boston: Beacon Press, 1960.

Hatzfeld, Helmut. *Estudios literarios sobre mística española.* Madrid: Gredos, 1955.

Hild, Joseph A. *Etudes sur les démons dans la littérature et la religion des Grecs*. Paris: 1881.

Imam, Syed M. *The Poetry of the Invisible*. London: Allen & Unwin, 1937.

Juden, Brian. *Traditions orphiques et tendances mystiques dans le romantisme français (1800–1855)*. Paris: Klincksieck, 1971.

Kiesewetter, Karl. *Faust in der Geschichte und Tradition*. Leipzig, 1893.

Knapp, Bettina L. *Dream and Image*. Troy, NY: Whitston, 1977.

Lang, Andrew. *Magic and Religion* (1901). Rpt. Westport, CT: Greenwood Press, 1971.

Lepinte, Christian. *Goethe et l'occultisme*. Paris: Les Belles Lettres, 1957.

Lowe, Joyce E. *Magic in Greek and Latin Literature*. Oxford, Eng.: Blackwell, 1929.

Maeterlinck, Maurice. *Le Grand secret*. Rpt. Paris: Fasquelle, 1950.

Malinowski, Bronislaw. *Magic, Science, and Religion and Other Essays*. Rpt. Garden City, NY: Doubleday, 1954.

Mead, George R. S. *Thrice-Greatest Hermes*. 3 vols. London: John M. Watkins, 1949.

Mercier, Alain. *Les Sources esotériques et occultes de la poésie symboliste.* (1870–1914). 2 vols. Paris: Nizet, 1969-74.

Pavia, Mario N. *Drama of the Siglo de Oro: A Study of Magic, Witchcraft, and Other Occult Beliefs*. NY: Hispanic Institute, 1959.

Péladan, Joséphin. *L'Art idéaliste et mystique*. Paris, 1909.

Reed, Robert R. *The Occult on the Tudor and Stuart Stage*. Boston: Christopher Pub. House, 1965.

Reitzenstein, Richard. *Hellenistic Mystery-Religions*. Trans. by John E. Steely. Rpt. Pittsburgh, PA: Pickwick Press, 1978.

Riffaterre, Hermine. *L'Orphisme dans le poésie romantique* . . . Paris: Nizet, 1970.

Roos, Jacques. *Aspects littéraires du mysticisme philosophique* . . . Strasbourg: P. H. Heitz, 1951.

Saurat, Denis. *Literature and Occult Tradition* (1929). Trans. by Dorothy Bolton. Rpt. Port Washington, NY: Kennikat Press, 1966.

Schuré, Edouard. *From Sphinx to Christ: An Occult History*. Rpt. NY: Blauvelt & Rudolf Steiner, 1970.

Seillère, Ernest. *Les Etapes du mysticisme passionnel* . . . Paris: La Renaissance du Livre, 1919.

Senior, John. *The Way Down and Out: The Occult in Symbolist Literature*. Rpt. Westport, CT: Greenwood Press, 1968.

Spurgeon, Caroline. *Mysticism in English Literature*. Cambridge, Eng.: The Univ. Press, 1913.

Thorndike, Lynn. *A History of Magic and Experimental Science*. 8 vols. NY: Macmillan, Columbia Univ. Press, 1923–1958.

Tuzet, Hélène. *Le Cosmos et l'imagination*. Paris: Corti, 1965.

Viatte, Auguste. *Les Sources occultes du romantisme*. . . Rpt. Paris: Champion, 1965.

Waelti-Walters, Jennifer. *Alchimie et littérature* . . . Paris: Denoël, 1975.

Watkin, Edward. *Poets and Mystics*. London: Sheed & Ward, 1953.

Welsh, Andrew. *Roots of Lyric: Primitive Poetry and Modern Poetics*. Princeton: Princeton Univ. Press, 1978.

Wilson Colin. *The Occult*. NY: Random House, 1971.

Wolff, Robert L. *Strange Stories and Other Explorations in Victorian Fiction*. Boston: Gambit, 1971.

Index

Alciphron 78
All's Well That Ends Well 166
Analogies 75, 78
Animism 77
Apology 104, 105, 108, 109
Apuleius 103
Aragon, Louis 134, 137, 140, 146
Artephius 192
Augustine, St. 105, 107
Axël 44, 45, 46
Bachelard, Gaston 140
Ballanche, P. H. S. 59, 63, 94
Baudelaire, Charles 61, 126, 149
Beethoven, Ludwig van 183, 184, 188, 191
Béguin, Albert 133, 135
Bely, Andrei 4, 17, 22, 23, 24, 26, 29
Biographia Literaria 79, 85
Block, Haskell M. 43
Boehme, Jacob 54, 180, 181
Bonald, Louis de 54, 58, 59, 60
Bourgeois vision 138, 139, 140, 141
Bourget, Eithne 119
Bourget, Jean-Loup 111
"Bloy and the Symbolism of History" 111
Bloy, Léon 111
Bowman, Frank Paul 51
Breton, André 87, 133, 148
Briusov, Valerii 26, 28
Carlyle, Thomas 135, 145
Caws, Mary Ann 147
Cendrier du Voyage 152, 153
Charney, Maurice 171
Christianity 84
Cocteau, Jean 141, 143
Coleridge, Samuel Taylor 75
Columbus, Christopher 115, 117, 118
Comedy of Errors 164
Crevel, René 146
Curses 80, 81
Cymbeline 167
"Dangerous Game of Dreams: Jean Paul and the Surrealists" 133
"Dark Framing and the Analogical Ascent" 147

Daumal, René 150, 151
De Deo Socratis 108, 109
Demeures Philosophales, Les 180
Description de San Marco 183
Demonology 108, 109
Destutt de Tracy 61
Dialogue avec 33 variations 183, 184, 186, 188
Drama, Symbolist 4, 43, 143
"Drama of the Unseen—The Turn-of-the-Century Paradigms for Occult Drama" 3
Dreams 76, 78, 133
Dupin, Jacques 151, 152, 153
Eckstein, Baron 59
Emmett, Dorothy 77
Emploi du temps, L' 183
Energy 75, 76, 77, 83
Entertaining Mr. Sloane 172
Flamel, Nicholas 180
Fleurs du mal, Les 126
Fourier, Charles 183, 186, 187, 191
Freud, Sigmund 134
Friend, The 76
Fussell, B. H. 161
Galatea 96, 98
Garat, Dominique-Joseph 56
Gaudon, Jean 87
Gautier, Théophile 65
Gerould, Daniel 3, 197
Ghosts 76, 78, 79, 81, 83
"Ghosts, Spirits and Force: Samuel Taylor Coleridge" 75
Goethe, Johann Wolfgang von 28, 43, 141
Golann, Cecil Paige 103
Gravir 151
Hamlet 166
Harding, Anthony John 82
Heights of Machu Picchu, The 150
Helbo, André 183
Hermes Trismegistus 108
Hesse, Hermann 143
Hugo, Victor 57, 61, 87, 144
Huysmans, Joris-Karl 33, 112, 113, 118
Jabir 180, 181

Joan of Arc 117, 118
King Lear 166
Kircher, Athanasius 180
Kosicka, Jadwiga 3, 197
Kuhn, Reinhard 133
Lahr, John 172
Lamennais, Félicité de 51, 59, 60
Lautréamont 138
Lawler, James R. 125
Letters (Coleridge) 78
Love 79, 70, 81, 82
"Love-in-Death: Gautier's 'morte
        amoureuse'" 65
Maeterlinck, Maurice 4, 12, 13, 14
Magi 108, 109
"Magic in the Life and Writings
        of Apuleius" 103
Maine de Biran 58
Maistre, Joseph de 58, 59, 62
Mallarmé, Stéphane 10, 51, 52, 61, 62,
        125, 144
"Mallarmé and the 'Poison Tutélaire'"
        125
Marvelous 138
Mercury 108
Metamorphoses (Apuleius) 104
Michelet, Victor-Emile 13
Miciński, Tadeusz 4, 6, 8, 16, 17, 18,
        20, 21, 22, 29, 30, 36, 38
Minder, Robert 134
Mobile 183
Modification, La 183
Montgolfier brothers 144
"Morte amoureuse" 65
*Mount Analogue: A Novel of . . .
        Climbing* 150
Mysterium Magnum 181
Napoleon 114, 117, 118, 119
" 'Neck Riddle' and Dramatic Form"
        161
Neoplatonism 108, 109
Neruda, Pablo 150, 155
Nerval, Gérard de 57, 61, 134
Nietzsche, Friedrich Wilhelm 83
Nodier, Charles 61
Notebooks (Coleridge) 76, 79, 82
"Numerology: The Butorian Imagination"
        179
"Occulted Discourse and Threatening
        Nonsense in Joe Orton's *Entertaining
        Mr. Sloane*" 171
"Occultism and the Language of Poetry"
        51
Oedipus 163
1001 Nights 181, 182
Oriental mystery religions 109

Orton, Joe 172
Passage de Milan 182, 183, 188
Péladan, Joséphin 112, 114, 115, 119
Pericles 162
Philosophical Lectures (Coleridge) 75
Picasso, Pablo 140
Pichoia, Claude 133
Pinter, Harold 173
Plato 28, 108, 109, 136
Poe, Edgar Allan 51, 52, 125
Poems (Coleridge) 77, 78, 79, 80, 81, 82
Portrait de l'artiste en jeune singe 179,
        180, 182, 183, 186, 188, 192
Przybyszewski, Stanisław 4, 5, 36, 38,
        39, 197.
Répertoire 179
Richter, Jean Paul 133
Riddle 161
Riffaterre, Hermine 65
Rimbaud, Arthur 62, 141, 145
Romeo and Juliet 166
Rose des vents, La 183, 184, 186, 188
"Rumpelstiltskin" 161
Saby, Bernard 191
Saint-Martin, Louis Claude de 52, 54, 55,
        62
Schuré, Edouard 13, 14, 32
Scriabin, Alexander 10, 12, 13, 24
Self 78, 79, 81, 82
"Speaking tables" 88, 91, 92
Spirits 79, 82, 84, 85
Sorcery 108
Statesman's Manual 76, 77
Steinmetz, George 54, 60
Stoker, Bram 66
Stravinsky, Igor 183
Strindberg, August 4, 17, 18, 38, 43 fol.
Surrealism 133
"Symbolist Drama: Villiers de l'Isle-
        Adam, Strindberg, and Yeats" 43
Taylor, Anya 75
Theurgy 108, 109
Tombeau de Baudelaire, Le 129
Troisieme dessous 191, 192
Trope, in a drama 164
Valentinus, Basilus 180
Verne, Jules 180
"Victor Hugo and Galatea's Flight" 87
Villiers de l'Isle Adam 43, 44, 45
Visibility 77
Visitors 36, 38, 39 177
Waelti-Walters, Jennifer 179
Waiting for Godot 170
Witchcraft 80
Wordsworth, William 78, 79, 80
Wyspiański, Stanisław 4, 8, 16, 17, 30, 32
Yeats, William Butler 43 fol., 83, 84

1508-7

5-03

DATE DUE

GAYLORD   PRINTED IN U.S.A.